Love,
greg,
maggie

MONTESSORI
PARENTING

MONTESSORI PARENTING
Unveiling the Authentic Self

WRITTEN FOR ALL PARENTS AND TEACHERS BY
DR. JIM AND SONNIE MCFARLAND

Shining Mountains Press
BUENA VISTA, COLORADO

Cover design by Michael Propp
Front and back cover photos by Jeannie McFarland Johnson

1st printing 2011 • 2nd printing 2011

ISBN 978-0-9754887-0-6

LCCN 2010916237

ATTENTION CORPORATIONS, UNIVERSITIES, COLLEGES, AND PROFESSIONAL ORGANIZATIONS: Quantity discounts are available on bulk purchases of this book for educational, gift purposes, or as premiums for increasing magazine subscriptions or renewals. Special books or book excerpts can also be created to fit specific needs. For information, please contact Shining Mountains Press, PO Box 4155, Buena Vista, CO 81211; phone 719-395-3969.

www.ShiningMountainsPress.com

We dedicate this book

to all of the children of the world

and all of the parents and teachers

who so compassionately support

each child's process of

Unveiling his Authentic Self.

CONTENTS

FOREWORD

Montessori Parenting: Unveiling the Authentic Self is a must read for all parents and teachers of young children. Dr. Jim and Sonnie McFarland have captured the essence of the Montessori philosophy especially the salient points that parents need to know to understand their children. Dr. Maria Montessori knew the real secret of childhood, which is articulated so well in this book written especially for parents.

Parents will learn about the VEIL Model that outlines children's natural process of development. The components of the model are: **V**olition, **E**ngagement, **I**ntegration, and **L**ove. These four aspects repeat themselves each time a child completes a cycle of learning. At the completion of each learning cycle the child is enthused because a portion of his Authentic Self is unveiled. This enthusiasm naturally motivates him to involve himself in the repeating cycles of the VEIL Model. Parents will understand that by trusting the child's natural process of development they are facilitating the manifestation of the child's potential; thus unveiling the child's Authentic Self.

Sonnie and Jim share practical ways to prepare the home environment so that it embodies Montessori philosophy in all the domains—physical, mental, emotional and spiritual. A variety of strategies from Maria Montessori, well-known psychologists, and current researchers are included in the book and provide excellent resources for parents. The Native American Medicine Wheel is used as a metaphor to help parents understand children's behavior and support children's journey of understanding themselves. This unique approach sets this book apart from typical parenting books.

An important point that most authors forget is the preparation of the adult. For adults to truly be present for their children and function as appropriate role models, they must first work on preparing themselves. Information on centering skills, parenting styles, communication strategies, facilitating inner discipline and understanding children's behavior are all tools given in the book to help parents enhance their repertoire of knowledge. Each chapter concludes with reflective questions for parents to ponder and personalize for their own children and unique situations.

Reading this insightful book will help parents understand the creative process of child development and thoughtfully facilitate the unveiling of their child's authentic nature. The child, who is allowed to unfold and blossom, will experience the joy and peace of actualizing his potentials. Indeed, within the heart of the child lies the hope for peace in the world that we all want for our children and grandchildren's futures.

—BETSY COE, PH.D.

PREFACE

"All people, especially children,
when manifesting the greater Self within,
are Shining Mountains, glowing with eternal promise."[1]

—DR. JIM MCFARLAND

Children come to us as loving souls whose ultimate purpose in life is to manifest their potentials and contribute meaningfully to the world. As parents we have the greatest influence on whether or not our child will be able to successfully unveil his Authentic Self and share the beautiful gifts hidden within him. Our most important responsibility is to recognize the essential beauty within our child and facilitate his natural process of development. To successfully accomplish this task, we must first understand our child's authentic nature and the inner resources within him that naturally lead him toward self-actualization.

Over a hundred years ago, Dr. Maria Montessori discovered some key principles and practices that transformed the lives of children in almost "magical" ways. She witnessed disgruntled, unruly and competitive children transform into happy, thoughtful and cooperative children. Her discoveries were so dramatic that it created a worldwide educational revolution that continues to this day. While these principles and practices are being successfully used in Montessori Schools, their benefit is not limited to Montessori educational settings. Understanding and implementing this wisdom in the home will bring the same type of transformation to the members of the family. We will see competitive behavior transform into cooperation, we will see selfishness transform into selflessness, and we will see rudeness transform into thoughtfulness.

The principles of *Montessori Parenting* do not imply that a child must attend a Montessori school for the ideas shared in this book to be useful in the home. *The philosophy, principles and practices are universal and applicable for all children and their families, regardless of their educational choices or cultural backgrounds.* If a child does attend a Montessori school, however, he will definitely benefit from having consistency between both his home and school setting. Teachers will also benefit from reading this book as it provides valuable information to share with parents so the children can benefit from a consistent approach at school and at home.

The Montessori approach to parenting is not a band-aid we apply to stop the bleeding or a tool we use to fix what is broken. Instead it is a holistic approach that includes all of the members of the family and addresses the physical, mental, emotional and spiritual needs of each person in the home. When someone in the family changes his behavior, it affects the behavior of all of the family members. Of course as a parent, when we change our behavior our entire family is influenced.

This book addresses the authentic nature of our child and how we can support the developmental processes that he naturally engages in to unveil his Authentic Self. In addition there are practical suggestions to help us prepare meaningful environments that support our child's natural maturation. To help us more consistently operate from our Authentic Self, the book offers practical suggestions to help us manage our physical, mental and emotional states so that we can more consistently act from wisdom and love. Understanding our parenting style and its effect on our child is included as well as thoughtful discussions on effective communication and inner discipline. Finally, the book offers insight into the root causes of our child's misbehavior and ways to help him reconnect to his Authentic Self and the resulting thoughtful behaviors.

The subtitle of the book, *Unveiling the Authentic Self*, not only implies the gradual unveiling of the child's Authentic Self but the unveiling of our Authentic Self as well as the Authentic Self of all members of the family. *The Authentic Self is the true nature of all people.* It is the Spirit that dwells in the heart and inspires wisdom, compassion and peace. Through her work Maria Montessori recognized the connection between nurturing the Spirit of the child and creating a peaceful world. In her words, "Only a sane spiritual rebuilding of the human race can bring about peace. To set about this task, we must go back to the child."[2]

It is our hope that the wisdom in this book will inspire and help us, as parents and teachers, to provide each child whose life we touch with the love and support he requires to unveil his Authentic Self, share his special talents and create a more peaceful world.

ACKNOWLEDGMENTS

As we reflect on the people who have significantly contributed to the completion of this book on parenting, the first people who come to mind are our parents: William Grant and Alice Marie Smith McFarland (Jim's parents), as well as Melvin Brent and Marjean Elggren Richards (Sonnie's parents). Because of our parent's ability to provide us with home environments encompassed with unconditional love, each of us has been able to experience our Authentic Self and use its wisdom to navigate through the various paths our lives have followed. In this process we continue to discover new potentials within ourselves and have the great joy of sharing our knowing with others.

In our discovery of the art of parenting, our two wonderful children, James Christian McFarland and Jeannie Marie McFarland Johnson have been our greatest teachers. Their pure love for us has inspired us to be our best for them. Because we are so "in love" with them, we have willingly gone through a process of continual transformation and self-reflection. We are definitely better people because of them. To this day they are our close friends, enthusiastic fans and supporters of our work.

Our grandchildren, Andrew Christian McFarland, Seraphim Imanoel McFarland and Alexander James Johnson continue the tradition of inspiring, as well as being teachers for us. Their love and light warms our hearts and motivates us to continue our work of helping parents and teachers unveil each child's Authentic Self.

In addition to the contributions of our family we recognize the knowledge and wisdom that has been shared with us by so many teachers throughout our lives from elementary, high school, under graduate, graduate and post graduate studies. We also acknowledge the many experts in the field of education, sociology, psychology, communication, parenting and spirituality whose work has inspired and enlightened us to be able to share what we do today.

During the writing of *Montessori Parenting* we acknowledge Barb Whitehead for her encouragement, especially when fatigue would set in. During the editing phase we want to extend appreciation to: Judi Bauerlein, Janet Engel, Tajali Theresa Tolan, and Pat Yonka who shared their valuable insights and refinements for the book. We acknowledge Dr. Betsy Coe for her wisdom and for the thoughtful ideas she shared in the Forward. Finally, we acknowledge Sharon Chang for her enthusiastic and generous support of the publishing of *Montessori Parenting: Unveiling The Authentic Self.*

PART I

Discovering the Authentic Child

PART I

Discovering the Authentic Child

"We know how to find pearls in the shells of oysters, gold in the mountains, and coal in the bowels of the earth; but we are unaware of the spiritual gems the child hides within himself when he enters the world to renew mankind."[1]

—MARIA MONTESSORI

What are these spiritual gems the child hides within himself? Maria Montessori discovered that every child is born with special gifts and talents, a unique creative spirit and an innate desire to manifest himself to the fullest degree. She called these gems the "spiritual embryo" of the child. She said,

> *The child becoming incarnate is a spiritual embryo which needs its own special environment. Just as a physical embryo needs its mother's womb in which to grow, so the spiritual embryo needs to be protected by an external environment that is warm with love and rich in nourishment, where everything is disposed to welcome and nothing to harm it.*[2]

When it is time for the child to live on Earth, its mother and father create a physical embryo that is nurtured in the mother's womb. In this warm environment miracles begin to take place for a period of nine months. During this short time this miniscule embryo develops naturally and spontaneously into a physical body, complete with skeletal, muscular and skin structures; a trunk to house respiratory, digestive, circulation and nervous systems; legs to move upon the Earth; arms to reach out; hands to touch and hold; a head to provide the child with eyes to see, ears to hear, a mouth to taste, and a nose to smell the beauties of the planet. Another vital part is the creation of a brain that provides the mechanics for the mind to assume its place as the mechanism allowing the child to think, learn, choose and create. Once this physical preparation is complete the child is born.

In spite of the meticulous physical preparation within the womb, something additional is needed to bring life into the infant's physical body. This gift travels on the breath and arrives as the child's spiritual embryo. Just as the physical embryo contains the parent's genetic particles, the spiritual embryo contains the genetic particles of the spiritual parent.

Each of us has our own way of viewing this source of Spirit. Some of the names used to describe this essence are: Higher Power, God, Brahman, Allah, Buddha-Nature, Mother Nature and Great Spirit. What we call this source is not important. What is important is that we acknowledge our connectedness to it and recognize our Spirit as our authentic nature. The more we connect to our authentic nature of love and use it as a compass in our lives, the greater will be our joy and success in our roles as parents and our lives in general.

Montessori realized that the child comes into the world with an active spiritual embryo that takes a long period of time to fully develop and that parents must understand what is taking place within the inner being of the child so they can provide a loving, nurturing environment that supports the delicate unfolding of the child's Spirit or Authentic Self. In her words,

We should regard this secret effort of the child as something sacred. We should welcome its arduous manifestations since it is in this creative period that an individual's future personality is determined.[3]

The child comes to us so closely associated with his Authentic Self that he is still connected and directed by it. He has an inner knowing, but he doesn't consciously realize what he knows. As parents, it is our awesome responsibility and opportunity to help our child identify with his authentic spiritual nature and learn to use it as his inner guide throughout his life. This is our greatest task as parents!

To be able to accomplish this task we must understand the child's authentic nature. In the first chapter we share some of Maria Montessori's amazing discoveries about the authentic nature of the child. In the second chapter we explore the child's connection to the universe and in the third chapter we provide a unique description of how the child's Mind and Spirit interconnect and support the unveiling of the Authentic Self.

CHAPTER 1

Montessori's Pathway of Discovery

*"The world which Columbus discovered was
a world without; Montessori discovered a
world within—within the soul of the child."[1]*

—E.M. STANDING

On January 6, 1907, over one hundred years ago, Dr. Maria Montessori started her first school in Rome, Italy which she called the Casa dei Bambini or the House of Children. At that moment in history we were gifted with an amazing discovery far greater than gold or silver for the world witnessed the discovery of the authentic nature of the child.

Prior to this time in many parts of the world, children were seen by adults as not having much capacity to learn until the age of six when formal schooling began. The daily care of young children was often left to someone other than the parents, or the children were left unattended all together. As a result very little stimulation was available to the developing young child. The general attitude of parents and care givers was that children were to be seen, not heard and that children were empty vessels that needed to be filled by those with greater knowledge and wisdom. Most parents saw themselves as the authority, expected obedience and attempted to control children through reward and punishment.

School teachers held a similar view of children and as a result the classrooms were stark, the desks immovable, and the seats hard and uncomfortable. Students' learning experiences were limited to listening to the teacher, watching what was written on the slate, copying assigned work and being tested on the material. The teacher's attitude was one of "I know and I must teach you!" When deemed necessary teachers punished children in ways that were humiliating to the students—hoping to "teach them a lesson."

Maria Montessori was born in 1870, and experienced firsthand the pain and frustration of being a student in the schools of that time. Early on she felt the shame and disrespect that teachers directed toward her and her fellow students. She experienced the agony of the social norms that wanted to prevent her, as a female, from following her mathematical and scientific interests. Rather than submit to the social pressure, she held true to her inner promptings, challenged the system, followed her intuition and made the discovery of the century—the secret of childhood.

During this past century, millions of children around the world have benefited from her perseverance and vision as they enjoy attending schools where they are respected and their learning experiences are spontaneous and joyful. The discoveries that Maria Montessori made are universal principles that support the natural development of children and are applicable to any educational setting as well as in the home. Following is a brief overview of how she came to discover the authentic nature of the child and the subsequent impact on the children of the world.

Early Life

Maria Montessori was born on August 31, 1870 in Chiaravalle, Italy. Her father, Alessandro Montessori, came from a recognized family, served in the military as a young man and later became a civil servant who was known for bravery, dignity and politeness. He saw life from a conservative point of view and therefore did not encourage his daughter's unfolding desires to be an independent woman, go to Medical School and promote revolutionary educational ideas. However caring and loving he was to her, he wanted her to embrace the traditional role of women which in those days meant that she would marry, be a mother, and if a career was desired, be a teacher.

Maria would become more like her mother, Renilde Stoppani, who was the niece of a renowned philosopher and scientist, Antonio Stoppani. Montessori resembled her mother in appearance and temperament. Both of them were attractive, charming and intelligent. Because of these qualities her mother understood, supported and encouraged Maria's compelling interests and quest for independence. The two of them remained close until Renilde's death in 1912.

When Montessori turned five, her father's work took the family to Rome where she began first grade at the State Day School. The schools of that time were quite unsatisfactory as the teachers had little understanding of how children learn and their primary method of teaching was drill, drill and drill. In many schools there were not enough books, pens, ink or other teaching materials. Many of the smaller schools only went to the third grade level, and if they went beyond third grade, boys were separated from girls. After elementary school, the curriculum for girls was of a domestic nature and the boys' curriculum was technical. Rules, regulations and expectations overrode any joy or spontaneous expression from the children. The teachers received little respect and were not paid a decent wage. Rita Kramer described the schools in this way.

> It was a system that could not have been better designed to
> quash individuality, but it failed to quash Maria's. And when she
> eventually turned her attention to education per se, it gave her a
> clear model of what a school should not be.[2]

Fortunately for Maria, she was able to attend elementary school until she was twelve. In spite of the challenges of her school experience Montessori did well and was sensitive toward her parents and classmates. Foreshadowing her future philosophy, she was always a peacemaker and defender of the underdog. While still young she did knitting every day for the poor, and befriended a neighborhood hunchback girl by taking her for daily walks. Once when a sharp disagreement occurred between her parents, she took a chair, placed it between them, climbed up on it, and joined their hands together to encourage them to make peace. Once when encountering classmates making a disturbance, she was bold enough to exclaim, "You! Why you are not even born yet." We are left to wonder that even at this tender age she was dimly aware of her future notion that child development was a succession of new births at consecutively higher levels.[3]

There was another time when her sense of personal dignity was offended. One of her teachers chastised her for looking directly and intensely into her eyes. The teacher told her that small children should not look at their superiors. Maria maintained her personal respect by never looking into the eyes of that teacher again. After reviewing these early years E. M. Standing, her biographer and collaborator, concluded,

> *Her whole life's work could be summed up as an effort to bring to an end the age-long struggle which has been waged and is still being waged between the child and the adult, a struggle which—as we shall see later—is no less real because it is carried on unconsciously.*[4]

By the time Maria completed her elementary studies she had developed a great deal of confidence and had an independent willfulness. Even though her parents wanted her to become a teacher and follow the more traditional career path for women, she would have none of it. She had a strong interest in mathematics and was determined to pursue this. After much struggle, she was admitted to the technical school for boys where she thought she might become an engineer.

In time her interests moved toward biology and she realized what she really wanted to do was study medicine. Her father was extremely resistant to this and did little to support her. The idea of a woman studying medicine was unheard of at the time and was viewed with scorn by many of the elite of Rome. Her mother, however, was one of the few who understood her daughter, stood beside her and encouraged her to break the stereotypical role assigned to women. In spite of the obstacles placed in her path, Maria Montessori persevered and proclaimed, "I know I shall become a Doctor of Medicine."[5] And so she did! After much struggle, she was the first woman to be admitted to the University of Rome Medical School.

Once Maria entered medical school she was met with additional resistance as her fellow male students were slow to accept her. As a woman she had to wait until all of the men sat down before she could take a seat in the lecture room. At that time, it was considered inappropriate for men and women to view the naked cadaver bodies together so she had to do her dissecting work at night with only the cadavers to keep her company. In the end Maria's indomitable will prevailed and in 1896 she graduated with respect from her colleagues and with honors from the University. She had become the first female to graduate from the University of Rome Medical School.

Early Professional Life

Dr. Maria Montessori would spend the next ten years pursuing an intense array of activities and learning with and from experts in the field of child psychology and education. Due to her attractive personality, fine looks, brilliant mind and dynamic way of speaking the young doctor was sought out often during this period and throughout her life to make public presentations. She was always received well and had intriguing and interesting material to present. She often defended the cause of working women, advocated for children, promoted educational opportunities for all and enthusiastically shared her revolutionary educational discoveries.

Soon after graduating she was appointed as the assistant doctor of the Psychiatric Clinic at the University of Rome. In this role she began her work with the "idiot" children, or so they were thought to be. One day she noted the disgust with which the children were held by their caregivers. When she asked why the children were held in such contempt, the woman in charge replied, "Because, as soon as their meals are finished they throw themselves on the floor to search for crumbs."[6] Dr. Montessori looked around the room to find it totally empty and bare. After some reflection it came to her that this behavior was not a medical or mental health problem for the children; rather it was a pedagogical problem. She recognized that their hands and their very souls were starved in this wretched environment. It was not food they craved when they went to the floor, but self-respect and meaningful activity. This experience touched Montessori's heart and guided her work with children throughout her life.

This insight provides a hint towards the core of Montessori Parenting developed throughout this book. Children can best manifest their authenticity and potentials when they are respected and have the opportunity to engage in stimulating physical environments as well as nurturing mental, emotional and spiritual environments. Montessori became intently immersed in pursuing this line of thought. She became convinced that with these deficient, as well as normal children, two things have to happen:

1. Adults need to change their perceptions of the child from one of lack and emptiness to one of potential and inherent dignity.

2. Children need nurturing environments complete with experiential activities and satisfying relationships.

In her research and study, Dr. Montessori became exposed to the work of two French doctors Jean Itard (1775–1835) and Edouard Seguin (1812–1880) who had independently reached similar conclusions to her own. Itard is credited as one of the founding fathers of special education and the first physician to claim that an enriched environment could compensate for developmental delays. His work was pivotal in bringing hope to the possibility of helping children with mental handicaps. Seguin studied under Itard and eventually refined the work of educating mentally deficient children. He created concrete sensory training materials so children could learn through all five senses and not be limited to seeing and hearing. Seguin successfully used these materials in schools for mentally challenged children.

Dr. Montessori was intrigued with the sensorial materials and began to use them with the mentally defective children in the Psychiatric Clinic. After working with the materials for a period of time she arranged to have some of the eight year old children take the State test. She was delighted that these children scored as well or even higher than children without mental challenges. It was at this point that her full attention turned to the study of education. During the academic school year of 1897–1898 she audited courses in the science of education and read the major works on educational theory. The ideas of those who had gone before provided a strong foundation upon which she would construct her educational philosophy and practice.

In 1899 she was invited to speak at a congress in Turin where she spoke to the need for all children, including mental defectives, to be educated. These ground breaking ideas attracted the attention of Dr. Guido Bacelli, the Minister of Education, who invited Montessori to give a series of lectures in Rome on the importance of educating mentally deficient children. As a result a special school was opened in Rome for the mentally challenged and Montessori was asked to direct the school which she did for two years. This was an intense period of observation, practice and study for the young doctor. She said the following about those two years. "Those two years of practice, are indeed my first and only true degree in pedagogy."[7]

Montessori continued to study and to teach Hygiene, Anthropology and Education at the University of Rome. She also managed to carry on a limited private practice in medicine. She knew she was progressing in a meaningful direction, but needed time to develop deeper understanding and have more experience with the children.

In addition to her academic and scientific abilities, she trusted in her mystical and intuitive abilities as well. She believed, "There is a divinity that shapes our ends," and that to be successful in life we must know how to "be obedient to events."[8] This faith would soon mature into one of her core beliefs that to be effective as a person, we must pay attention to our experience and trust our inner voice. When she lectured her manner was gracious and electric. Her friend and colleague, E. M. Standing, commented on this. "One of the reasons why Dr. Montessori's lectures had such a widespread appeal was that she never treated educational problems on a purely technical or utilitarian level. Her appeal was always to the spirit."[9]

Period of Discovery

In 1906, at the age of thirty six, Montessori was offered the chance to further test her emerging beliefs that every child has untapped hidden potentials and that all children would benefit from a new form of experiential education. This experiment would begin with a strong faith in children's inner potentials and a basic trust in their ability to direct themselves in the process of unveiling their authentic nature.

This amazing experiment started in San Lorenzo, a dirty, crime-ridden slum area of Rome. The Roman Real Estate Association decided to minimally fix up enough of the many dilapidated apartment buildings to ultimately house about one thousand people. They were motivated by the accolades they might receive for carrying out this "urban renewal" project and the money they could make by only doing basic renovations. When the project was completed they wanted to ensure that the property would be kept up, so to accomplish this they only allowed employed married couples to rent the facilities. This answered one concern, but it didn't answer the concern of what to do with the children who would be left without supervision while their parents worked. Their main concern was that the unattended children would physically harm the apartment buildings. They decided that the best thing to do would be to have someone come in and take care of the children. The person they thought to ask was Dr. Maria Montessori.

In spite of criticism from her colleagues, Montessori enthusiastically accepted this offer. She saw this as an opportunity to use the educational materials that had been so successful with mentally challenged children with normal children. In addition she wanted this to be a place where parents could be involved so they would have a better understanding of how to support the development of their children. Involving parents in the children's education was a new idea for the culture.

On January 6, 1907 the Casa dei Bambini (Children's House) opened its doors to fifty children between the ages of two and six. The space allotted for the children was on the ground floor of one of the apartment buildings. The only furniture provided was a few rough tables for children, an adult desk and a set of locked cabinets. Montessori received money from some of the society women to purchase toys and materials for the children. In addition, she brought in the sensory materials that she had used with mentally challenged children. Montessori hired another woman to actually be in charge of the children on a daily basis so that she could regularly observe the children and direct the teacher according to what she saw. She said, "I merely wanted to study the children's reactions. I asked her not to interfere with them in any way as otherwise I would not be able to observe them."[10]

The first children arrived frightened, crying and resistant. In spite of this, Montessori respected each of them and helped them feel safe. Rather than speaking harshly, criticizing or demanding obedience from them, she thoughtfully talked to them and patiently demonstrated simple hygiene and practical living skills to help them be more independent. She relates a time when she showed the children how to blow their noses. They were so excited and impressed with her demonstration that they actually started clapping.

Over the next few weeks the children's behavior moved from disinterest and rebellion to enthusiasm and interest as they began to learn practical living skills and work with the sensory materials Montessori had provided. The children looked healthier, their self confidence increased, and their behavior toward one another became cooperative rather than competitive. This wave of change was just the beginning of Montessori's path of discovering what the children were capable of doing and being. Following are some of her initial insights into the authentic nature of the child.

CONCENTRATION AND REPETITION

One day when Montessori visited the classroom, she noticed a three-year old girl intently working with one of the sensory materials that required her to place specific graded cylinders into their corresponding sockets in a wooden block. This required her to remove the cylinders from the block, mix them up, and put them back into their proper places. Montessori noticed that the child was repeating this exercise over and over again. Wanting to know how much concentration the child actually had, she asked the teacher to have the rest of the children march and sing, but this did not disturb the girl's concentration. Montessori then gently lifted the chair the girl was sitting in and placed the child and the chair on the low table where she was sitting. The child holding on to the materials placed the objects on her knees and continued to repeat the exercise many times. After more than forty two repetitions she stopped. Montessori described it this way, "Then she stopped as if coming out of a dream and smiled happily. Her eyes shone brightly and she looked about. She had not even noticed what we had done to disturb her."[11]

Through this experience and many others like it Montessori discovered that children have a great capacity to focus their energy and repeat an activity over and over again until they are satisfied or master the concept. She also recognized that children have the ability to concentrate for long periods of time, and when they come out of this state of concentration, they have connected to their authentic nature of peace and calm.

LOVE OF ORDER

Another discovery Montessori made was that children between the ages of one and six are in a sensitive period for physical order because this is how they learn to organize their mental world. When the school first opened the teacher distributed the learning materials to the children and, when they were finished, she returned the materials to a locked cabinet. Montessori observed that the children would then follow the teacher to see where she put them. Montessori interpreted this to mean that the children wanted to be able to put their own work back in the cabinet. From that time on, the children were allowed to return their own work to the cabinet.

OPEN SHELVES AND FREEDOM OF CHOICE

Another similar insight came one morning when the teacher didn't arrive on time and visitors came to see the school. The children took the initiative to take the visitors into the school, and because the cabinet had accidentally been left unlocked the night before, the children opened the doors, took out appropriate activities and began to thoughtfully work on their chosen tasks. From this point on, Montessori realizing that the locked cabinet was not necessary, put all of the activities on open shelves for the children and offered them the freedom to select activities that they were interested in and prepared for.

CHILDREN PREFERRED WORK

Originally there were both toys and educational materials available for the children to select. Time and time again, the children demonstrated that they would rather work with the educational activities than play with the toys. She came to the astonishing realization that the children found a deep inner satisfaction when they were engaged in meaningful work.

NO NEED FOR REWARD AND PUNISHMENT

As Montessori observed the teacher using rewards and punishment to attempt to control the children's behavior, she saw that they did not respond positively to either. The rewards of candy or small prizes did not seem to affect them. She observed that many times they would leave the reward and engage themselves in their work of choice. As far as punishment, she observed that when children were humiliated or shamed for their behavior, it only created more animosity within them. Her insight was that the best form of discipline is the inner discipline that comes from children being meaningfully engaged in work. She observed that when children are engaged in work that interests them, they naturally control their impulses so they can concentrate on their work. As they do this they experience inner satisfaction emanating from their Authentic Self. From this place, there is no desire to misbehave. She came to believe that "naughtiness" is an unnatural state—a place of disconnection from the child's true nature. She called this disconnection a "deviation" from the "normal" state of authenticity.

JOY OF SILENCE

A small baby was the spark that shed light on children's love of silence. One morning Montessori came into the classroom carrying a sleeping four month old baby. The baby was very still and she wanted to share this beautiful stillness with the children. She pointed out how softly the child was breathing. In a joking manner she told them, "None of you could do so well."[12] Spontaneously the children began to imitate the breathing of the baby and sit with complete stillness, silence and joy. From that time forward, special times of silence were practiced in the classroom because it brought such joy to the children. When in silence they were connecting to their Authentic Self.

FREEDOM TO MOVE AND LEARN

From the beginning Montessori recognized the importance of movement in the learning process. She discovered that children remember more when they are able to physically involve themselves through movement and the use of their five senses. To facilitate this need to move she designed materials that utilized both movement and the senses. In addition, she designed furniture, shelving and materials that were child size and moveable so the children could be comfortable, freely move about the classroom and easily use the concrete materials provided for them. In addition she brought both plants and animals into the classroom so the children could be engaged in their care.

FREEDOM AND DISCIPLINE

Freedom never meant chaos in the Montessori classroom. What she meant was that children should have the freedom to act constructively within well-defined limits. When asked by others if by freedom she meant anarchy she replied, "A room in which all the children move about usefully, intelligently, and voluntarily, without committing any rough or rude act, would seem to me a classroom very well disciplined indeed."[13] The children were free to move about the classroom, select their work and stay with it as long as they had interest in it. If a child became unfocused the adult in the classroom, would give him time to re-engage on his own; however, if this didn't happen, the child would be respectfully redirected into meaningful work. The teacher's responsibility was to guide the children and make certain that they made appropriate choices that would further their development and education. Montessori recognized that when children were engaged in constructive work that corresponded to their readiness their natural goodness came forth.

CONTINUOUS LEARNING

In addition to the above insights, Montessori continued to discover what the children needed and what they were capable of accomplishing. A classic story is how the children learned to read and write. The shared attitude of the time was that children should not be allowed to write or read before the age of six. However, some of the children began asking Montessori to show them how to do it. When the children's parents, many of whom couldn't read or write themselves, also began to ask her to help their children learn how to read and write she began to explore this possibility.

To begin this process she created two separate sets of alphabet letters. One was a set of cardboard letters that the children could manipulate and the other was a set of sandpaper letters which were mounted on a little wooden block. These were designed to allow the children to trace the letters with their index and middle fingers of their writing hand. As children began to work with these letters, they were given the phonetic sound of the letter rather than the name. The children were attracted to these letters and worked with them. Then one day a child made the connection that he could build words by listening to the sounds in each word and laying out the corresponding letters on the rug. This was an exciting discovery.

The next level came one day when Montessori was up on the roof terrace with a group of children. She gave one of the boys a piece of chalk to draw a picture on the tiles of the roof. Once he had completed this request, he shouted out, "I can write, I can write." He then knelt down on the tiles and wrote out the word "*mano*" which means "hand" in Italian. He was so enthusiastic that other children came to watch his great accomplishment. Then several of them asked for a turn with the chalk and they, too, successfully wrote words. In Montessori's words, "The first word written by my little ones aroused within themselves an indescribable emotion of joy."[14]

Montessori watched the children explode into writing and saw them writing words over and over again, but they still could not read. Then six months later it happened! She wrote a short sentence on the chalkboard which said, "If you love me, give me a kiss. If you can read this, come to me." On the fourth day a young girl went up to her and said, "Eccomi (Here I am")[15] As each child realized that his ability to write gave him the ability to eventually read another explosion into reading occurred. The children had discovered a new means of silent communication—writing and reading.

The World Hears of the "Miracles"

Dr. Montessori was a master observer of children. She brought both her scientific observational skills as well as her intuitive skills to her work and through this combination was able to see in children what others could not. Over the years she continued to develop educational materials and activities that met children's needs and interests, and because they were satisfied, motivated and respected, they manifested an entirely different set of behaviors than had been seen before. According to Montessori this happened because, "The children found no obstacles in the way of their development. They had nothing to hide, nothing to fear, nothing to shun. It was as simple as that."[16] In this special environment, the children moved from being sullen, uninterested and rebellious to joyous, curious and cooperative children. Montessori had discovered the intrinsic qualities of children. Within one year, the public began to flock to the Casa dei Bambini to witness firsthand this miraculous discovery. The word was out, "New Children have been born!"

Many people began visiting the Casa dei Bambini to view for themselves this new form of education and its positive effect on the children. Most people went away amazed and told others of the miracles that were taking place. Newspaper articles were circulated which brought additional visitors from various professions and levels of society. This educational experiment even attracted Italy's Queen Margherita who visited the Casa a number of times. She was heard to say, "I prophesy that a new philosophy of life will arise from what we are learning from these little children."[17] This type of reaction not only happened in Italy but people began to visit from various other European countries as well. Interest in this new educational phenomenon soon went beyond the shores of Europe to such countries as the United States, Canada, Argentina, New Zealand, India, China and Japan.

In 1909 Dr. Montessori wrote her first book, *The Montessori Method*, which described the philosophy, activities and practices being used in her schools. It was translated into over twenty languages. During this same time period she offered her first training course for about one hundred people. Many of these people opened Montessori schools throughout Italy and in other countries. The same magical transformation of the children took place in these new schools as well. By 1911, just four years after opening the first Casa dei Bambini, the Montessori system was adopted in the public schools of Italy and Switzerland.

At this same time, an influential journalist in the United States, S.S. McClure, reported on the first Montessori School that Anne George had opened in the United States in October of 1911. The same amazing results were duplicated in the American school and McClure made sure to let his American audience know of its success. This drew the attention of such public figures in the United States as, Thomas Edison, Alexander Graham Bell, his wife Mabel Hubbard Bell and Margaret Wilson, the daughter of President Woodrow Wilson. In fact in 1912 the Bell's opened a Montessori school for their two grandchildren and a few children from their neighborhood in Washington D.C. By 1913 there were nearly a hundred Montessori Schools in the United States.

In 1913 Montessori was invited to the United States to do a series of lectures under the direction of McClure. Her first lecture was in Washington, D.C. and was attended by over four hundred people. While there she visited with the US Commissioner of Education, who indicated that he would like to see the Montessori system introduced into the public schools. When in New York, she lectured at Carnegie Hall to a packed house of five thousand people. While in Philadelphia she met and visited with the famous Helen Keller. She traveled for three weeks and all along the way enthusiasm grew for this new approach to educating children.

Montessori returned to the United States in 1915 to demonstrate her work at the Panama-Pacific International Exposition in California. While at the Exposition she set up a demonstration class in a glass covered pavilion so that people could actually see a Montessori classroom in action. The experience went very well and she was awarded one of the two gold medals offered in the field of education. She returned one last time in 1917 to give a teacher training course in southern California and visit schools in the area. World War I began and she never returned to the United States to oversee, guide or offer teacher training. Due to this and other events the interest in Montessori education in the United States declined significantly. It wasn't until the late 1950's that the enthusiasm and interest in Montessori education began an ongoing Renaissance.

From 1915 until 1939, Montessori's popularity in other parts of the world continued to increase and she spent most of her time lecturing, offering teacher training, and overseeing the proliferation of Montessori schools in Europe and other places such as India. In 1939, as World War II was festering, she accepted an invitation to live in India where she established schools, offered teacher training and deepened her practice. During the seven years she resided there she had the opportunity to work with older children and further develop the elementary and adolescent programs. While there she connected with Mahatma Gandhi who deeply admired her work with children. They both believed in the dignity of the child, agreed that character building should be a major goal of education and that the way to bring this about was through meaningful work. Montessori not only felt physically at home in India, she also experienced a deep philosophical connection to the wisdom of the East which is further discussed in Chapter 3.

In 1946, following the end of World War II, Montessori returned to Amsterdam to live and continue her work until her death in 1952. In this same year she was nominated for the third time to receive the Nobel Peace Prize for her significant contribution to the education of children.

Conclusion

Over the past fifty years Montessori education has had a rebirth and resurgence throughout the globe. The second wave of Montessori education in the United States began with a single preschool established in 1958. Currently in the United States, there are over 4,400 Montessori schools that include head start programs, private, public, charter and magnet schools. There are schools that offer infant/toddler, preschool, lower elementary, upper elementary, middle school, and high school education. Enthusiasm for the Montessori approach to teaching children has also exploded onto the international scene where there are over 8,000 Montessori Schools on all six continents. At this point in time Montessori education is the largest single pedagogy or science of teaching in the world today and the educational success story of the century.

On January 6, 2007, there were a number of celebrations worldwide to commemorate the 100th Anniversary of the opening of the original Casa dei Bambini. The aim of the centenary celebration was to continue to fulfill Montessori's core mission: To place all the children in our world at the center of society and to assist them in becoming the transforming elements leading to a harmonious and peaceful humanity.[18]

Montessori professionals are committed to carrying on the philosophy and practices that Maria Montessori developed on her pathway of discovering the authentic child. In addition to their work in the schools, Montessori educators are also committed to helping parents implement this philosophy and practice in the home. The more Montessori professionals and parents collaboratively offer the children a consistent approach, the easier it will be for the world's children to manifest their authentic nature and lead us to a more "harmonious and peaceful humanity."

Suggestions for Follow Through

■ Find a special journal or notebook, put a picture on the front that inspires you and dedicate it as your Parenting Journal. Use it frequently to record your observations and reflections in your role as a parent.

■ Close your eyes and remember what it was like to be a small child. Remember a person (parent, relative, teacher, etc) who made you feel special. Record the following:

1. List the emotions and qualities that you felt when you were in that person's presence.

2. List the behaviors and qualities he/she demonstrated in your presence.

■ Reflect on what qualities and behaviors you want to consistently demonstrate to your child. Record this in your journal.

■ Write and complete this sentence in your journal. When my child remembers me, I want him to say that I was _____

_____.

CHAPTER 2

The Child's Place in the Universe

"We shall walk together on this path of life, for all things are part of the universe and are connected with each other to form one whole unity. This idea helps the mind of the child to become fixed, to stop wandering in an aimless quest for knowledge. He is satisfied, having found the universal center of himself with all things."[1]

—MARIA MONTESSORI

Imagine that you are in a beautiful garden with lovely trees offering patterns of sun and shade to the green grasses, the flowers, and the nests where many birds care for their young. Be aware of the many varieties of flowers, each of which has its own unique shape, color, fragrance and inspiration for you. As you look closer, be aware of the tiny insects climbing along the flower petals, the bees gathering nectar and the butterflies brushing the flower's stamens to participate in the fertilization process. While enjoying this fascinating dance become aware of the symphony of natural sounds in nature's amphitheater. Behold the chirping sounds of the sparrows, the cawing of the crows, the buzzing of the hummingbirds, and the cooing of the doves as well as the water gently falling into the glistening water of a small pond. Are you not in awe?

In such a transcendent moment, one may experience a brief glimpse into the amazing interconnectedness of the web of life. The earth, the sun, the water and the air are the four dynamic elements that make plant, animal and human life possible on our planet. Each element is necessary to sustain the whole and a higher cosmic power is the creator of it all. For us to be the most effective parents and teachers of our children, it is imperative that we embrace an awareness and appreciation of the physical as well as the spiritual interrelationship of all life and our part in it. Montessori described the importance of helping children center in the reality of their spiritual nature.

> *If the work of man on the earth is related to his spirit, to his creative intelligence, then his spirit and his intelligence must be the fulcrum of his existence, and of all the workings of his body. About this fulcrum his behavior is organized and even his physical economy. The whole man develops within a kind of spiritual halo.*[2]

It is important that we see our task of parenting in a holistic framework that includes the authentic nature of the universe, the child and ourselves. The framework we use includes the physical, mental, emotional and spiritual dimensions of both the child and the adult. In this chapter, we discuss children's inherent goodness, Maria Montessori's philosophical view of the cosmos, the principal of holistic synergy, and the perennial question of "Who Am I?" Through this discussion we show that the authentic nature of both adults and children is intimately connected to the spiritual nature of the universe. With this realization, we develop a new paradigm of deeper respect for ourselves, our children and life which creates a preventative cushion allowing uninterrupted growth for the child. The attitudes, tools and techniques of parenting become more natural as we are filled with an increased power of love and wisdom.

Children's Inherent Goodness

To appease the materialists, logical positivists, behaviorists and technocrats, whose thinking has dominated the modern age, we adults often restrict ourselves to a limited view of human nature and our children. Too often educators see children as animals to be conditioned and trained, machines to be programmed and fixed, parts on an assembly line to be put together and manufactured, or empty buckets to be filled. We tend to ignore children's emotional and spiritual natures and often view them as challenges to be dealt with, sinners to be saved, emotional cases to be cured, or deviants to be contained. This limited view of the child results in a negative or incomplete view of human nature that inhibits the full development of children's potentials and talents. It is far more beneficial for us to see the child as naturally and enthusiastically prepared to realize his potentials and fulfill his cosmic task.

Centuries ago Plato's idealism of human nature was almost buried by Aristotelian rational thinking. This rational, logical scientific thinking of Aristotle has made it possible for us to create amazing physical inventions in our world; but, in the process we have often neglected the idealistic spiritual authentic nature of humans as seen by Plato.

Maria Montessori's contribution to the modern world was to see children anew in the original glory that the ancient ideal has always maintained. She affirmed that, "Man is a sculptor of himself, urged by a mysterious inner force to the attainment of an ideal determined form. Growth may be defined as a seeking after perfection, given by an impulse of life."[3] In the next chapter we discuss more fully the role of the inner guide and vital life force as it relates to the child's development. Montessori re-introduced an awareness of the child's Authentic Self to our educational process, parenting methods and cultural awareness.

It is imperative to clarify our personal views of our child's essential nature because these underlying core beliefs determine how we relate to our child. The personal belief system we embrace actually creates a self-fulfilling prophecy for our child. What we reflect to him becomes the mirror through which he views and defines himself. Seeing our child from a positive point of view allows and calls forth his spiritual nature of goodness and love.

For over 100 years Montessori philosophy and practice have been successfully implemented by people of all spiritual and religious persuasions throughout the world. Recognizing the authentic spiritual nature of children is a universal principal not limited by religious persuasion. Aline Wolf reminds us that, "Spirituality is a basic quality of human nature; the practice of a particular religion is the way that many people choose to give voice to their spirituality."[4]

In order to understand and practice Montessori philosophy in the home, and see our child's inherent goodness, it is important to adopt a view of human nature that reflects our child's authentic spiritual nature. Affirming the child in this manner requires our delving into the question of the intrinsic nature of humanity and life—a deep philosophical and metaphysical question. We all have a metaphysical point of view or paradigm of how we view life. In this book we discuss what Maria Montessori believed as well as our own personal beliefs. We do not ask you to adopt either approach; instead, we encourage you to reflect on your own belief system to see if it reflects a consistent and positive view of your child.

Montessori's Philosophical View
of the Cosmos

Dr. Maria Montessori was a scientist and also a mystic. She was a brilliant woman who studied the sciences in great detail to learn all she could about the physical nature of life. Her studies included chemistry, physics, zoology, botany, biology, math, anthropology and psychology. Throughout her life she was dedicated to uncovering life's mysteries.

In addition to her pursuit of scientific knowledge, she was a woman of great faith who believed in a spiritual connection within all beings. From an early age Maria Montessori displayed compassion for others and a strong inner knowing that she had a mission to fulfill. Of course, she did not know the exact nature of her work, but step by step, followed her intuition and prepared herself for what was to come. It was the combination of her quest for scientific understanding coupled with her compassion and faith that allowed her to facilitate the process of unveiling the child's true nature.

Through Montessori's scientific study, observation and intuitive knowing she came to see the universe as one connected whole. "All is strictly interrelated on this planet.... We may compare it with a tapestry: each detail is a piece of embroidery; the whole constitutes a magnificent cloth."[5] In addition to Montessori's view of the universe, there are a number of scientists, such as Pierre Teilhard de Chardin, who also see the spiritual connection between all elements of the universe. Brian Swimme, a current metaphysical scientist said the following about Teilhard de Chardin's work.

> *His most important achievement was to articulate the significance of the new story of evolution. He was the first major thinker in the West to fully articulate that evolution. Teilhard de Chardin in the West and Sri Aurobindo in India really arrived at the same basic vision, which is that the unfolding of the universe is a physical evolution and also a spiritual evolution.*[6]

By definition the word "cosmos" is "the universe as an ordered system." Montessori recognized this order. As a scientist Dr Montessori affirmed the interconnection of the physical universe, and, as a spiritual person, she connected it to a divine source of creation. She saw that all things in the universe exist as an individual part that cannot exist alone as separate from the whole. Everything is dependent on everything else for the cosmos to exist. She recognized that when something happens to a single part of the whole, all parts are affected. Today the terms used to express this interconnection of all aspects of life have been referred to as deep ecology, string theory, systems theory or holistic theory.

We can better understand and nurture our child's process of development by seeing it unfold as a series of systems interconnected within many other systems. A child's behavior is not linked to a single cause but by many systems interacting simultaneously such as his physical, mental, emotional and spiritual systems, his social (family and/or peer) system or even the weather system. For example, a child may start crying (emotional reaction) because he falls down (physical system) and when he sees his mom (family system) he expects comfort (mental system) and begins to relax (physical system) and feel calmer (emotional system). When comforted by mom (family system) he feels love in his heart (spiritual system).

Montessori's faith in the child's divine birthright formed the foundation of her belief in the spiritual nature of the child as well as all nature. She believed in both Creationist and Evolutionary theories. She did not create a quarrel over intelligent design vs. evolution. She saw the cosmos as being inherently divine in one interconnected whole and humanity evolving through a natural, divinely inspired evolutionary process. She recognized that children are more than biological zygotes or products of a physical evolutionary process. She saw them as being endowed with a spiritual embryo. Just as the children's physical bodies evolve through a natural process of growth, she recognized that their mental and spiritual natures also evolve naturally through specific patterns and sequences. She saw the human journey as a cosmic adventure where all things are connected in a beautiful cosmic whole.

In her work with children Montessori clearly described the evolution of physical life, the interconnection and interdependence of all life forms as well as their specific purpose for being created on the planet. Included in this view is the idea that each child comes to earth with a unique purpose or cosmic task to fulfill. This knowledge is important for children as it gives them a sense of purpose and connection to all life. As she worked with the children she saw them respond enthusiastically to the concept of an interrelated, purposeful web of life that she called the "cosmic plan." She explained its importance in the following excerpt:

> If the idea of the universe be presented to the child in the right way, it will do more for him than just arouse his interest, for it will create in him admiration and wonder, a feeling loftier than any interest and more satisfying. The child's mind then will no longer wander, but becomes fixed and can work. The knowledge he then acquires is organized and systematic; his intelligence becomes whole and complete because of the vision of the whole that has been presented to him.... He is satisfied, having found the universal center of himself with all things.[7]

The child is the integration and synthesis of all aspects of the cosmos—the universe, consciousness, body, mind, emotions and spirit. The child's cosmic task is to create this unity and realize his unique contribution to life. When this endeavor is blocked and he is unable to bring these aspects of his life into harmony, his ability to unveil his authenticity is diminished. Montessori believed that, "It is not a good thing to cut life in two, using the limbs for games and the head for books. Life should be a single whole."[8] The single whole is the power of love within the child that also encircles all of life's creations. She realized that love springs from the child and the child springs from a higher being, which is also love.

Giving children a view of the interconnectedness of the universe instills love in their heart, enthuses them to the core and provides them with gifts of respect and gratitude for all life. Montessori concludes that "The fundamental principle in education is correlation of all subjects, and their centralization in the cosmic plan."[9]

Holistic Synergy

The concept of "holistic synergy" is often explained as, "The whole is greater than the sum of its parts." Each part changes the whole; as the whole changes the part. What does this mean and how does it relate to parenting? A wind chime hangs silently in the garden until a slight breeze gently touches one chime that touches the next chime, the next and the next until a beautiful symphony is resonating on the wind. The individual "parts" are the chimes and the "whole" is the symphony resonating on the wind. Another example is an orchestra where individual musicians with their unique instruments contribute their specific "parts" to the group. When this happens the "whole" becomes an amazing harmonic hum or cosmic vibration where the whole is definitely greater than the sum of its parts.

The family structure consists of individual people who live, work and play together. When these activities are done in a spirit of love and harmony, there is a special glow or feeling of euphoria that emanates in the family. This glow is the "whole" that is greater than the sum of each of the "parts" (family members). In this state, things flow smoothly and cooperation abounds. Parents learn to look to themselves, as well as other influences, to create a nurturing climate for the child.

Why are celebrations so effective? It is because we usually come to the occasion with an open heart and a sharing attitude. We willingly set aside our daily worries and open ourselves to the joy of the celebration. Is it possible to live everyday as a celebration? In other words, can we set aside our worries and walk in awareness and gratitude throughout each day? The more we can do this, the more we, and the members of our families, will experience the joy and satisfaction of the synergetic glow.

The concept of synergy also relates to how children learn most effectively. They learn, not by absorbing single unrelated concepts but, by interacting with related concepts within their environments. As these related concepts or "parts" come together in the subconscious mind, almost as by magic a new idea is created as the "whole." An example of how this happens can be illustrated by the Pink Tower Principle. Within all Montessori early childhood (3 to 6 years of age) classrooms there is an activity called the Pink Tower which consists of ten cubes ranging in size from 1 cm to 10 cm. When using this work the child creates a relationship between the random cubes or "parts" by placing them vertically in sequential order from the biggest to the smallest. By doing this he creates a Pink Tower. Beyond the simple building of a tower, the child grasps what is even greater than the sum of the parts—he discovers the greater "whole"—the qualities of gradation. When the cubes are parts, they are just parts; when combined they form a *tower*, a whole new entity. When the cubes are assembled in relationship to one another, the child *experiences* the concepts of gradation such as big, bigger and biggest as well as small smaller and smallest.

Montessori early childhood classrooms are designed with holistic synergy in mind. Each new educational concept in the areas of: practical living, sensorial exploration, math, language, geography, history, science, art, music and peace education has corresponding concrete materials. These materials are sequentially (easiest to hardest) placed on the shelves in their corresponding area of study. A child is attracted to specific activities in the environment based on his unfolding interests. As he learns a new concept, the impressions are stored in his subconscious mind. As he continues this process of indirectly absorbing various concepts or "parts," his subconscious mind simultaneously makes connections to form a larger "whole." The child experiences great jubilation when he suddenly discovers that he knows something new. An example of this is when a child suddenly realizes that he can read. When asked how he learned, he will say, "I learned it all by myself," or "I just know how." It is this holistic synergetic process of connecting individual patterns to higher levels of abstraction that creates the child's intelligence and expands his consciousness. This process of learning how to learn aids the child throughout his life. As a teacher, there is no greater joy than being in a classroom when 20–25 children are thoughtfully engaged in their self-chosen work of learning. The harmonic hum or synergy in the classroom is magical!

We can have many links on a chain, but the links are only useful when they are attached to one another. Likewise, three sticks scattered on the ground are just three sticks scattered on the ground; however, when we lash them together to form a triangle, an entirely new structure is formed that does not represent the sum of the sticks. With a triangle we can construct a skyscraper. An individual part connected to a larger whole creates an entirely new kind of entity. A child unveils his Authentic Self by making meaningful connections with life. This concept is elaborated throughout the book.

The more we develop our ability to see life from a systems point of view and observe our own conditioning, the more effective we will be as parents and teachers. To nurture the authentic nature of the child we must go beyond the parts and see the holistic pattern of child development. When we understand, accept, and apply these principles, we greatly enhance our educational and parenting skills.

Who Am I?

Once, a friend of ours (Mike) went to a concert with his friend (Joe) who worked the sound system. At the conclusion of the performance, Mike waited outside the stage door for Joe to come out. A wide-eyed young woman approached Mike with a pen and program in hand looking for an autograph. She asked Mike if he was a "somebody," and he quickly answered that he was a "nobody." The young woman left disappointed and our friend, Mike, began to reflect on what he had just said. He realized that he had told the young woman that he was a "nobody." This was not accurate! He realized that he was neither a "somebody" nor a "nobody." The next question he asked himself was, "If I am not "somebody" and I am not a "nobody," then who am I?" This is the oldest question of man? Who am I?

When parents are asked the question "Who are you?," they quickly respond by saying, "I am Mary." "I am John." "I live here." "I do that." "I have this." "I am a parent." etc. It quickly dawns on them, however, that there is something more, something deeper and intrinsic in the core of their being. We are not defined by what we eat, think or do; we are not our zip code, SAT score, bank account or any other external factor. These things say, of course, something important about us, but they do not define our essential nature. How we define ourselves and how we define our child greatly influences how we relate to our child.

Montessori states that "The energy that can help mankind is that which lies within the child. We must insist upon the attainment of the ancient ideal contained in the saying, "know thyself!"[10] The Delphic oracle, as well as all the sages, philosophers and poets down through ages likewise cry out. "Know Thyself." Shakespeare sums up the plea when he says "To thine own self be true, and it must follow, as the night the day, thou canst not then, be false to any man."[11]

What then exactly is our "inner" nature? What are the energies, the essence and the true inherency of our inner being? Who are we? Seriously, who are we really?

Dr. Montessori was not an alchemist. She did not attempt to start out with a gross material and turn it into gold. She started with gold. By seeing children as already gold, she discovered that they are not human beings trying to be spiritual but spiritual beings placed here on earth to learn how to be human. This is accomplished by consciously developing their potentials here on earth.

Because of her strong faith in the innate goodness of each child, she was able to free herself of the common adult attitudes of her time that blocked and prevented the fullest manifestation of the child's authenticity. Her strong faith and belief in the divinity within each child allowed her to discover the unique characteristics of the developing life of the child's personality. Montessori speaks of "two faiths that can uphold man: faith in God and faith in himself. And these two faiths should exist side by side."[12]

Montessori was not the first to recognize a divine source of creation dwelling within humanity and all creation. Many spiritual traditions, philosophers and sages have also identified the authentic nature of children and all humanity as being connected to Divinity, not different and separate.

The Christian Bible states that God and man are connected and therefore inherently good.

> *So God created man in his own image, in the image of God created he him; male and female created he them.... And God saw everything that he had made, and behold, it was very good.*[13]

Jesus prayed,

> *That they all may be one; as thou, Father, art in me, and I in thee, that they also may be one in us.... And the glory which thou gavest me I have given them; that they may be one, even as we are one.*[14]

In the Torah of the Jewish tradition we find:

> *So God created man in his image, in the image of God.*[15]

In the Muslim Quran we read:

> *Behold I thy Lord said to the angels: "I am about to create man, from sounding clay from mud molded into shape; When I have fashioned him, and breathed into him My Spirit, Fall you down in obeisance unto him SO the angels prostrated all of them together.*[16]

43

In the Hindu tradition we hear this from Swami Rama:

You are not just the reflection of God; you are a replica of God. If God means creator, then the creator's creativity is in you. If God means beauty, then that beauty is you, and is in you. If God means love, then that love is you. If God means the power to be and the power to become, then that power is you. Therefore, you have the capacity to become whatever you wish.[17]

In the Buddhist tradition this concept is illuminated in *The Teaching of Buddha.*

Buddha-nature exists in everyone no matter how deeply it may be covered over by greed, anger and foolishness, or buried by his own deeds and retribution. Buddha-nature cannot be lost or destroyed: and when all defilements are removed, sooner or later it will reappear.[18]

Conclusion

Maria Montessori saw the divinity within adults as well as children and recognized how powerful it is when adults realize who they really are and who the child really is. When we embrace and act from our Authentic Self we connect to our source of inner wisdom that guides us to know how to best nurture our child. To know who we are is to know what to do.

When adults see the child as a sacred being, deep respect automatically follows. It has been scientifically shown, that when teachers see their students as being capable, the students perform at higher levels. This phenomenon is called "the self-fulfilling prophecy." The deeper our faith and trust in the child's Authentic Self, the more effective we will be as parents and teachers.

Maria Montessori brought a combination of great faith in the human Spirit, scientific understanding of child development and observation skills to her first school. Within a short time, she began to see results that she had never witnessed before and was continually amazed at what was being revealed to her by the children. In her words,

> *One day, in great emotion, I took my heart in my two hands as though to encourage it to rise to the heights of faith, and I stood respectfully before the children, saying to myself: "Who are you then? Have I perhaps met with the children who were held in Christ's arms and to whom the divine words were spoken? I will follow you, to enter with you into the Kingdom of Heaven." And holding in my hands the torch of faith I went on my way.*[19]

Suggestions for Follow Through

■ **Observe the synchronicity of nature**. Find an inspiring place to sit in nature. Take some deep breaths, clear your mind and observe the beauties around you. Watch how the various aspects of life that you observe are connected to one another. Record your observations and/or draw what you see.

■ **Reflect on the miracle of birth**. Find a quiet place, take some deep breaths and revisit the emotions and inspiration you experienced at the birth of a child. Reflect on the miracle of life that entered with the first breath taken by the infant. Write down your feelings and reflections in your Parenting Journal.

■ **Frequently express your love**. Consciously and frequently tell your children how special they are and how much you love them. Let them know they have a special Light of Love or Spirit within them that is their authentic nature.

■ **Demonstrate to your children that they have a spirit of light and love within them**. In Sonnie's book, *Honoring the Light of the Child: Activities to Nurture Peaceful Living Skills in Young Children*, Activity One—entitled "See My Love" gives a step by step procedure and concrete materials to demonstrate this vital concept to the children.[20]

CHAPTER 3

The Child's Authentic Nature

*"The child's true constructive energy, a dynamic power,
has remained unnoticed for thousands of years. Just as men
have trodden the earth, and later tilled its surface,
without thought for the immense wealth hidden in its depths,
so the men of our day make progress after progress in civilized life,
without noticing the treasures that lie hidden
in the psychic world of infancy."[1]*

—MARIA MONTESSORI

Just as men have tilled the earth's surface and not noticed its hidden treasures, parents and teachers often see only the surface nature of the child and ignore the authentic nature hidden deep within. When we inaccurately identify children's nature by what we see them demonstrate on the surface through their behavior, we limit children's mental and spiritual growth. To fully nurture the hidden potential buried in the child's soul, we must learn to see what lies beneath the surface of the child's personality.

As described earlier the child's Authentic Self is connected to a divine source in an inclusive field of Cosmic Consciousness. Montessori realized that, in its deepest essence, the child has a divinely created "spiritual embryo" which will forever remain his connection to the universal good, the protector and forbearer of potentials and the empowerment to fulfill his purpose throughout life.

Montessori often referred to the mysteries surrounding the phenomenon of the spiritual embryo as the "secret of childhood," and refers to this divine essence in many ways throughout her writing, such as: "Spirit," "psychic entity," and "inner teacher." In Western Europe she was ahead of her time when she recognized the authentic nature of the child as an embryonic spiritual essence that is universal and connected to a divine source. "The newborn child should be seen as a 'spiritual embryo'—a spirit enclosed in flesh in order to come into the world."[2]

Through her work she recognized that within the child's spiritual embryo there are innumerable potentials as well as an inner guide and vital life force prepared to assist the child in the manifestation of these potentialities. Her observations revealed a dynamic inner structure that, if properly nurtured by parents and teachers, encourages children to realize their potentials and become balanced, fulfilled adults. Our purpose in writing this chapter is to more fully describe the dynamic authentic nature of children so parents and teachers will better understand how to nurture children's growth and development. We describe the general functions of the Mind and Spirit and show how each function relates to the authentic nature of the child.

The Internal Functions of Mind and Spirit

Through her life and work Dr. Montessori recognized that the child's Spirit and creative intelligence needed to be the fulcrum around which all his behavior is organized if he is to fulfill his full potential. She once expressed that, "Today, even our Western ideas have become receptive to this idea which has been prominent in Indian philosophy."[3] While in India Montessori was exposed to and found that she had an affinity with Eastern thought as expressed by the Theosophists, Gandhi, Tagore and other great teachers of the ancient Vedantic tradition. It appears that her ideas about education and the authentic nature of the child are compatible with Eastern philosophy and psychology even though her educational philosophy and child psychology were formed independently of these traditions. Her experiences while living in India reinforced, validated and encouraged her own thinking. While there she was immersed in a spiritual milieu that was built on the same fulcrum as her own—the spiritual connection of all life.

As we describe the concept of the authentic nature of the child in this chapter, we draw from our own study of Eastern philosophy and psychology. Many years ago, when we were first exposed to the ideas of Montessori education, we simultaneously had the good fortune of meeting and studying with the venerable Swami Rama of the Himalayas. Swami Rama was a sage and yogic master who came to America to share and integrate the ancient science of yoga with Western thought. One of his many contributions was to share a holistic model of the mind that clearly describes the Mind's inner functions and its connection to the Spirit or Authentic Self. We immediately noted the similarities of Dr. Montessori's view of the spiritual embryo and the model of the mind as presented through Yoga Psychology.[4] While her thoughts are not exactly the same in all aspects, the overlap and compatibility between the two models is striking. By sharing this model of the mind and integrating it with Montessori's view, we hope to add clarity and authority to Montessori's conclusions. Her cosmic view of the child might have been new to the Western world, but it resonates strongly with the Eastern wisdom of the ages.

The spiritual embryo that Montessori describes consists of both the mental and spiritual characteristics of the child. The following model illustrates the various functions of mind within all of us and its connection to the spiritual realm. Please note that this is a functional representation of the mind, not a visual map of the brain. In other words, we can take a concrete picture of the eyes and ears; however, we can't take a visual picture of the function of "seeing" or "hearing" any more than we can take a visual picture of spirit or the vast expanse of consciousness. Modern imaging techniques can capture more and more of the physical world of brain and its electro-chemical activity, but the deeper energy forces can only be understood by observing their functions and results. The following model is meant to visually clarify the various functions of Mind and its relationship to the Spirit or Authentic Self.

Map of the Mind and Spirit

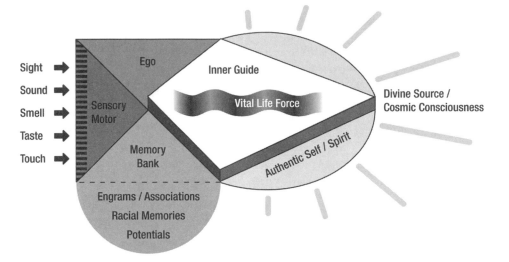

Mind Aspects:

1. Sensory-Motor
2. Ego
3. Memory Bank
4. Inner Guide.

Sensory-motor, ego and the inner guide are considered "conscious mind" and the memory bank is considered "unconscious mind."

Spiritual Aspects:

5. Authentic Self or Spirit
6. Vital Life Force
7. Cosmic Consciousness

No one aspect of mind can stand alone as there is a holistic, dynamic interconnection between them. The spiritual aspects are always present as the all-knowing presence of Divine Light and Love. Following is a brief description of each of the functions of Mind and Spirit, their patterns of interaction, and how each affects the child's development.

Sensory-Motor

The sensory-motor aspect of mind is considered lower mind and has the function of bringing the external world into our awareness through the five senses of seeing, hearing, tasting, smelling and feeling. The sensory-motor function acts as a screen that reflects upon our conscious awareness what our senses are experiencing. This is somewhat like a television screen that reflects images to us from another source. In addition, as the myriad of impressions, thoughts and memories, originating from our unconscious or memory bank, spontaneously bubble up to our consciousness, they are also registered on the sensory-motor screen. While a vast amount of sensory stimulation and unconscious material bombards the sensory-motor aspect of mind, it does not have the capacity to discriminate or decide what to do with the incoming information; the best it can do is register the impressions and react from habit or instinct. The first tendency is for it to react from a place of doubt or fear. Once the sensory-motor aspect receives direction from the ego, memory or inner guide it then has the capacity to engage the motor responses of the body and carry out the plan. Only the inner guide has the function to thoughtfully discriminate and make wise choices.

Maria Montessori keenly understood the vital role the sensory-motor function plays in a child's learning process and personality development. She saw that it: 1) absorbs the input of sensorial impressions *from* the external environment into the memory bank and 2) coordinates the motor activity *within* the external environment. She said, "At the moment that tentative life flowers into consciousness, putting the senses in contact with the environment, the muscles are activated in the perpetual effort of realization."[5]

She observed that children from birth to six have a unique capacity to absorb directly what they experience in their environment through their senses. Adults admire their environment; they can remember it and think about it; but the child absorbs it.... The child does not "remember" sounds but he incarnates them.[6] She called this unique characteristic of the young child the "absorbent mind." While the sensorial impressions are automatically received through the senses, "The individual is by no means mechanically enslaved to its senses (like the animals).... The child is specially favored. His senses, which also have a guide, are not limited like those of the animals."[7] Fortunately the child has an inner guide to organize and direct the sensorial impressions received through the sensory-motor function of mind.

The five senses of sight, smell, sound, touch, and taste are the receptors of all sensorial input and deliver environmental information to the child's mind. As sensorial impressions enter the memory bank they are unconsciously ordered to create the intelligence and personality of the child. This early period of sensory input is one of "adaptation"[8] and is driven by inherent potentials, instincts and habits of the unconscious mind. During this period, from birth to six, children literally incarnate their language, cultural customs, and family patterns directly from their environment. Swami Rama speaks to this accumulation of sensory data, "Even before the more advanced conscious aspects of the mind come into being, 'chitta' (memory bank) is accumulating, like an immense lake bed, a huge pool of sensory impressions and data."[9]

The sensory-motor function also acts as the coordinator of the body's motor activity when engaged in external exploration. When it receives impressions from the memory bank, ego or inner guide, it immediately coordinates the appropriate motor responses. For example: When a young child sees an object that interests him the sensory motor function coordinates the movement necessary to reach the object. Once the child has the object in his possession, under the direction of the sensory-motor function, he continues to explore the various sensorial aspects of it. As the child experiences various sensations, impressions are embedded in his subconscious mind. These impressions automatically search to make associations which form the basis of the child's intelligence. This is what Montessori meant when she said that the hand feeds the mind of the child.

Montessori recognized the important role sensory input has in building the intelligence of the child. "There is no doubt that children love light and flowers and watching animals, which is understandable because we know that they are acute observers who can order the images of what they perceive."[10]

Ego

The ego function of mind establishes the concept of individual identity, or a sense of "I-ness." It has the function of determining what incoming sensory or memory data is worth paying attention to, i.e., "This is important to me" or "This is unimportant to me." While developing a strong sense of "I-ness" is important for us to be effective in the external world, we must learn to ground the ego in the greater wisdom of our inner guide. If we are not grounded in our inner guide's deeper awareness, ego can take over the controls and run our show in a self-centered manner. When this happens ego becomes judgmental and likes to tell us that we are better or worse than others or that we should have things our way. It wants to be right, puts up defenses when challenged, and continually reinforces our separateness from others. Learning to use the ego in a balanced, constructive way is important because it significantly influences the creation of our personality and our ability to interact effectively in the social world. Maturation is the process of eliminating false identification with ego to embrace our Authentic Self.

Prior to the age of two, children cannot differentiate what is coming into their sensorial awareness from who they are. Around two years of age the child begins to see himself as separate from other people and the sensory stimulation in the environment. He is developing the ability to identify sensory input as "my thought," rather than "me." For the infant or toddler, the child "is the rose," as the child's ego develops the child says, "I see a rose."

This initial stage of ego development has come to be known by many as "the terrible twos" because children's behavior can seem demanding, stubborn and erratic. By understanding what the child is experiencing, it makes it easier for us to work through these challenging times. The child's sense of "I-ness" is beginning to manifest itself and seek independence, separateness and uniqueness; however, because the ego has not developed enough to create intelligent use of the incoming sense data the child can become very disturbed when things don't make sense to him.

The first identity crisis of life occurs as the child seeks to find out who he is separate from others. He is just beginning his journey from complete dependence on others to a life of independence and ultimately interdependence. The child is driven by the natural urge to be separate and independent, and is entering new territory that can be uncomfortable and unsettling. At this age children are attempting to find order in life and since they learn best through concrete objects and repetitive activity they may get upset when items or routines are changed. It is for this reason that when something is out of place or not done in the manner the child has defined as the way it is, frustration takes over and he may express this by displaying negative emotions and temper tantrums. If we react to this emotional response with a strong power statement such as, "Just eat it!" we are likely to find ourselves engaged in an unpleasant power struggle. At this stage in a child's life it is important that we are as consistent as possible and when we can't do things or have things in the same place give him advanced warning or an explanation before he becomes upset. As his identity becomes more established around the age of three, he will be able to handle change with more grace.

The undeveloped ego primarily adapts to lower functions of the mind such as pleasure, pain, fear or habit. The ego has little ability to decide directly or assign meaning to incoming information. It only has a shallow reaction of: "What is in it for me?" or "How can I stop hurting?" A child obviously needs to develop a confident self identity to be effective in life. However, if he has learned to rely primarily on such things as identifying with what he can or can't do better than someone else, or what material items he has, he may be limited by his ego's self image throughout his life rather than his authentic identity. If on the other hand he learns to identify with his Authentic Self he will naturally exude confidence as well as compassion for others.

Without the input of the inner guide, the sensory and ego impressions are primarily unregulated and disconnected. Unbridled sensory input can be seen as a phone bank whose operator is out to lunch; no one knows what to do with the incoming calls. An undisciplined ego is like a dull and unimaginative drone that does his job without understanding the whys and wherefores of incoming information. It is the next higher level of consciousness that channels calls and other input to their appointed places. The inner guide has the function of discriminating and deciding what information is true or false, real or unreal, useful or irrelevant, beautiful or ugly.

Memory Bank

The memory bank is located in the unconscious or subconscious mind and is a huge storehouse containing our working conscious memory as well as our subconscious racial memories, engrams and potentialities. While these characteristics are tucked away and inaccessible to our conscious mind, they strongly influence our learning, development, behavior and personality. Montessori broke down the concept of the memory bank into two parts: 1) she called the unconscious, "mneme" and, 2) that which we consciously remember as "memory." All the experiences through which an individual passes in life are retained in the mneme, not only the infinitesimal part that enters the consciousness (memory).[11]

One of the most startling discoveries that Montessori made was to come to a clearer understanding of how a child learns and matures. She observed that there are dynamic forces determining the development of his personality, intelligence and talents that are hidden within his memory bank or unconscious mind. While others had some idea of the contents and workings of the unconscious mind and how it related to the child's development, she took this knowledge to a new level. She came to understand how these inner forces worked together and how each contributed to the growth of the child. The three components of the subconscious that she identified were: racial memories, engrams and potentials. Following is a discussion of each of these subsets of the memory bank and how they relate to children's growth and development.

RACIAL MEMORIES

At the deepest level of the unconscious mind are what Montessori referred to as "racial memories" which "help all living things reproduce their own species and perpetuate manners of living."[12] It is the part of the subconscious that holds the patterns of behavior from species to species. In the human, it is what attracts the child to absorb and incarnate human life rather than animal life.

ENGRAMS

Montessori significantly contributed to solving the mystery of how children learn. She realized that everything that is experienced is embedded in the unconscious mind. "In order to gain something from life, we must retain traces of experiences undergone, and here memory comes to our aid.... This subconscious memory has marvelous mobility, and everything is there on record though we are not consciously aware of it."[13]

As stated earlier, the senses gather data from the external environment and send it to the unconscious mind to be stored. Montessori states that these experiences are refined once they enter the subconscious and become memory traces which she called "engrams."

> *It is not an accumulation of memories that is left in the mneme, but a power to recall experiences to the conscious memory.... Thus it is not the experiences in themselves, but the traces of them left behind in the mneme, which makes a mind powerful; such traces being known as engrams....*[14]

As engrams form in the memory bank they spontaneously seek to organize themselves by connecting with other engrams to create networks or associations based on such things as commonalities and contrasts. These associations are the mental equivalent of the physical synapses that form in the brain when new input is received. Montessori recognized that the deepest and most effective learning is a process of increasing the number of engrams and their corresponding associations in our subconscious. In appropriate environments these associations accumulate rapidly and the thoughts and ideas can be recalled into conscious memory when necessary. "The subconscious is full of these engrams, by which intellect grows much more than by conscious memory."[15]

She makes the point that this process of forming associations in the subconscious is extremely powerful and much more effective than the process of rote memorization using the conscious mind. When a child's interest is aroused through sensory stimulation and the impressions enter the unconscious mind, the mind spontaneously calls forth all those related memory traces or engrams to form a new or expanded idea. This is how the intellect grows.

> *Thus it may be said that every human being does his most intelligent work in the subconscious, where psychic complexes are the construction of engrams.... These do much more than create an association of ideas, for they organize themselves to carry out work which we are unable to do consciously.... It could only happen because the engrams did not sleep, but in association had done the work and forced it into the consciousness.*[16]

POTENTIALS

Montessori identified another element found within the spiritual embryo and contained in the unconscious memory bank that she called "nebulae of sensitivities" and compared them to the nebulae of the universe. "The nebulae of sensitiveness direct the newborn babe's mental development just as the genes condition the fecundated egg in the formation of the body."[17] Just as nebulae are potential stars, so the child's nebulae of potentials are the future possibilities inherent within each child. She described the nebulae as many "specialized kinds or stages" or "potentialities" which lead the young child towards development and self-fulfillment at the appropriate time. "The mental organism is a dynamic whole, which transforms its structure by active experience obtained from its surroundings; it is guided thereto by an energy of which the nebulae (potentials) are differentiated and specialized kinds or stages."[18]

She recognized that children's primary drive, motivated by the vital life force and guided by the inner guide, is to manifest these potentials. Through her work she discovered that there are specific and predictable times when these inner sensitivities are ready to develop. She called these times, "sensitive periods." and observed that when a child is ready to develop a specific potential he involves himself in this process intently until it is mastered.

Carl Jung recognized the presence of potentials in the unconscious mind and named them "archetypes." According to Jung, the archetype "is an irrepresentable unconscious, pre existent form that seems to be part of the inherited structure of the psyche.... The archetype in itself is empty and purely formal, nothing but a preformed faculty, a possibility of representation which is given a priori."[19]

Jung sounds like Montessori speaking when he goes on to say, "Archetypes were, and still are, living psychic forces....Always they were the bringers of protection and salvation, and their violation has as its consequences the 'perils of the soul'.... They are (when repressed), the unfailing causes of neurotic and even psychotic disorders."[20]

The Authentic Self, as we are describing, is what Jung calls the "Inner Child." According to his psychology; if the conscious mind splits off or represses the inner, Authentic Self, it does not destroy the truth, it merely inactivates it. The conscious mind then denies or falsifies the true self. In technical terms, then, this is how authenticity is lost. Jung concludes, "If, then, the childhood state of the collective psyche is repressed to the point of total exclusion, the unconscious content overwhelms the conscious aim and inhibits, falsifies, even destroys its realization. Viable progress only comes from the cooperation of both."[21]

In other words, both the inner and outer child must be preserved, holistically, not split apart. Montessori recognized the harm being done by adults not recognizing this truth when she said, "No social problem is as universal as the oppression of the child....No slave was ever so much the property of his master as in the case of the child."[22]

Nurturing children's authenticity is accomplished, not by adults teaching them and pouring adult wisdom into their minds, but by creating environments at home and school that attract him and match his unfolding potentials. The more a child's inner sensitivities match his environment, the more likely he is to creatively engage himself in the activities available to him and to manifest his inner potentials.

Inner Guide

The inner guide is the power of discrimination that observes and evaluates incoming sensorial and memory impressions, helps balance the ego and makes decisions as to what action to take. These decisions range from what outfit to wear to one's purpose in life. At the deepest level of the inner guide, we find pure reason, intuition, wisdom and knowing coming from the Authentic Self. The ancient yogic sages used the Sanskrit word *Buddhi* to refer to our inner guide. The importance of this concept in India is reflected by noting that it is from this word that Buddhism takes its name. The Buddha, or awakened one, is the one who knows that he knows. The lower mind can know, but *Buddhi* knows that it knows.

The inner guide is our personal link to the Authentic Self and provides a vantage point of reflection for our conscious mind. It helps us to step outside of the cycle of action and reaction. This activity can also free us from the bonds of cause and effect. It is like a Sage, or source of wisdom, within us.

We speak of it colloquially when we refer to such experiences as "intuition," "conscience," "hunches," "gut feeling," "in my heart," "something tells me," "inspiration," "creative muse," or even good old "I just know." The inner guide is the portion of our mind that is directly connected to our Authentic Self. It is the seat of our ability to see clearly and observe our lower mind's thinking processes.

Even though we all have this wisdom source within us we often marginalize it when we rely on our lower mind to make decisions for us. Our culture tends to be suspicious of inner knowing; consequently we tend to de-emphasize it. Regardless of what we call this inner knowing it is helpful to affirm that we have inner resources available to help us make wise choices that exist beyond our lower mind. Swami Rama describes the inner guide, or *Buddhi*, as a bridge between our conscious and unconscious mind: "simply create a powerful bridge between your conscious and unconscious mind. Fill your unconscious with the light of your Buddhi, which is infused with the power of right understanding and decisiveness."[23]

The sensory-motor, ego and memory bank, as well as the physical brain and nervous system, are all very important to the growing child. However, these lower functions of mind and body are like the hardware of a computer. Without the software and programming, total efficient functioning is not possible. The child's inner guide provides this software for the organizing, decisive, coordinating function of his mind and body. Without the inner guide the child would be swept along by sensory overload, ego attachment and a chaotic memory bank.

The inner guide is growth oriented and is the key to the child's positive, beneficent maturation. It offers meaning as well as a framework for the child's experiences, thoughts and emotions. Montessori recognized the bridge between the conscious and unconscious mind and saw the inner guide as a mysterious power that guides, oversees and directs the child's self fulfillment. She states that the child is "Directed by a mysterious power, great and wonderful... (the child matures) because he is endowed with great creative energies."[24] We can be at peace in the knowledge that there is an inner guide within the child. Therefore, we are well within our bounds of reason to trust in the child's natural learning process.

Every child comes into the world more attuned to his inner guide, which can unveil his Authentic Self. During the first six years of life each child has the unique capacity to be led before being influenced by the rational mind, social mores and stifling conventions. During early childhood children have a delicate sensitivity to the Spirit that must be honored, protected and supported by the adults in their lives. As the child matures and develops all the functions of his rational mind, it is our role as adults to encourage him to make thoughtful decisions. The result will be right action that comes from the child listening to his inner guide rather than his lower mind of sensory stimulation, ego and memory.

Vital Life Force

Within the unconscious mind of the child Montessori recognized the presence of a vital force that she called "horme." She observed that this inner force motivates children toward independence and the full manifestation of their hidden potentials and compels them to construct themselves into the persons they were born to become.

> *A vital force is active within him, and this guides his efforts towards their goal.... The horme belongs to life in general, to what might be called the divine urge, the source of all evolution. This vital force for his growth stimulates the child to perform many actions, and if he is permitted to grow normally, without being hindered, it shows itself in what we call the "joy of life." The child is always enthusiastic, always happy.[25]*

The life force is that which sustains, supports and directs all life on earth. In partnership with Cosmic Consciousness it keeps all life flowing harmoniously. This vital life force travels on the breath and enters the physical body at birth. When the life force leaves the body, people and animals experience death.

Dr. Montessori was a contemporary of the most prominent thinker of her day, Professor Bergson. His masterwork, entitled *Creative Evolution*, was published in 1907, the same year Montessori opened the Casa dei Bambini. It is from Bergson that Montessori received the term *elan vitale*. They shared the idea that a vital force sustains all life, including the physical body. Nietzsche called this force "The Will to Power." Other world cultures recognize this vital life force. For example the Chinese call it *Chi*, the Hindus call it *Prana* and the Polynesians call it *Mana*.

Dr. Wayne Dyer, a contemporary writer and speaker referred to this inner life force in the following way. "We're here in the perfect body for our time...and it's a living, breathing miracle in every way. It's guided and being directed by an invisible force that directs everything and everyone, in the universe. It beats our heart, digests our food, circulates our blood, grows our hair, and repairs our cuts and bruises, all independent of our opinions."[26]

This invisible force of life within the child provides energy for growth and maturation. A lighter way to talk about it is to say that children come into the world equipped with a set of batteries that do not have to be replaced, but do need to be maintained and charged regularly. As one weary mother said, "If they are serious about renewable energy sources, they should check out my two year old."

Without this creative power or vital impulse the child would not have the motivation to continue the work of self fulfillment. It is the child's driving impulse that motivates him to absorb his environment and create his individual personality. Montessori states that, "The baby is next endowed with an urge, or need to face the outer world and absorb it. We might say that he is born with 'the psychology of world conquest.' By absorbing what he finds about him, he forms his own personality."[27]

The dynamic, interconnected functions of the Mind and Spirit can be illustrated by comparing the various aspects of the mind to a chariot. The sensory-motor function takes in the view, the memory bank collects the information, the ego is the passenger, but it is the inner guide that holds the reins and steers the chariot. The life force is the horse providing the power. It is the energy that pulls us forward to fulfill life's purpose. The work of the life force is a prime example of holistic dynamism in action. It interacts and interpenetrates all the functions of the conscious and unconscious mind. It is the horse power of the chariot; it stimulates the senses to absorb life's experience; it is the brain's motor to process incoming information and it is the ego's urge to construct a full-functioning personality. Working in conjunction with the inner guide, it provides the energy to carry out choices. Finally, it is the work of the life force to assist the child in the unveiling of his Authentic Self.

Authentic Self or Spirit

The Authentic Self is the pure individualized Spirit dwelling within each one of us, as our personal expression of Cosmic Consciousness. The Authentic Self is nothing less than our true nature of love! It is the individualized divine light that moves human beings to fulfill their potentials and become consciously aware of their authenticity. It is the source of all of the positive virtues such as love, joy, faith, courage, honesty and compassion. It is the part that, when followed, brings us peace and purpose to our lives. It is the place where the inner guide taps into pure wisdom to guide us along life's unfolding path to fulfill our cosmic task.

Montessori not only saw love at the core of human nature, but as an energy force that holds the universe together. She describes it in the following way,

> *Love is much more than we have said so far. In man's mind it has been exalted by fantasy, but in us it is no other than one aspect of a very complex universal force, which…rules the world, keeps the stars in their courses, causes the conjunction of atoms to form new substances, holds things down on the earth's surface. It is the force which regulates and orders the organic and the inorganic and which becomes incorporated into the essence of everything…, like a guide to salvation and to the endlessness of evolution. It is generally unconscious, but in life it sometimes assumes consciousness, and, when felt in man's heart, he calls it "love."*[28]

We take Montessori at her word. These are not just rhetorical, flourished or flowery speech, but what she believed about God, Man, and the Universe. So, if God is love, the child is love, and life is love. Who then are we? It wouldn't be a stretch to claim that we are love and light.

Montessori was keenly aware that the children were inspired from within by the power of love. She saw it as the driving force within each child that internally motivates him to fulfill his potentials and realize his destiny. She saw love as the key to unveiling the Authentic Self. Margaret Stephenson, reaffirmed this by saying, "It is only the power of love that can enable the adult to come close enough to the child to understand him. Love and humility will unlock for us "the secret of childhood' and enable us to understand the inner significance and true meaning of Dr. Montessori's work."[29]

Cosmic Consciousness

*Love is conceded to man as a gift directed to a certain purpose,
and for a special reason, and in this it resembles everything lent
to living beings by the cosmic consciousness. It must be treasured,
developed and enlarged to the fullest possible extent.*[30]

—MARIA MONTESSORI

Cosmic Consciousness is the source of all life and love. It is a dynamic energy that touches all that is and all we are. As described in this chapter all of the aspects of mind and all of the spiritual aspects are connected and form a dynamic whole that includes the Cosmic Consciousness. It is reassuring to know that the spiritual embryo of the child doesn't come from nothing. By acknowledging that the child's spiritual embryo is connected to Cosmic Consciousness we can trust that there is a natural path prepared for the child to unveil his Authentic Self and fulfill his cosmic task.

Dr. Maria Montessori discovered this pathway and developed a holistic, child-centered approach that facilitates the unveiling of the Authentic Self. Through her keen observations of children she discovered what is necessary for them to be naturally motivated to move through the Unveiling Cycles and attain self-mastery.

The ancient Sanskrit word, *Namaste,* means *The Divinity in me, honors the Divinity in you.* This salutation is often used when people in India greet one another. It is more than a salutation; it is an affirmation of the pure personhood that is shared between people. The idea of connecting with our children through the Namaste Principle is the core of Montessori Parenting.

Conclusion

Through Montessori's many experiences and keen observations of children in supportive environments, she was convinced that the unfolding spiritual embryo of each child is to be trusted. Too often, we as adults, with our preconceived ideas, think that we must lead the child because we know what is best. While our intentions may be worthy, our actions can stand in the way of children's natural development. Montessori said it clearly, "We should help the child therefore, no longer because we think of him as a creature, puny and weak, but because he is endowed with great creative energies, which are of their nature so fragile as to need a loving and intelligent defense."[31]

This does not mean that we abandon children. It means that we learn to understand, watch over and assist them in their development. Often this requires us to change our view of children and what is motivating their actions. When we see our children as divine beings striving to develop their human potentials, rather than willful children purposely annoying us, we will approach them from an entirely different perspective. Instead of making assumptions as to their reasons for doing things and reacting to that, we find ourselves developing greater understanding about what they are attempting to do. Instead of reacting negatively to the children, we find ourselves looking for ways to help them meet their needs in more appropriate ways. Through this process we see ourselves developing greater patience and deeper wisdom.

The function of the nurturing parent is to recognize and trust the child's inner vitality, to promote it rather than diminish it, and to guide rather than dominate. Montessori Parenting begins with recognition, acceptance and respect for the child's Authentic Self. Montessori maintains that, "When we understand the inner nature of the child, we trust the child and become selflessly centered on the child and less on ourselves." She concludes by saying, "Our first teacher, therefore, will be the child himself, or rather the vital urge with the cosmic laws that lead him unconsciously."[32]

One last word from the great sage, Yoda, of *Star Wars*, "Let the force be with you!"

Suggestions for Follow Through

▨ **Sit by your child's bedside while he is asleep.** Breathe deeply, let your thoughts be still and quietly observe your child in peaceful sleep. Be aware of the thoughts that come from your intuition or inner knowing. Who is this child? Record your reflections in your Parenting Journal

▨ **Practice observing your child without judgment.** Just watch! Record what you see in your journal.

▨ **Reflect on your role and responsibility as a parent.** Why did you choose to become a parent? What are your desires for your child? What are your responsibilities to your child? Record your reflection in your Journal.

▨ **Make a love light pin for each member of your family.** A love light pin is a concrete representation of the spirit of love within each of us. It is made by cutting out a 2" diameter circle in yellow felt and gluing a jewelry pin to the back of the circle. Give a pin to each member of your family as a reminder that you see the light of love within them. Look for occasions to wear your pin and invite your children to wear their pins whenever they wish to express their love in that way.[33]

PART II

Unveiling the Authentic Child

PART II

Unveiling the
Authentic Child

*"The effort to force the child's natural development
can only do harm. It is nature that directs.
Everything depends on her and must obey her exact commands."[1]*

—MARIA MONTESSORI

We all know that the rose bud has an internal pattern that guides its natural blooming process and if we attempt to force the opening of the bud we damage or destroy the rose within. So it is with our children. The inherent forces within each child also guide and direct the opening life of the child's soul; and if adults attempt to force this delicate unfolding, we may, although unintentionally, damage this natural process and thwart the child's growth.

> *To recognize this great work of the child does not mean to diminish the parent's authority. Once they can persuade themselves not to be themselves the builders, but merely to act as collaborators in the building process, they become much better able to carry out*

their real duties; and then, in the light of a wider vision, their help becomes truly valuable. The child can only build well if this help is given in a suitable way.[2]

—MARIA MONTESSORI

The task of growing up is the child's life-long process of achieving self mastery and finding purpose and meaning in life. Montessori recognized that each child comes into this world with a precise internal pattern that guides his development. She also recognized that each child has all of the necessary tools to accomplish this task. Our role as parents, therefore, is to support this internal developmental process by respecting it and thoughtfully preparing physical, mental, emotional and spiritual environments that provide nourishment for the child's positive self construction. Dr. Montessori reminds us that, "It is necessary, then, to give the child the possibility of developing according to the laws of his nature, so that he can become strong, and having become strong, can do even more than we dared hope for him."[3]

Each child comes to the earth as a pure spiritual being endowed with many talents and gifts. However, at birth an invisible veil is drawn on the child's awareness of who he really is. Fortunately, the child's Authentic Self, inner guide and vital life force retain the knowledge of the child's authentic nature. Their primary purpose is to guide the child in the discovery of his authenticity and the fulfillment of his cosmic task. As parents we can collaborate in this process of self-actualization by implementing the philosophy and principles prescribed by Dr. Maria Montessori in our homes.

The Unveiling Cycle

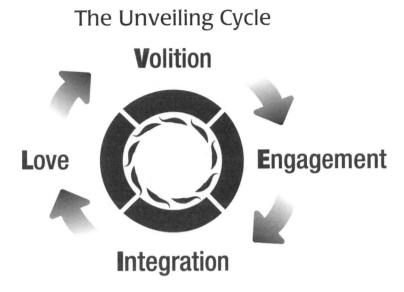

Volition

Love

Engagement

Integration

To bring greater understanding to the principles and processes involved in children's natural development toward self-actualization, we designed a model called, *The VEIL Model*. This model has four interacting phases that continually repeat themselves as children interact with their environments and complete learning cycles. The four phases are:

Volition—**E**ngagement—**I**ntegration—**L**ove.

The VEIL acronym represents the veil that hides the child's Authentic Self and at the same time, provides the pathway for children's authenticity to be revealed. Each time a child is motivated to engage in an appropriate activity (*Volition*), receives sensory stimulation (*Engagement*) and assimilates the information (*Integration*), he experiences a moment of realization and catches a glimpse of who he is and what he is capable of (*Love*).

The more this Unveiling Cycle is repeated, the greater is the child's ability to recognize his authenticity and realize his potentials. He enters into an upward cycling spiral towards self-actualization.

The Unveiling Spiral

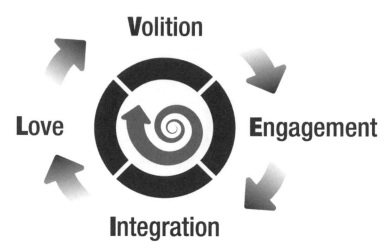

In the next four chapters we explore these four phases and include the key factors of Montessori philosophy and practice that support the natural unveiling of the authentic child.

CHAPTER 4

The Volition Phase

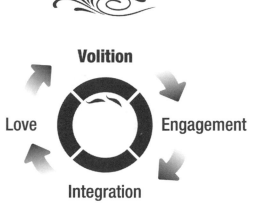

Volition is the first phase of the VEIL Model and focuses on four qualities embedded within the child's authentic nature that naturally motivate him toward self-actualization and fulfillment. The qualities of the Volition Phase are:

1. Need Fulfillment
2. Quest for Self Mastery
3. Sensitive Periods
4. Compelling Interests

Need Fulfillment

One of the strongest motivating forces within children, as well as all human beings, is to fulfill their basic needs. Abraham Maslow, a leader in the field of humanistic psychology, identified the following Hierarchy of Needs:

PHYSIOLOGICAL NEEDS

The need for physical survival is the most powerful and basic of all needs. This includes the need for food, clothing, shelter, sleep, water, and oxygen. When children's basic needs such as hunger or sleep are unfulfilled his behavior is often challenging until this need is met.

SAFETY NEEDS

Children seek to make sense of the world and find their place in it. As a result they need a world that is predictable, safe and secure. They respond best to consistency, fairness, healthy boundaries and predictable routines. According to Maslow, "Freedom within limits rather than total permissiveness is preferred; in fact it is necessary for the development of well-adjusted children."[1]

LOVE AND BELONGING NEEDS

Children thrive in an atmosphere of love, affection and belonging. Maslow found that, "the absence of love stifles growth and the development of potential."[2] They have a deep need to know they are loved, accepted and understood by the members of the family and that they have a meaningful place in the group. Trust is born when the needs for love and belonging are met. However, when these needs are not met children figure out ways to get recognized and their chosen behavior can be quite challenging, as discussed in Chapter 16.

ESTEEM NEEDS

Maslow describes two categories of esteem needs: 1) self-esteem, and 2) esteem from other people. The child's need for self-esteem is a desire to experience self confidence, competence, independence and mastery. The need to experience esteem from other people includes such things as acceptance, recognition, attention and appreciation from others. When this need is met, children operate from a state of confidence and well being which propels them into the qualities of self-actualization.

If it is unmet, children struggle with new challenges, taking risks and being creative.

SELF-ACTUALIZATION NEEDS

Maslow described this need as "the desire to become more and more of what one is, to become everything that one is capable of becoming."[3] This need, driven by the vital force, propels children to fulfill their inner potentials and become the people they were born to be. The qualities children manifest at this level include: meaningfulness, self sufficiency, effortlessness, playfulness, richness, simplicity, order, justice, perfection, individuality, aliveness, truth, goodness and beauty. When children experience this level, they are expressing their authenticity.

Maslow's research indicates that need fulfillment begins with the most basic physiological needs and moves sequentially to the next need level as the current need is fulfilled. This Hierarchy of Needs can be seen as a pyramid with the basic needs at the bottom and the higher level needs at the top. Children and adults, motivated by the life force within, move step by step through each need level in order to realize their authenticity. Maslow described this process as "meta motivation."

Maslow's Hierarchy of Needs

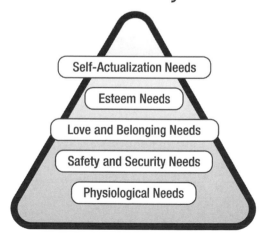

It is important to remember that children's need levels fluctuate from moment to moment depending on the situation and circumstance. For example, a child can be behaving in a concentrated, self assured and thoughtful manner (self-actualization) and then become threatened by a person or event. As the child registers the threat to his safety and security, he is thrust back into the lower need level of safety. Until this safety need is met, he will manifest a different set of behaviors than he demonstrated at the higher level of self-actualization. To return to the former state of self-actualization, he must again climb the pyramid ladder of needs by feeling safe, being reassured that he is loved and belongs, and experiencing positive self-esteem. Then he can enjoy self-actualization once again. As adults it is our responsibility to provide for the child at each level of the Hierarchy of Needs so that his Authentic Self may experience self-actualization routinely. Montessori reminds us that, "It is not enough to ensure for the child food, clothing and shelter. On the satisfaction of his more spiritual needs the progress of humanity depends—the creation indeed of a stronger and better humanity."[4]

Quest for Self Mastery

The vital life force is the compelling energy that not only sustains the life of the child, but propels him toward self mastery, meaning and purpose in life. Montessori observed over and over again the spontaneous, joyful activity arising from children as they purposely engaged themselves in their quest for self mastery. This quest begins from a state of complete dependence, moves through co-dependence, counter-dependence, independence and completes itself in a state of interdependence.

From birth to about nine months of age a child is totally dependent on his parents to meet his needs. The primary task during this period is for the parent and child to develop a bond of trust and love. Around nine months, until the child is approximately three years of age, there is a "push-me, pull-me" scenario going on. This is a time of counter-dependence where the child begins to separate physically and psychologically from the parent. During this time the child begins to crawl, walk and explore his surroundings. If he gets too far away and becomes frightened, he immediately returns to the safety of the parent. If all goes well during this stage of development the child successfully reconciles his longing for bonding and oneness with the need for separateness and individual selfhood.

Around the age of three children's counter-dependence naturally moves toward independence and they are able to more easily separate from their parents. During this stage of development children develop a strong desire to do things by themselves and resist too much adult control. The first signs of over control come when children want to carry out practical living tasks alone and become emotionally upset when well-intentioned adults do it for them. "The child seeks for independence by means of work: an independence of body and mind. The child's first instinct is to carry out his actions by himself, without anyone helping him, and his first conscious bid for independence is made when he defends himself against those who try to do the action for him...."[5]

All children need to feel capable, experience control in their lives, and develop their capacities on their own. As children experience mastery of their environment, they develop a sense of confidence and well being in what they can do and what gifts they can offer. Regardless of the age, children are naturally motivated by the vital life force and are eager to learn and master the concepts offered them. If this interest is encouraged and appropriate activities are made available for their use, children naturally and joyfully engage themselves in the learning process throughout their lives. However, if children are deprived of the opportunity to become independent, due to excessive adult control, they begin to manifest behaviors of defiance, non cooperation and they lose their enthusiasm for learning. "We must clearly understand that when we give the child freedom and independence, we are giving freedom to a worker already braced for action, who cannot live without working and being active. This he has in common with all other forms of life, and to curb it makes him degenerate."[6]

Defiant, non-cooperative behavior can be reversed when parents trust the child's vital life force, provide attractive environments that meet the child's evolving interests, establish reasonable structure, and remove the obstacles to his being able to engage freely in the activities that interest him. It is through meaningful engagement in the learning process that a child touches the roots of his Authentic Self and displays the characteristics of happiness, joy, and enthusiasm.

The need to achieve independence continues throughout the early childhood, elementary and adolescent years. During early childhood children's primary focus is to become physically independent. The elementary years are a time for intellectual mastery, while adolescents focus on obtaining emotional independence.

Self Mastery does not stop with children's ability to act independently in life. Around the age of five children's quest for independence begins to include the first seeds of interdependence. This is where they learn to share, cooperate and have compassion for others. This is a time when they are very sensitive to having things fair and just. Elementary children begin to move from self interest to realizing that all people and all life need one another to exist. As children move into the elementary years they have active imaginations and want to discover the connectedness and interdependence of the universe and the meaning of their place in it. This is the time to encourage and expand their interests through such things as reading, clubs, artistic activities and travels. Engaging children in stimulating conversations about many topics will have impact on them throughout their lives. Modeling curiosity and a love of learning is probably the most powerful influence a child can have at this age.

During the adolescent years students reach a new stage of claiming their emotional independence that can sometimes be challenging. This is a time similar to the two-year olds' claim to independence. Like the toddler who is moving from being an infant to a young child, the adolescent is moving from being an elementary-aged child to a young adult. This is a time when what his peers think of him is far more important than what his parents think. Adolescents can vacillate between seeming overconfident and independent to feeling insecure and confused. During this time they are simultaneously developing their interdependence by learning how to effectively work, cooperate and "hang out" with their friends. This is also a sensitive period for them to discover what they can contribute and how they can be meaningfully engaged in the adult culture. Providing opportunities for them to engage in adult activities, such as mentoring, service learning, or employment is an excellent way for adolescents to explore possibilities and learn to handle responsibilities.

The culminating state of self mastery is the attainment of both independence as well as interdependence. Children who gracefully move through the levels of dependence, co-dependence, counter-dependence, independence and interdependence are most likely, as adults, to find meaning and purpose in their lives by contributing their talents and being responsible global citizens.

Sensitive Periods

Between birth and six years of age, children go through a unique process of developing their potentials and skills. This process involves the vital life force, inner guide, the absorbent mind, the child's physical development and his experiences within the environment. Montessori observed that young children pass through specific periods of sensitivity, which can last for months or years. During these sensitive periods the child's attention is focused intently on the mastery of specific skills. When this happens they block out other stimulus, repeat the same routine over and over again until they accomplish satisfactory perfection in the process and then move on to master another function. Montessori speaks to the importance of adults being aware of this process and cooperating with it. "If the child is prevented from enjoying these experiences at the very time when nature has planned for him to do so, the special sensitivity which draws him to them will vanish, with a disturbing effect on his development, and consequently on his maturation."[7] Some of the most noticeable sensitive periods are:

SENSITIVITY TO LANGUAGE

The acquisition of language is an example of a sensitive period. At birth, children have no ability to speak but by the age of two most children are able to speak their native tongue. This happens because of the motivation of the vital life force, the potential for language acquisition within the subconscious mind, the ability of the sensory motor mind to absorb the language spoken around him and the physical development of the vocal chords. Over the course of two years, the child's physical organs develop so that he can form words; simultaneously his subconscious mind quietly connects and refines all the necessary elements of language such as meaning, accent, and grammar. When this process is complete, around the age of two, the child has mastered his native tongue.

SENSITIVITY TO SMALL OBJECTS

During this time of sensitivity, children are drawn to small objects and will spend concentrated time observing and manipulating small objects and exploring nature's mysteries. Allowing them time to do this is important for the development of concentration, fascination and imagination.

SENSITIVITY TO ORDER & PRECISION

Young children are searching to understand life by absorbing what they see and experience in the environments surrounding them. If the environments are orderly, they have a much easier time of categorizing and seeing the inter-relationship of objects. Similarly, children need consistency in people and routines so that they know what to expect. Sudden changes in their environments or routines often upset children because their need for security is threatened.

SENSITIVITY TO EXPLORING WITH TONGUE AND HANDS

Young children primarily explore their environments through the sensory stimulus of taste and touch because this helps them absorb the qualities of the objects they encounter. In addition, the combination of the motor (hand) and sensory (taste) activity directly affects the neurological structures of the brain and affects the formation of the child's intelligence. Preparing an environment that is safe for them to touch and taste is important.

SENSITIVITY TO MOVEMENT

During the first three years of a child's life, he progresses from a helpless to active being. The child is compelled to reach out, turn over, sit up, crawl, stand and then walk which is the crowning glory! It is exciting to watch children find their mobility. They love to walk and encouraging them to take walks in nature is a marvelous experience for them. This need for movement continues throughout childhood as it is a key to their being able to bring the sensory stimulus of their environment into their consciousness in the most effective manner. This is covered in more detail in the next chapter.

SENSITIVITY TO SOCIAL RELATIONSHIPS

At the age of five, children begin to develop intense interest in understanding their relationships with others. They want to understand fairness, cooperation and community building so they can relate positively with others. This sensitivity to social relationships continues through the elementary years and into adolescence.

SENSITIVITY TO INTERCONNECTEDNESS

Elementary age children have a natural desire to understand the interconnectedness of the universe, solar system, earth's elements, plants, animals and humans. At this age children love to know how life formed and how each part of the universe is related and dependent on each another. This is the reason why cosmic education, as referred to in Chapter 2, is so successful for elementary children.

Even though the sensitive periods, as described above, find their greatest intensity in the early childhood years (birth to six), the fulfillment of potentials continues throughout life motivated by the energy of the vital force, the inner guide, the imagination and the stimulus of the environment.

Compelling Interests

Children's interests are motivated from within by a combination of a deep love for life, the vital force, inner potentials and previous positive experiences registered in the unconscious mind. These internal factors compel children to spontaneously interact with and learn from their environments. Montessori spoke of this phenomenon when she said, "The environment must be rich in motives which lend interest to activity and invite the child to conduct his own experiences."[8]

A child's natural tendency is to love and be attracted to his environment. This natural involvement with a healthy environment is the food for growth and development—a natural vital urge. The Nobel Laureate, Herbert Simon further describes this process. "Children left to themselves in a rich environment find, and attend to, stimuli that are at the right level of complexity for them—in which they can find interesting pattern. With experience, they learn to discover and enjoy more and more complex patterns. We say that they have curiosity."[9]

When children find themselves in a rich environment filled with objects and elements of interest to them, they naturally and enthusiastically engage themselves in absorbing, observing, manipulating, and learning from the stimulus. When engaged in this way, they focus intently, demonstrate enthusiasm and remember what they have learned. Research confirms that children are more engaged, have greater memory retention and enjoy the learning process more when they are engaged in an area of interest to them.[10]

While most children are naturally attracted to learn from their environment, there are some children, for various reasons, who are not naturally drawn to the activities in the environment. Instead they see it as fearful and tend to shy away from engaging themselves. When this is the case, it is more important than ever to make the environment as attractive as possible, ensure that there are activities of interest to the child, and gently introduce the activities to him. At the moment we sense that he is engaged, it is important that we quietly and gradually remove ourselves so he can begin to feel the satisfaction of engagement and self-direction. Our challenge here is to reawake the child's love for his environment.

Edward T. Clark Jr. in his article entitled "The Search for a New Education Paradigm" summed up the necessity for interest based education. "One thing can be said about the curriculum without danger of contradiction. If it is not inherently interesting, substantive, provocative, and relevant, effective learning will not occur. No amount of money, training, classroom management skills, organizational strategies, teaching methodologies, or external reinforcements can lead to effective learning without a curriculum that stimulates the interest and captures the imagination of the students…."[11]

Conclusion

The four areas described in this Phase of Volition are naturally engrained in the psychological wiring of our children. It is not up to us as parents to start the child's engine as it is ready to start at birth. Our role is to provide the fuel and thoughtful guidance so that it can be activated.

Our children are naturally motivated to fulfill their needs, seek self mastery, respond to their sensitive periods and follow their compelling interests. What they need from us is respect, understanding and environments that allow them to engage in meaningful activity.

Suggestions for Follow Through

Observe your child's natural Volition. Be consciously aware of what motivates his activity. Observe without interference and hold the following questions.

■ Is my child being motivated by his needs of preservation, safety, belonging, esteem or self-actualization?

■ Is my child being motivated by his quest for independence and self mastery in his environment? If so, is he striving for physical, mental or emotional independence?

■ Is my child being motivated by a specific sensitive period at this time such as language development, movement, small objects, a sense of order, a desire for justice or making connections?

■ Is my child being motivated by one of his compelling interests? If so, what attracts and naturally draws his attention?

Record what you observe in your parent journal.

CHAPTER 5

The Engagement Phase

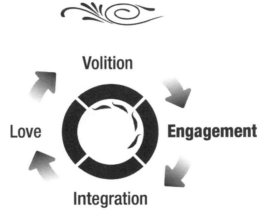

Engagement, the second phase of the VEIL Model, is the process that allows children to receive and take in stimuli from their environments. The four qualities that naturally facilitate the Engagement Phase:

1. Absorbent Mind to Inquiring Mind
2. Meaningful Work
3. Movement
4. Freedom of Choice

Absorbent Mind to Inquiring Mind

As mentioned earlier, children's minds from birth to six have the unique capacity to absorb directly what they experience in their environments.

This capacity is vital to the young child's development and personality formation. "There is in the child a special kind of sensitivity which leads him to absorb everything about him, and it is this work of observing and absorbing that alone enables him to adapt himself to life. He does it in virtue of an unconscious power that only exists in childhood."[1]

Montessori called this unconscious power the "absorbent mind" and contrasts it to the mind of adults. "Adults admire their environment; they can remember it and think about it, but the child absorbs it. The things he sees are not just remembered; they form part of his soul. He incarnates in himself all in the world about him that his eyes see and his ears hear."[2]

This process of absorbing the environment through the five senses is driven by children's love for and natural passion for observing their environments. Have you ever watched a young child observe a bug crossing the sidewalk? As you know, he totally absorbs himself in watching the tiniest details of the bug—its movements, its shape and its colors. In this moment of deep concentration and observation, the child absorbs many of the bug's characteristics which automatically embed themselves directly into his memory bank where they form impressions (engrams) and create patterns of relationship (associations). Montessori referred to this as the child's process of incarnation or the construction of his personality. "It is the child's way of learning. This is the path he follows. He learns everything without knowing he is learning it, and in doing so he passes little by little from the unconscious to the conscious, treading always in the paths of joy and love."[3]

The absorbent mind allows a direct route between the child's sensorial impressions and the memory bank where the impressions are organized into meaningful patterns. The sense impressions are absorbed as whole gestalts and do not pass through the process of rational thinking. Montessori claims that "nothing that is formed in infancy can ever be wholly eradicated…What the child absorbs, remains, a final ingredient of his personality."[4] In a real sense what children absorb from their environments in the earliest years of life determines who they will become as adults. Research estimates that the majority of a child's basic personality is determined by the age of six. This concept speaks strongly to the need for parents to provide thoughtfully prepared environments for children and model the desired characteristics we want them to absorb.

If the absorbent mind automatically receives the various stimuli in the environment, what happens to the child when this special quality of absorbency expires around the age of six? Fortunately, the motivation to engage and learn from the environment now takes the form of an inquiring mind. The inquiring mind is a curious mind and naturally wants to learn about its surroundings and life. At this time the child's mind develops the ability to reason and consciously remember what he is learning. The child is gifted with an active imagination and loves to learn by exercising his ability to imagine. This love of learning can be done nicely through the use of stories, inquiring questions, and other creative activities. With this new way of learning, children have the ability to use their imaginations, see interrelationships and begin the process of abstraction—moving from the concrete materials to abstract concepts. If properly nurtured, a child's natural love of learning will continue throughout his lifetime.

Meaningful Work

A key component that motivates the child to engage in the environment is his natural love for working within his environment. The task of self construction and the corresponding unveiling of his authenticity are often referred to as "the work of the child." For adults the word, "work" often brings up thoughts of drudgery and unpleasantness. "I *have* to go to work." The adult's work is usually seen as an end product; however, to a young child, work is something he naturally loves to do because it is his opportunity to create his personality and practice his skills of self mastery through interaction with the motives in his environment. Rather than seeking an end product through his work, the child immerses himself in the process of experiencing his physical, mental, emotional and spiritual environments as a means of discovering who he is and what he is capable of doing. This work of receiving information from the environment continues throughout life, but never so strongly as during the early childhood stage.

It seems, therefore, 'natural to man' that the child should begin by absorbing the environment and accomplish his development by means of work, of gradual experiences in his surroundings. He nourishes and develops his human qualities first by this unconscious absorption and then by his activities directed to outward things. He constructs himself; he forms his characteristics by nourishing his spirit.[5]

—MARIA MONTESSORI

The child's work of self construction is motivated by the life force's urge to help the child manifest his inner potentials. This work is simultaneously directed by the child's inner guide to encourage the child's self-actualization. This compelling energy of self construction must be directed in a meaningful manner. "If the child lacks the external means to adapt, he has no way to utilize the great energy that is his. Moreover, he is impelled instinctively towards activity that utilizes all his energies because in this way he can perfect his faculties. Everything depends on this."[6]

As children are allowed to follow this guidance and work constructively with appropriate activities in their environments they become centered happy and fulfilled. Their authenticity shines through. "In children, the drive for activity is almost stronger than that for food....If we give them the right environment, we see little unhappy nuisances transformed into happy active children."[7]

Movement

As the newborn infant leaves the comfort of the womb he is met with a variety of sensorial stimulation such as seeing light, hearing voices, smelling aromas, feeling touch and tasting milk. These sensations are literally his first connection to the external world and serve as the means to help him develop his intelligence. However, receiving the sensorial impressions alone is incomplete; it must be coupled with movement within the environment.

There are two forms of movement going on in the life of the young child. There is movement motivated automatically by the cerebellum part of the brain that directs the development of gross motor movement such as turning over, sitting up, crawling and walking. Secondly, there is a form of movement that is directed by the child's intelligence and utilizes purposeful movement with the hands to receive and learn about the environment: "movement has great importance in mental development itself, provided that the action which occurs is connected with the mental activity going on."[8]

This process begins when a child sees something in his surroundings is attracted to it and reaches out with his hands to interact with it. This act is an important connection for the child because, at this moment he consciously realizes that, through his own volition, he can contact and interact with his environment. Through the movement of reaching out the child begins to develop both his muscular as well as neurological structures, which, in coordination, begin to form the intelligence of the growing child. The hand is the first physical appendage that reaches out to help the child receive the environment into his psyche.

The child not only becomes conscious of his movement but also subconsciously absorbs the qualities of the object. As a child uses his hands to work with and manipulate physical objects in his environment, he literally builds his mind's intelligence by forming engrams and associations that are related to such concepts as: shape, texture, color, weight, relationships. As each new impression embeds itself into the child's subconscious mind, physical neural pathways are established in the brain of the child as billions of nerve cells organize themselves into the neural structures of cell bodies, dendrites, axons and synapses which allow perception, thinking and remembering to take place. The more the child's intelligence expands, the more he is motivated to consciously learn. Montessori spoke strongly about this when she said, "Scientific observation shows that intelligence is developed through movement; experiments in all parts of the world have confirmed that movement helps psychic development, and that development in turn expresses itself in further movement, so there is a cycle, which must be completed, because mind and movement belong to the same unity."[9]

Current research confirms that there is a positive correlation between movement and learning in several areas. According to Angelina Lillard, "There is an abundant research showing that movement and cognition are closely intertwined. People represent spaces and objects more accurately, make judgments faster and more accurately, remember information better, and show superior social cognition when their movements are aligned with what they are thinking about or learning."[10]

Giving children the freedom to move about and explore their surroundings is essential if we are going to provide optimal intellectual development for our children.

Freedom of Choice

Children have more receptive energy for learning when they have some control and freedom to choose what they do. As mentioned earlier, the inner guide is directly connected to the child's Authentic Self and thoughtfully leads the child toward maturation and fulfillment. It meticulously guides the child to make choices that are purposeful and meaningful to his natural development. Montessori calls on adults to respect and trust this phenomenon within the child. "Mothers, fathers, politicians: all must combine in their respect and help for this delicate work of formation, which the little child carries on in the depth of a profound psychological mystery, under the tutelage of an inner guide."[11]

Trusting in the child's inner guidance is important if we, as adults, are to feel comfortable enough to gracefully allow our children to make choices on their own. Of course, this process of choice making is related to the level of the child's maturation and the nature of the choice. First of all, young children respond well to making choices between a few possibilities rather than many. For example, it works best to ask a young child if he wants to have peas or corn for dinner instead of asking him what vegetables he wants to eat. It is also easier for a child to make thoughtful choices when his belongings are organized and limited in number. Too many choices actually overwhelm children. For choice making to be successful it is also important that the child is able to make choices among activities that match his skill level. If something is too difficult for a child it will be discouraging.

As discussed earlier, the child is naturally motivated by specific sensitive periods and unfolding interests within the environment. When he is allowed the freedom to follow these unfolding interests he does so with great enthusiasm and joy. As we follow the lead of the child and give him the opportunity to make choices for himself, he develops self confidence and strengthens his skills of listening to his inner wisdom of authenticity. Montessori reminds us that "the child must learn by his own individual activity, being given a mental freedom to take what he needs, and not be questioned in his choice. Our teaching must answer the mental needs of the child, never dictate them." [12]

When we make unnecessary choices for the child we contribute to the loss of his authenticity. We may think we are helping a child when we make the majority of his choices, but the opposite is happening. Instead of him appreciating our help, he receives the message that we don't trust him, that he is weak, and that he needs to rely on us or other outside sources for direction in life. When we make choices for him, he forgets how to access his own inner knowing and his sense of identity and authenticity become unstable.

If this pattern continues into adulthood it can have harmful effects on the life of the child. Rather than being comfortable with his Authentic Self, he learns to rely on others to define who he is and what he should do. He moves from relying on his parents and teachers to relying on his peers and other cultural influences for his decision making and identity. Rather than making decisions from his inner wisdom, he learns to make them from his lower mind of sensory stimulation, memory, emotion and ego because his anchor of authenticity has become unstable. This can result in the child assuming a false identity which is the basis of addictive behavior.

Angelina Lillard, in her book, *Montessori, The Science Behind the Genius*,[13] discusses a number of scientific studies that confirm that children, as well as adults, experience feelings of well being, perform tasks more effectively, and are more persistent as well as creative when they have some control over the choice of their work. In other words, when children are allowed to make choices they are more engaged, focused and successful in what they do. When a task is successfully completed, often visible signs of enthusiasm, satisfaction and joy can be observed. We believe that the reason this happens is that the child, following his inner wisdom and concentrating his mind, connects with his Authentic Self, which manifests itself as happiness and joy.

It was upon witnessing children independently making choices and spontaneously working in the classroom with little adult direction that first attracted and amazed observers to Montessori classrooms and made the Montessori approach to education famous. Fidelity to this *"special psychic force at work,"*[14] for the past one hundred years, has made Dr. Maria Montessori's insights the educational success story of the century. The key to Montessori parenting, likewise, is to trust and respect the inner wisdom of children and follow their lead.

Conclusion

The Engagement Phase brings sensory input into the mind of the child. The absorbent minds of young children and the inquiring minds of older children naturally attract them to stimulating environments where they naturally engage in activities that interest them. Once engaged in meaningful work, children receive sensory information that automatically embeds itself in their memory bank and further increases their intelligence and character. Movement within the environment increases children's ability to engage themselves and more thoroughly experience their surroundings. Freedom of choice is an internal motivator that encourages children to engage themselves in the learning motifs of the environment.

Suggestions for Follow Through

Observe what is motivating your child's Engagement in the environment. Watch your child, without interference, and ask the following questions.

- Is my child automatically bringing in information through his absorbent mind (ages 3—6) or is he seeking information due to his natural curiosity and inquiring mind?

- Is my child receiving information by engaging in meaningful work he has chosen to do?

- Is my child receiving information through movement such as engaging his hands or other parts of his body to receive information from the environment?

- Is there a difference in my child's receptivity and engagement when he is offered the freedom to make a choice?

Record what you observe in your parent journal.

CHAPTER 6

The Integration Phase

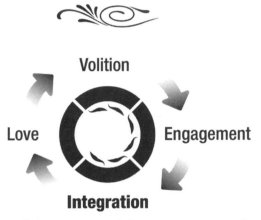

Volition

Love   Engagement

Integration

The third phase of the VEIL Model is Integration or how children assimilate and process information that is received from their environments. The four qualities of the Integration Phase are:

1. Concentration
2. Repetition
3. Emotional Safety
4. Meaningful Context.

Concentration

Developing the ability to concentrate is an important skill that helps the child integrate what he receives from his surroundings. Without concentration, the mind is easily distracted by sensorial sensations, memories, imaginations and general wanderings. The power to concentrate implies that all of these distractions are quieted and the child can focus his full attention on the present moment and listen to his inner guide as he engages himself in his work. Montessori observed the great benefits of concentration among the children. "Each time that such a polarization of attention took place the child began to be completely transformed, to become calm and more intelligent."[1]

The state of concentration can be compared to the state of meditation where an individual is able to focus on the present moment with full attention. The result of this is a feeling of calm, well being and love. Children experience this when they become meaningfully engaged in an activity for long periods of time. During this process children are absorbing or taking in the meaning of their learning experience, responding to their inner guidance, forming new concepts and making connections in their unconscious mind.

Montessori discovered that concentration occurs naturally when children are totally engaged in an activity or work. She used the word "normalization" to describe the child's being in touch with his Authentic Self. She said, "Normalization comes about through 'concentration' on a piece of work. For this we must provide 'motives for activity' so well adapted to the child's interests that they provoke his deep attention.... The essential thing is for the task to arouse such an interest that it engages the child's whole personality."[2]

This delicate state of concentration needs to be respected and protected by parents and teachers. When we see a child engaged in an activity with this kind of focus, it is imperative that we do our best not to interrupt this flow of energy within the child. If it is absolutely essential that we talk to a child during this time of concentration, it is important to move gracefully in his presence and gently call his name so he can slowly switch his attention to us.

Another possible pitfall is to see a child doing something well and say "Good job!" While our intention is to encourage him, by saying this during the period of concentration, we actually stop his flow of concentration. This is where we need to develop our own ability to concentrate so we can observe what the child is doing before interrupting him. Montessori was extremely sensitive to the sanctity of the child's periods of concentration and the adult's need to respect this "great work of the child." "If…a teacher respects the freedom of the child and has faith in him, if she has will enough to forget all she has learned, if she is modest enough not to consider her intervention essential, if she knows how to wait patiently, then she will see a complete change in the child.[3]

She goes on to describe the change that can be seen in a restless child when he finds an activity that draws his deepest attention. "He is agitated until he seeks something within the depths of his mind that he has not yet found for himself…. It must hold his entire attention; he must concentrate and consecrate his entire being, at the same time, he must be free from everything that goes on around him. This is what we call the great work."[4]

Once the child has completed his task of concentration, he displays a deep sense of joy and satisfaction. The child has had a wonderful period of experiencing his Spirit and takes great pleasure in this. Montessori observed that,

> *The child who concentrates is immensely happy; he ignores his neighbors or the visitors circulating about him. For the time being his spirit is like that of a hermit in the desert: a new consciousness has been born in him, that of his own individuality. When he comes out of his concentration, he seems to perceive the world anew as a boundless field for fresh discoveries.…Love awakens in him for people and for things.…The spiritual process is plain: he detaches himself from the world in order to attain the power to unite himself with it.[5]*

Repetition

Children's ability to integrate, assimilate and remember what they are learning depends on a number of things, including the process of repetition. As we know, the sensorial impressions entering the child's mind form engrams that automatically search for related engrams to establish associations in the subconscious mind. This process is simultaneously carried out on the physical level through specific functions in the brain.

As the brain receives sensorial stimulation from sight, sound, smell, taste or touch, it forms neurons from the millions of cells in the brain. Each neuron, equivalent to the engrams formed in the subconscious mind, consists of a cell body, dendrite spines and an axon. Signals from neighboring neurons are picked up by the dendrites and, when a relationship is found, a message to connect is sent through the axon. Because the neurons do not actually touch one another, the message to connect is sent over a gap, called a synapse. The synapse actually makes the connections to the related neurons and, over time, a magnificent "neural highway" develops. This highway is the equivalent of the associations forming in the mind and is the process by which the child's intelligence is created.

Dr. Jane Healy, an expert on the developing mind of the child speaks eloquently about this amazing process, "Each child weaves his own intellectual tapestry, the quality of which may depend on active interests and involvement in a wide variety of stimuli. The home environment provides the raw materials for the masterpiece."[6]

Research has shown that a primary factor in increasing the formation of these neural networks or associations is directly related to the child's active interest and involvement in the learning process. Another factor is repetition. As a child repeats an activity he increases the power of his memory by strengthening and enriching the synaptic connections in his brain.

Children naturally and spontaneously repeat activities until they have mastered the task at hand, then all of a sudden they are finished. From the outside it may seem random, but within the life of the child, his inner work is complete and he is ready to move on to a new task. All the while, what has been associated in the mind remains and continues to search out new connections. This phenomenon explains why a child "all of a sudden" knows a concept that was unknown previously. His sub-conscious mind has been busy at work assimilating the variety of stimuli entering the mind by forming engrams and making associations. At a certain point, specific related engrams connect up and form an entirely new concept (holistic synergy in action). An excellent example of this is when a child "all of a sudden" speaks words. How did this happen? There were no language classes to teach the child how to talk.

It happened internally and naturally within the depths of the child's subconscious mind.

Two additional characteristics of repetition that affect the child are the development of inner discipline and constructive habits. When a child is in the process of repetition, he naturally inhibits movements that are not serving his purpose of assimilating the task at hand. This willing inhibition on the part of the child is an important step toward the positive development of self discipline. Habits are also formed by the repetition of physical and mental activity. The more an act is repeated the stronger it becomes as it embeds itself into the memory bank. Soon it becomes automatic and outside of conscious thought. Helping children establish constructive habits at an early age serves them throughout their lives.

Repetition and concentration are closely related. Repetition is made easier, and has a greater impact, when a child is in the state of concentration where he has access to the direction of his inner guide. As parents and teachers it is important to be sensitive to the child's need for both repetition and concentration. To unnecessarily interrupt the child, may result in the child displaying traits of anger and frustration. Prolonged insensitivity to the child's need for concentration and repetition can result in the child having a short attention span or other learning challenges.

Emotional Safety

When I was in high school, I took a speech class where one of the assignments was to prepare a dramatic interpretation and perform it before judges at a competitive speech meet. I carefully prepared for this experience but when I stood up to deliver the dramatic piece, I dramatically forgot everything, including my name. My mind was blank. What had happened?

In looking back on this experience I came to understand that when I looked out on the audience and realized that I was going to be judged, fear overtook my rational mind and erased all memory of what I was doing there. This dramatic moment in my life taught me how powerful the emotion of fear is.

Daniel Goleman, a leading expert in the field of emotional intelligence, describes the process taking place in the brain when we are faced with situations that trigger fear-based emotions: "the signals of strong emotion—anxiety, anger, and the like—can create neural static, sabotaging the ability of the prefrontal lobe to maintain working memory. That is why when we are emotionally upset we say we "just can't think straight"—and why continual emotional distress can create deficits in a child's intellectual abilities, crippling the capacity to learn."[7] In his book, *Emotional Intelligence*, Goleman talks about the three parts of the brain: the reptilian, limbic and neo-cortex and how they interact to either support learning or sabotage it.

The reptilian brain is the primitive part of the brain that regulates our basic life functions such as breathing, digestion and metabolism. Its responsibility is to keep the body functioning efficiently without conscious thought. If a threat is perceived, the reptilian brain automatically responds by assuming a fight or flight mode to assure survival. When this happens, it sends its troops of adrenaline and other chemicals into the body to defend against the perceived attack. All other activities such as rational thinking and memory retrieval are over shadowed and ignored.

The limbic brain is the center for our emotional responses from love to fear. It is the part of our brain that fosters nurturing of our young as well as loathing of our enemies. This is the place where hormones are regulated and, while it is not quite as independent of conscious thought as the reptilian brain, it too can get carried away with irrationality.

The crowning jewel of the brain is the neo-cortex or thinking brain. It is the area of the brain that is the control center. It is the place in the brain where intelligence is formed, where the neural highways of learning are created, where sensory stimulation is put together and comprehended. This is the place that allows reflection, planning, and strategizing. This is the place where we can think about what we are feeling and make decisions about our actions. This is the part of brain that connects to the inner guide function.

When the three brains are working harmoniously our experience is generally one of centered calm, relaxed demeanor and clear thinking.

However, when life's challenges face us, we often find ourselves unable to focus, overcome by emotion, and unable to think clearly. What happens then? Goleman gives us a clue: "the emotional areas are intertwined via myriad connecting circuits to all parts of the neo-cortex. This gives the emotional centers immense power to influence the functioning of the rest of the brain—including its centers for thought."[8]

Within the limbic portion of the brain are two almond-shaped clusters of interconnected structures called amygdala glands. They are the seat of passion, they store all emotional memories and they register the significance of all incoming emotions. The normal pathway for environmental stimulation to enter the brain is for it to first register on the thalamus gland whose job is to route information to both the amygdala glands and the neo-cortex or thinking brain. Because the distance between the thalamus and the amygdala glands is but a synapse away, they get the information first and begin assessing the input earlier than the thinking brain.

If the amygdala glands sense a threat, they sound an alarm and immediately connect with the reptilian brain so that triggers "the secretion of the body's fight or flight hormones, mobilizes the centers of movement, and activates the cardio-vascular system, the muscles and the gut."[9] In a very real sense, the amygdala glands can hi-jack the sensorial information from the thinking brain and take over all rational thinking. In instances when the amygdala glands are *not* threatened, incoming sensory input finds its way to the thinking brain and does its natural work of creating networks of connected neurons to create the mind's intelligence.

How does all this relate to the need for emotional safety in the child's learning process? Simply put—when a child is emotionally upset, his capacity to learn and remember is thwarted. Since the natural process of learning depends on the free flowing act of neurons connecting to one another in the thinking brain, any distractions coming from the amygdala glands' negative reaction impedes the learning process. According to Goleman, "When emotions overwhelm concentration, what is being swamped is the mental capacity cognitive scientists call 'working memory,' the ability to hold in mind all information relevant to the task at hand."[10]

There are various levels of negative emotional reactions ranging from extreme fear to low level anxiety. When children experience any of these negative feelings, it takes a toll on both their capacity to formulate new concepts and remember what they have learned. On the other hand, there is research to show that when children have the benefit of supportive and appropriately stimulating environments their capacity for brain development is enhanced.

An interesting study using rats illustrates this concept. Two sets of rats were given identical mazes to master over a period of time. One set of rats were treated with extra care and shown emotional support by the people involved. The other set's human contact was limited to meeting their minimal needs. The first set of rats successfully completed the maze before the second set did. Upon analysis, the brains of the first set of rats actually showed that there was a thicker coating of myelin on the axons of the neurons which resulted in stronger synaptic connections than the second set of rats. This study illustrated that the rats that were treated with extra care thought more clearly and made their way through the maze more quickly than the rats that did not receive extra attention.[11] How does this relate to a child?

Providing nurturing emotional environments during childhood is extremely important because this is the time when the child forms the majority of his intelligence and the time when his emotional impressions are being recorded in his amygdala glands. What a child experiences in the first years of life remain embedded in his emotional memory forever. Emotional safety for children is best achieved when parents and caregivers demonstrate respect and offer encouragement. When children experience this positive regard they develop self confidence and the courage to attempt new things. Jane Healy sums it up nicely:

> *The bottom line here seems to be that infants need safety, love, and conversation from their parents, or from capable, consistent caregivers. They need an environment that stimulates them to do their own exploring, manipulating, and wondering. A calm caring home with reasonable limits but without excessive fear of punishment is a good one for brain building.[12]*

Meaningful Context

Research has shown that children integrate and assimilate information from their environment more easily and effectively when what they learn is related to concepts previously presented to them. This information makes sense when we relate it back to the understanding of how learning takes place in the brain—environmental stimulus enters the brain and forms neurons that automatically search for connecting links with other neurons. If information coming into the brain is totally unrelated to former knowledge it may form a new neuron, but because it is unrelated to former knowledge, it is not as strong and as deeply embedded in the memory. Montessori spoke of this phenomenon nearly 100 years ago. "Here then is an essential principle of education: to teach details is to bring confusion; to establish the relationship between things is to bring knowledge."[13]

Four ways in which we can provide meaningful contexts for our children's learning are:

1. relate new experiences to former ones

2. make the purpose and meaning clear

3. place concepts in a greater whole

4. provide opportunities for children to the share their knowledge with others.[14]

Another way to talk about relating new experiences to former ones is to see learning as a series of stepping stones. In Montessori classrooms the entire learning environment is designed so that each concrete learning material is arranged on a shelf in sequential order from the simplest to the most complex. In this manner the concepts learned are related to one another and progress step by step to the next level of difficulty.

In the home it is important to be aware of what the child has experienced and provide new input that is connected to former concepts and offers a new dimension. To be able to do this, we must watch for teaching moments. An example of this was when my ten year old granddaughter was studying about the country of Norway in school and called me excitedly on the phone to ask me about her ancestors who came from Sweden and Denmark. When she came to visit, she enthusiastically sought out and enjoyed reading stories about her great, great, great grandparents who sailed to the United States to pioneer the west. Had I just asked her to come and read these stories, without any prior connection to previous knowledge and interest, she most likely would not have had the same level of enthusiasm, if she had any interest at all.

When something interests us, it is much easier and pleasant to learn more about it because the new knowledge holds meaning for us. One way to do this is to make abstract concepts clearer by the use of concrete materials or symbols. For example, we find that young children respond beautifully to the abstract concept of "love" when we give them a love light pin which is a two inch yellow felt circle they can place over their heart center. Prior to giving them the love light pin, we talk with them about the beautiful light of love within them and illustrate it by shining a flashlight on the heart center of a tissue paper template of a child's body.[15]

When we present new ideas in the context of the greater whole, the ideas will be assimilated and remembered more effectively because we provide the child with hooks (neurons) that he can use to connect the new knowledge. In other words, if we want to help a child know where he lives, give him a globe or map of the whole world, show him the continents, go to the country where he lives and finally point out his town. Stories can also be an effective tool to create a greater whole and trigger the child's imagination.

When children share what they have learned with others it not only reinforces their own memory patterns, it also adds meaning because of the social implications it holds. When a child helps another child, his own learning is reinforced and he experiences meaning because he has assisted another person. When children are given the opportunity to share what they have learned with their peers, they are naturally motivated to study and solidify their presentation because they are motivated to do a good job in front of their friends.

Angelina Polk Lillard sums up the importance of learning within a meaningful context when she says that there are, "many studies showing that embedding learning in a meaningful context is associated with better learning, more interest, and greater embracing of challenges than embedding learning in the abstract contexts that school materials too often use."[16]

Conclusion

The Integration Phase is where the child's mind assimilates and orders incoming data. The child's ability to integrate sensory input in his subconscious mind is facilitated by his ability to concentrate his full attention on the task at hand. Repetition is the quality that embeds sensory input deeply into the memory bank so that new learning can take place. Emotional safety frees the mind from fear and allows the natural integration of environmental stimuli. Finally, when new information can be connected to previous learning, it is more easily integrated and remembered.

Suggestions for Follow Through

Observe your child's natural processes of integration. When you see your child focusing on a particular activity, observe how he is assimilating the incoming sensorial stimulation. Observe and hold the following questions.

■ Is my child concentrating his full attention on the activity? What happens to his focus when he is interrupted? Observe how he feels when he finishes his activity uninterrupted. If you need to interrupt your child, how can you do it with the least amount of disruption?

■ Is my child repeating the same actions over and over again? Is there something that visibly takes place when he stops the repetition?

■ Is my child feeling emotionally safe? What happens to his ability to concentrate and engage in repetitive activity when he is threatened?

■ Introduce something new to your child that is related to something he is already familiar with (a meaningful context). Observe his engagement. At another time, introduce something new to your child that has no apparent connection to past knowing. Observe his engagement. Is there a difference in his ability to assimilate the new information?

Record what you observe in your parent journal.

CHAPTER 7

The Love Phase

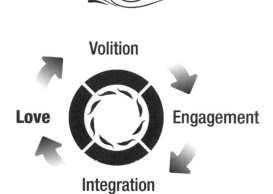

The fourth and culminating phase of the VEIL Model is Love. This is the mastery phase when children experience the joy and satisfaction of completion. This joy embeds itself in the memory bank of the child and serves as the seeds for future Volition. The successful completion of a cycle motivates him to reach out and learn something new—to begin the Unveiling Cycle all over again. Each Unveiling Cycle creates a spiral that continues to unveil the child's Authentic Self. Four of the basic elements of the Love Phase are:

1. Normalization

2. Authenticity and Self-Actualization

3. Creativity

4. Self Discipline.

Normalization

When a child is encouraged to live and work in harmony with the natural laws of child development, as described in the Unveiling Cycle, he naturally manifests positive psychological characteristics such as enthusiasm, thoughtfulness and joy. Montessori saw this state of equilibrium as the normal state of a psychically healthy child and called it "normalization." "Only 'normalized' children, aided by their environment, show in their subsequent development those wonderful powers that we describe: spontaneous discipline, continuous and happy work, social sentiments of help and sympathy for others."[1]

Montessori recognized that when children are deprived of the experience of organizing their personality through the natural Unveiling Cycle, they begin to manifest negative behaviors. Because this state is not "normal," she referred to it as being a "deviation" from the norm. When a child is misbehaving it is not that the child is bad, but that he is suffering from being out of touch with his normal state or his Authentic Self. Instead of operating and being guided by the magnanimity of his Spirit, he falls victim to the instability of the lower mind of sensory input, ego and memory. This can be a painful and frustrating place for children causing them to manifest a variety of negative behaviors such as disinterest, stubbornness, and fighting. Montessori recognized this when she said,

> *The naughtiness of small children is a manifestation of defense or of unconscious despair at not being able to 'function'....Naughtiness can also be a form of agitation caused by mental hunger when the child is deprived of the stimuli of the environment or by a sense of frustration experienced when he is prevented from acting in the environment. The 'unconscious aim' then moving ever farther from its realization creates a kind of hell in the life of the child who becomes separated from a leading source and its creative energies.*[2]

The leading sources of the child's creative energies are the inner guide and vital force located within his Authentic Self. Montessori witnessed over and over again that when a child, suffering from a state of deprivation, becomes meaningfully involved in work, experiences deep concentration and reconnects with his Spirit, his defects of character fall away. "But when the attractions of the new environment exert their spell, offering motives for constructive activity, then all these energies combine and the deviations can be dispersed. A unique type of child appears, a 'new child'; but really it is the child's true 'personality' allowed to construct itself normally."[3]

Authenticity and Self-Actualization

The more a child successfully moves through the Unveiling Cycles the deeper he connects to his authenticity. Montessori witnessed this phenomenon with awe. "And each time that such a polarization of attention took place, the child began to be completely transformed, to become calmer, more intelligent, and more expansive; it showed extraordinary spiritual qualities, recalling the phenomena of a higher consciousness, such as those of conversion."[4]

This transformational process that Montessori witnessed can be compared to what Abraham Maslow described as self-actualization or the process of fulfilling our greatest potential and becoming all that we are capable of becoming. We were fascinated to compare how his definition of "peak experiences" relates to Montessori's description of the joy children experience when accomplishing their great work of concentration.

It looks as if any experience of real excellence, of real perfection, of any moving toward the perfect justice or toward perfect values, tends to produce a peak experience.[5]

—ABRAHAM MASLOW

One is tempted to say that the children are performing spiritual exercises having found the path of self-perfectionment and of ascent to the inner heights of the soul.[6]

—MARIA MONTESSORI

Maslow points out that self-actualization is not a permanent state of being but rather a gradual accumulation of experiences and qualities described below:[7]

- Experiencing fully, vividly, selflessly with full concentration and total absorption.

- Making growth choices rather than fear choices

- Allowing Self to emerge

- Being honest and taking responsibility for one's own actions

- Listening to one's own inner voice

- Actualizing one's potentials

- Being surprised by joy—"peak experiences" or transient moments of self-actualization

- Opening up to one's Authentic Self and letting go defenses

From our perspective, these are the same experiences and qualities children manifest as they naturally move through the Unveiling Cycles. Each step along the way creates opportunities for them to master these eight qualities and lead them to a life of authenticity and self-actualization.

Another correlation between Montessori and Maslow's work are the characteristics that are manifested when people act from authenticity or a state of self-actualization. These shared characteristics are: truth, goodness, beauty, wholeness, synergy, aliveness, uniqueness, perfection, necessity, completion, justice, order, simplicity, richness, effortlessness, playfulness, and self-sufficiency.[8]

What a joy it is to know that through conscientious attention on the part of parents and teachers, we can provide children with the type of home life and education that nurtures their authenticity and their abilities to be who they were born to be. "All have a tendency, however vague and unconscious, to raise themselves up; they aspire to something spiritual."[9]

Creativity

Creativity comes because of an inner desire to bring about newness, novelty or discovery. This gift is an inborn potential available to all human beings. Whether it is developed or not depends on the quality of the parenting, education and environmental influences a child has in his life. What, then, does it take to foster creativity in children?

A leading expert in the field of creativity, Mihaly Csikszentmihalyi, refers to the process of creativity as "the flow experience." He makes a point that it is not *what* people do, but *how* they do it that determines the level of creativity.[10] Following is a description of what it takes for one to be in the flow of the creative process:[11]

- There are clear goals every step of the way

- There is immediate feedback to one's actions

- There is a balance between challenges and skills

- Action and awareness are merged

- Distractions are excluded from consciousness

- There is no worry of failure

- Self-consciousness disappears

- The sense of time becomes distorted

- The activity is carried out for the pure joy of it

You will no doubt recognize a correlation between these aspects of creativity and the natural laws propelling a child's own creative process of unveiling his authenticity. For humans to be creative they must develop such qualities as: self confidence, humility, trust, courage, flexibility, curiosity, determination, spontaneity, concentration and selflessness. They must be able to be in process rather than working for an end product.

For children to develop these qualities, they must be encouraged to engage themselves in appropriately stimulating environments, be allowed to freely make choices from their center of authenticity, be protected from distractions, and be left alone to concentrate and engage in their work. By being actively engaged in this continuous unveiling spiral, children tune into their Authentic Self and naturally manifest the necessary qualities to be creative individuals throughout their lives.

Csikszentmihalyi spoke to the central role authenticity plays in the development of creativity when he says, "What allows certain individuals to make memorable contributions to the culture is a personal resolution to shape their lives to suit their own growth instead of letting external forces rule their destiny."[12]

Montessori recognized the Authentic Self within all people and saw it as the creative seed of hope for a better future. "Both the individual and society have this in common: a continuous tendency to progress. Whether on the outer or inner plane, there is a tiny light in the unconscious of mankind, which guides it toward better things."[13]

Development of the Will

During each cycle within the Unveiling Spiral children naturally develop their power of will, which is a combination of the vital force and the inner guide. The vital force is the energy of impulse and the inner guide is the voice of discrimination or inhibition. Impulse by itself leads to erratic and meaningless activity. Inhibition by itself leads to timidity and dependence on others. Before the will is fully developed, young children swing back and forth between the two extremes of impulse and inhibition. As they are allowed to follow their internal laws of development they naturally find the balance between the two and the will is formed.

It is important to remember that will is the force within the child that nudges him to engage meaningfully in life and become an active participant in it. To think of "breaking a child's will" in order that they will obey an authority, is detrimental to the child's life and work. According to Dr. Montessori, "the will is a force which impels activities beneficial to life. Nature imposes on the child the task of growing up, and his will leads him to make progress and to develop his powers....

Conscious will is a power which develops with use and activity. We must aim at cultivating the will, not at breaking it."[14]

Through her work and observation of children, Montessori witnessed three stages that children pass through in the development of their will.

STAGE ONE: ATTENTION AND ATTRACTION TO THE ENVIRONMENT

This first stage of will development begins when the child is attracted to a certain object in his environment (impulse) and naturally eliminates other stimulation (inhibition) to give full attention to the discovery. When he reaches out to touch or caress the object (impulse), he begins to unconsciously coordinate his movements by eliminating unnecessary ones (inhibition). The act of making choices on his own (impulse) requires that he let go other choice possibilities (inhibition). As he unconsciously decides to focus, persevere and concentrate on an activity for a period of time, he begins to unconsciously create his inner will. When he repeats this activity willingly over and over again, he not only reinforces his learning, but also strengthens his will to master the task. With mastery comes a wonderful sense of satisfaction and empowerment which positively reinforces the joy of engaging constructively in purposeful activities within the environment. Each time this engagement happens the child's will is strengthened. Dr. Montessori describes how the power of concentration influences the development of a child's inner discipline.

The more the capacity to concentrate is developed, the more often the profound tranquility in work is achieved, then the clearer will be the manifestation of discipline within the child....A single instance will form the discipline of a child, and self-disciplined children are on the way to a natural psychic development.[15]

STAGE TWO: CONSCIOUS SELF DISCIPLINE

In the second stage the child moves from unconscious will development to conscious self-discipline. Realizing the benefits of involving himself in constructive work the child chooses self-discipline as a way of life. He naturally wants to make thoughtful decisions and cooperate with the people in his environment. He develops the ability to accept responsibility for his own actions and willingly complies with the limits of reality. He takes great joy in seeing what he is capable of accomplishing and consciously chooses to be in touch with his authenticity and inner guidance.

STAGE THREE: OBEDIENCE

In this final stage of will development the child, being filled with love for himself, others and the environment willingly takes direction from caring adults who he sees as having his best interest in mind. At this point, the child is primarily operating from his Authentic Self because his ego is not threatened by another person giving him direction.

Montessori was thrilled to witness this amazing process of will development:

> *Now the little child who manifests perseverance in his work as the first constructive act of his psychical life, and upon this act builds up internal order, equilibrium, and the growth of personality, demonstrates, almost as in a splendid revelation, the true manner in which man renders himself valuable to the community.*[16]

Conclusion

The Phase of Love is a joyous one. When a child is 1) motivated to select a new activity (Volition), 2) receives input from the environment (Engagement), 3) successfully assimilates the information (Integration) he feels great joy (Love) because he has experienced the inner satisfaction of discovering something new. He catches a glimpse of his authenticity, potentials and talents. He experiences what Maslow calls a "peak experience."

Having had a taste of this deep happiness, he is naturally motivated to engage in another Unveiling Cycle so he can create or discover something new. No one has to tell him to act because he has a natural desire to do so.

The greatest creation in life is the process of Unveiling the Authentic Self. What a joy it is to know that children are wired for success. If we, as adults, can let go our preconceived ideas that we must create the child and instead honor his natural process of development through repeating the Unveiling Cycles, the children will manifest their greatest potentials and lead us to a brighter future. Montessori said it this way:

> *When prejudice is vanquished by knowledge, then there will appear in the world a 'superior child' with his marvelous powers which today remain hidden. Then there will appear the child who is destined to form a humanity capable of understanding and controlling our present civilization.*[17]

Suggestion for Follow Through

Observe your child's expression of Love upon completion of a learning cycle. Be aware of your child when he is engaged in learning a new skill or concept. Do not interrupt his learning process or Unveiling Cycle in any way. Simply observe the first three phases of Volition, Engagement and Integration, as previously described, and watch his expressions in the fourth phase of Love when he successfully completes the learning cycle. Hold the following questions:

- When my child successfully completes a task what emotions does he manifest?

- After successful completion of a learning cycle, what is his behavior like?

- Do you observe elements of creativity or a desire to share what he has learned?

- Do you observe your child developing confidence in his abilities and being internally directed to continue the process of taking the next step to engage in another cycle of learning and unveiling his authenticity?

Record what you observe in your parent journal.

PART III

Creating Nurturing Home Environments

PART III

Creating Nurturing Home Environments

*"Scientific observation then has established that education
is not what the teacher gives; education is a natural process
spontaneously carried out by the human individual, and is acquired
not by listening to words but by experiences upon the environment."*[1]

—MARIA MONTESSORI

Dr. Maria Montessori recognized that the most effective way to educate a child is to provide him with environments that meet his physical, mental, emotional and spiritual needs. When environments are prepared to meet these needs, he is drawn to the activities within the prepared environment and naturally engages in the process of unveiling his Authentic Self through the VEIL Model.

For thousands of years, people thought that the best way to pass knowledge on to children is for adults to tell them what they need to know. With this idea comes the assumption that children must pay attention, listen intently and repeat back what is said to them. This model is based on the idea that children are empty vessels that must be filled by those that know.

The Adult

The Child

When Dr. Montessori stepped onto the educational stage she added a third dimension to the educational process—the Environment. She illustrated this concept using a triangle.

The Child

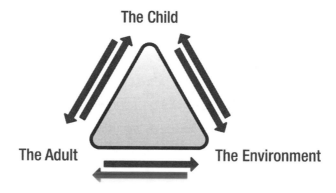

The Adult   **The Environment**

The Adult—(1) observes the developmental needs and interests of the Child, and (2) prepares the Environment to attract and provide concrete activities to match the child's needs and interests.

The Child—(1) trusts and follows the direction of the Adult, and (2) is attracted to the activities provided in the prepared Environment.

The Environment—(1) calls to the Child to engage in the activities provided, and (2) provides feedback to the Adult as to what activities are meaningful to the child and which ones need to be changed to meet the unfolding needs and interests of the Child.

Maria Montessori pioneered the concept of learning from concrete materials and experiences within an environment. Her work was a forerunner of what we now call "experiential learning." Throughout her lifetime, she designed complete sets of materials covering the major subject areas of practical living, sensory awareness, math, science, language, geography, history, culture, music, and art for children from three to twelve years of age. She also developed lessons and activities for adolescents that are based on their unique developmental stage.

Montessori's approach to education awoke the educational community during her time and continues to grow in popularity today as children consistently benefit from the process of being able to interact and learn directly from the activities of their prepared school environments. Making the effort to prepare our child's home environment will create a similar phenomenon and we will joyfully witness the continuous unveiling of our child's Authentic Self. Aline Wolf sums it up beautifully, "The role of the adult is not to teach but to prepare the environment that will facilitate the work of the child's inner teacher."[2]

In Parts I & II we focused on the nature of the *Child* and how he unveils his authenticity through the VEIL Model and its accompanying four phases of the Unveiling Cycle. Now in Part III we explore another element of the Montessori Educational Triangle—the *Environment*. In Part IV we explore the third aspect of the educational triangle—the *Adult*.

In the following four chapters we offer concrete suggestions to enhance the physical, mental, emotional and spiritual aspects of the home environment. Thoughtful preparation of the home will not only enhance the learning of our children but also their sense of well being, confidence and cooperation.

Montessori sums up the importance of examining our home environments: "The child thus incarnate is a spiritual embryo which must come to live for itself in the environment. But like the physical embryo, the spiritual embryo must be protected by an external environment animated by the warmth of love and the richness of value, where it is wholly accepted and never inhibited."[3]

CHAPTER 8

Creating the Physical Environment

For a moment remember how you are affected when you move from one home to another and all of your belongings are packed or scattered around. My recollection is one of feeling unorganized, unsure and overwhelmed with a variety of other disturbing and unproductive emotions floating around. Once I begin to put things in place and bring order to my physical possessions I begin to feel a sense of calmness and even excitement about creating a new space for myself and family. Children are even more dramatically affected by their physical surroundings than we are because their environments provide, not only physical sustenance and safety, but they also provide the means for children to construct their thought processes and unveil the Authentic Self. Following are specific suggestions designed to enhance the physical environment in the home.

Create Order

As discussed in Chapter 4, The Volition Phase, children, especially between the ages of birth and six, are in a sensitive period for order. They literally use their external environments to organize the internal functioning of their minds. In these first six years children absorb the stimuli surrounding them and form their patterns of thinking from what is available to them. When homes are cluttered and disorganized, children's natural processes of learning from their environments are hindered and they can easily become frustrated and overwhelmed. By thoughtfully organizing children's physical belongings, they are able to make accurate associations, increase their learning capacities, and interact with confidence because they know where things are and what to expect.

Once children move into the second level of development, age's six to twelve, they continue to benefit from an organized environment, even though their focus for order becomes internalized in the structuring of their mental concepts. Of course, at this age, children are capable of taking more and more responsibility for the order of their environments. Following are specific suggestions:

ORGANIZE CHILDREN'S BELONGINGS

Children benefit from knowing where their belongings are and how to use them. Their belongings include such things as their clothing, toys, art supplies, collections and their hygiene items such as comb, brush, toothbrush, towel and washcloth. Even in infancy, it is good to let children know what you are doing for them. For example, when you are dressing them gently speak about what you are doing. "It is time to get dressed. Here is your blue shirt. Let's put it over your head. Now let's put on your pants...." By doing this you are respecting the child by letting him know what is happening to him, you are encouraging the development of his vocabulary and you are helping him develop a pattern of how to do things in a sequentially successful manner.

When children become mobile, their belongings need to be accessible to them and in predictable places. This is a time when they want to be actively involved in the selecting and putting away of clothes and other items. Limiting their belongings to a manageable number greatly facilitates this process of maintaining order in their environment.

REMOVE THE TOY BOX

The toy box is a clutter box for children. To get to a specific toy, children must pull out toy after toy until they find what they want. By the time they find a toy of interest there is already a clutter pile of toys on the floor. The additional clutter can affect their play and when it is time to put the toys away, it is often an overwhelming process for them to do alone.

DISPLAY TOYS ON SHELVES

When toys are organized and displayed on low shelves so children can reach them, it is easier for them to make thoughtful decisions as to what they want to do. Organizing the toys so that small related objects, such as model cars, are all together in a container such as a basket or on a tray is helpful. Placing related items next to each other on the shelf reinforces connection and relationships and makes it easier for the child to know where to get the toy and where to put it when he is finished with it.

LIMIT THE NUMBER OF TOYS

Too many toys create chaos for children. Too many toys make it hard for children to thoughtfully choose what to play with. Too many toys challenge children's ability to concentrate. Too many toys make it difficult for children to put the toys away. Limit toys to how many can fit comfortably on the shelves and are of immediate interest to the children. Keep the toys they are not using out of sight and when you see that they have lost interest in one toy, take it away and bring out another one. This keeps the toy shelf fresh and interesting. Of course, as children get older, they can be involved in the decision as to what toys should stay and which ones should be put aside for the time being.

PROVIDE ROUTINES

Very young children (up to 3 years old) need as much order and routine as possible because they are working on the important task of making sense of the life around them. Because of this they can become extremely upset when the usual routines they are used to are changed. Have you ever seen a two-year old throw a tantrum when you vary the order in which you feed him? The reaction to a change in routine may not be as extreme as children get older, but they, too, appreciate the stability and reassurance of routines. To quote our ten year old granddaughter when we suggested a change to something she had come to expect and appreciate: "But Grandma, we always do it this way!" When it is necessary to change the expected routine, give children advance notice of what will be happening instead of what they have come to expect.

Facilitate Children's Independence

As discussed earlier children, around the age of two, begin to assert their independence and want to do things "all by themselves." When this need is frustrated, children often express their frustration through temper tantrums or resistive behavior. Children are extremely interested in modeling adult behavior and learning the practical life skills they see the adults in their lives doing. Young children are interested and excited to learn how to dress themselves, pour their own milk, eat with utensils and clean up after themselves. Older children follow this interest with more advanced activities such as cooking, baking, caring for plants, gardening etc. It is important to encourage children's independence in the home by providing many opportunities for them to become involved in practical life activities.

To begin focusing on this, become aware of what you are doing for your child and see if there is a way to design the activity so he can accomplish it by himself. It may be that a small foot stool makes it possible for your child to get a drink of water or assist with food preparation. Putting the dishes at your child's reach facilitates his ability to assist in table setting and snack preparation. By making things readily accessible you free him from the frustration of needing to wait for help and give him a vote of confidence as you let him know that you trust his ability to do it by himself.

Children engaged in practical life activities satisfy and develop their keen sense of order as they are shown step by step how to successfully accomplish the task at hand. This requires a thoughtful demonstration of how to move from one step to the next. Demonstrating how to pour a glass of juice may require as many as ten different steps. For example demonstrate how to: 1) get a glass, 2) carry it carefully to the table, 3) open the refrigerator, 4) thoughtfully carry the child-size juice pitcher to the glass, 5) hold the pitcher with one hand on the handle and one hand under the spout, 6) pour the juice into the glass, 7) clean up any spills with an available sponge, 8) replace the pitcher in the refrigerator,

9) drink the juice, and 10) put the used glass on the sink to be cleaned later. As you are demonstrating various tasks, move slowly and keep your talking to a minimum so the child can focus on what you are doing.

Because practical life is a real and rewarding experience, children naturally focus on what they are doing and develop their capacities to consciously concentrate and direct their energies. They also develop their eye/hand coordination as they engage in the physical process of accomplishing a given task. Children's desire to be independent continues throughout their lifetime so creating home environments that facilitate this quest for self mastery is vital. Following are practical suggestions to encourage children to become engaged in the ongoing practical life in the home:

ACTIVITIES IN THE KITCHEN

The kitchen is a treasure house of possibilities for children to become happily engaged. Let's start with the refrigerator. Organize it so that children can easily help themselves to healthy snacks and drinks. Make sure that the juice or milk is in a child-size pitcher so they can successfully pour the liquid. When you are ready to cook a meal ask your child to retrieve the vegetables that will be needed. Provide a place for him to safely help cut and prepare some of the vegetables for the meal. Children as young as three, with proper demonstration and supervision, are capable of cutting bread, fruit, cheese and vegetables. Providing children with their own special aprons for food preparation helps protect their clothes and also gives them a special sense of purpose in their work. It is helpful to have a small table and chair in the kitchen so the child can prepare the food. If this is not possible provide a special foot stool for your child so he can reach the counter or a booster chair so he can reach the table.

Our son, Christian, worked next to my side when he was very young as I baked cake, cookies, muffins and bread. He had his own measuring cups and spoons and, of course, a special apron I had made with a football appliquéd on it. During our baking times we talked about what it takes to make a cake become a cake. By the time he was eight years old, he was making our family cakes from scratch by himself from no recipe. It was amazing. On a similar note, our grandchildren, Andy and Sera, helped with the cooking and baking in our home during their visits throughout their elementary years. Now as young adolescents, they prepare the family meal together once a week.

When Christian and our daughter, Jeannie were less than three feet tall, we actually moved the plates and glasses to shelves low enough for them to reach so they could independently get a drink or snack as well as help set the table. We demonstrated how to carry the glass plates and glasses thoughtfully so the glassware would not break. Carrying plastic dishes doesn't provide children the opportunity to learn to concentrate because there is no consequence when a plastic plate drops on the floor.

Providing materials that allow children to clean up after preparing food or when accidentally spilling something empowers the children and helps us avoid shaming them. These materials must be easily accessible for the child and a size that he can successfully handle. These items include: a sponge, a small bucket for water, a drying cloth, a broom, a dust pan and brush.

ACTIVITIES IN THE BEDROOM

Earlier we discussed the importance of providing storage for children's belongings because of their need for order in their lives. Now let's focus on how that same effort of organization enhances their need to be independent and empowered in a constructive manner.

Look at your child's bedroom and see if he can get to all of his clothes without your assistance. Are the drawers organized in a way that is clear to your child? Are they low enough that he can open and close them without fear of the dresser falling over? Are the clothes hung low enough that he can reach them? Is there a place for the child to place the clothes that need to be washed? Once these items are in place, your child will be able to engage in the care of his clothes. With your assistance, he can learn to look at his clothes to see if the clothes are clean enough to wear again or if they need to be put in a laundry basket. He can learn to fold his clothes and put them away. He can begin to select the clothes he wants to wear, one step at a time. Initially you can give him a choice of two items and then, as he learns more about what is appropriate to wear together and for the weather, he can begin to make choices from a greater variety.

When our children were in preschool, we had a bedtime routine that worked very well. We engaged them in the process of selecting clothes for the next day. Sometimes we talked about the weather and what clothes would be appropriate. Sometimes we talked about what goes together and what doesn't. In the beginning we gave them the choice of two outfits so they were not overwhelmed. Once they decided what they wanted to wear, they would lay the clothes (including underwear, socks and shoes) out on the floor in the shape of their body. The next morning, they loved to surprise us by coming into the bedroom all dressed.

Older children also respond to having their bedrooms organized for their needs. When Andy and Sera came to visit us, the first thing they would do is go to their bedrooms and unpack so they could feel comfortable and "at home." If the laundry basket was not in the room, they would remind us to get it.

ACTIVITIES IN THE BATHROOM

The more children can do for themselves, the more willing they are to do the task. Such things as taking baths, brushing teeth and combing hair can happen naturally if the bathroom is set to help children do as much as possible by themselves.

The first thing to determine is whether your child can reach the sink and toilet by himself. If not, provide a foot stool. Make sure that he can reach his toothbrush and toothpaste. Of course, it is good for you to be present while he is very young so that you can make sure he is able to do a thorough job of brushing his teeth. Helping him to understand the importance of teeth brushing will help keep him motivated to do the job.

During toileting, make sure that he can reach the stool and the toilet paper easily. As soon as possible, empower him to complete the tasks of toileting all by himself. A friend of mine shared her 2 ½ year old son's reaction when she told him that he had to wipe himself. She said that the child looked shockingly at her and said, "You mean I have to wipe my own bottom for the rest of my entire life?" Mom said, "Yes!!!"

Taking a bath can be a most enjoyable experience for children. Having some items for your young child to play with while in the tub adds pleasure and fun to the bathing process. When it is time to wash and shampoo hair, do your best to make it a pleasant experience. Place a towel hook at your child's level so he can take it down and put it back on his own.

Create a place within your child's reach for his comb and brush. Give him demonstrations on how to comb and brush his hair. Encourage him to be aware of when he may need to use these skills. Have a full length mirror in either the bathroom or bedroom so your child can see himself. A newborn baby benefits by having a small mirror in the crib and then, as he is learning to crawl and then walk, it is helpful to have a mirror low enough that he can continue to see his reflection and develop a physical self image.

ACTIVITIES IN THE LIVING AREAS

In the family gathering areas such as the family room, living room and dining room, you can enhance your child's sense of awareness, appreciation and independence by providing the following activities.

Children naturally love plants and you can nurture this love further by providing them with the tools to care for them in your home. A child-size watering can, water sprayer, cotton balls and tongue depressor placed on a tray are all you need. Demonstrate how to gently wash the leaves by spraying them with water and wiping them. Show how to water the plant and then place a tongue depressor or other marker in the soil to mark that the plant has had a drink. Depending on the ages of your children, they can assist with the dusting, cleaning of glass, vacuuming, mopping and sweeping. As children get older their responsibilities should increase in proportion to their desire to be independent. It is important to provide child-size brooms and mops so the children can easily handle them. In general, provide child-size implements for children's successful use.

ACTIVITIES IN THE YARD

Children love to help with outside activities. Providing child-size rakes, shovels and other gardening equipment can be an inspiring and fun activity to share with your child. It is good to also provide gardening gloves and hats when needed. As children get older, you can have meaningful times of sharing as you show them how to use hammers, screw drivers, saws and other equipment. Allowing children to paint big surfaces is fun for them as well. Sera and Andy enjoyed working by Grandpa's side as he helped them build a tree house in the big willow tree in our yard. Of course, following the construction they enjoyed painting it, decorating it and giving it a name—"Andy and Sera's Tree House of Friends."

Make the Home Comfortable and Beautiful

As we design our homes, we carefully think about how to make it comfortable and beautiful for us. We put the pictures at a height that we can see readily while sitting or standing. We make sure that the chairs and couches are comfortable for our bodies and that the tables are both attractive and functional for us. Have we done the same for our children?

Have you ever sat in the middle of the floor of your living room and looked around to see how it looks from your young child's point of view? When you do, you will most likely see table legs and table tops, chair seats and chair legs, couch cushions and pillows all of adult size. Are there comfortable places for your child to sit in all of the family gathering places? Are there pictures they can enjoy at their eye level? Are there attractive objects they *can* touch and explore? Are there child activities they can be involved in? When we make the rooms in our home "child friendly" and beautiful, children experience respect and this adds to their sense of well being and calm.

When you have very young children in the home who want to explore everything around them, it is important to remove those items that are either dangerous to the child or would break your heart to have them harmed. Children's natural tendency is to touch and feel—they mean no harm. By removing that which is not appropriate for them to handle, we avoid saying, "Don't touch!" Of course, even young children can learn to treat the items in the home with respect if we kindly request them to, "Please leave the vase on the table." or "Let me show you how to touch this very gently."

Teach Self-Management Skills

Your child's physical body is certainly a vital part of his physical environment. Helping him understand how his body works will empower him throughout his life. When your child knows that the respiratory and muscular systems can be used to help him reconnect to his Spirit he begins to develop the ability to observe himself and consciously manage his body, mind and emotions. This skill leads to the ability to move from victim consciousness to empowerment consciousness.

Children benefit from actually seeing scientifically correct pictures of the respiratory and muscular systems so they can have a clear mental image of what is going on inside of their bodies. When they see that their lungs are large and protected by a rib cage, it is helpful to have them locate their rib cage and experience it with their hands. After surveying the size of the rib cage and the ribs themselves, have them keep their hands on the rib cage and breathe in deeply so they can feel how the rib cage expands and contracts. Involve the child in a discussion about the importance of oxygen. Some of the highlights are that it gives his body more energy, helps his mind think more clearly and calms his emotions so he can connect with his Authentic Self or Spirit of love. Let him know that there is a special way to breathe that will increase the amount of oxygen he brings into his body. Show him how to do diaphragmatic breathing.

The process of breathing from the diaphragm begins by having your child exhale the carbon dioxide in his lungs. The most effective way to empty the lungs is to have your child contract his abdominal muscles and exhale. When his lungs are empty have him expand his abdominal muscles and inhale oxygen. When your child uses diaphragmatic breathing he will increase the amount of oxygen in his body and begin to experience the benefits of calming down. On an on-going basis practice deep breathing with him and when you see him struggling and "out of sorts" remind him to use his deep breathing.[1]

A similar approach can be used to help your child learn to consciously relax his muscles. Show a picture of the muscular system and have him explore the various muscles in his body. Demonstrate how muscles can either be tense or relaxed just by sending a message from the mind. Ask your child to tense his muscles then ask him to relax his muscles. Next have your child lie on the floor and close his eyes. Let him know you are going to ask him to tense the muscles in his body one at a time. Begin by asking him to tense specific muscles starting with the muscles of his toes. Continue moving up the body asking your child to tense each of the main muscle groups. Once they are completely tense, ask him to relax the muscles and breathe deeply. Next, tell him you are going to ask him to relax the same muscle groups so he can see the difference. Repeat the process of moving up the body one muscle group at a time, but this time ask him to relax each muscle group and periodically remind him to take deep breaths. Again, when you observe that your child is stressed, remind or help him, consciously relax his muscles by sending messages to the muscles and deep breathing.[2]

Utilize the Power of Touch

The power of touch is one of the most effective ways to help your child relax and experience his center of calm. When Jeannie and Christian were infants we began gentle infant massage and proceeded to regularly offer back or shoulder rubs as they settled down for the night. It is not necessary to have a degree to give a child a tender massage. All it takes is compassion and a willingness to sense what your child's body may need. This can be as simple as a warm hug or as extensive as a full body rub. As our children got older they could sense when we needed a shoulder rub or hug and, because they had enjoyed both of these at an early age, they already knew how to do it. It is important to recognize that some children do not respond well to touch and in these cases we need to be sensitive to their needs.

Conclusion

Physical environments are concrete and surround children at all times. As discussed earlier, the physical environment is the primary vehicle for children to engage in the Unveiling Cycle and reveal their potentials and authenticity. It is, therefore, important to take the time and make the effort to thoughtfully design our home environments to be as responsive as possible for our children.

Suggestions for Follow Through

■ **Bring greater independence to your child**. Observe what you are doing for your child and determine if there is something you can do to the physical environment that will empower him to do it by himself. Be aware of your child's response to having more independence.

■ **Change clutter to clean**. Look for ways to reorganize areas in your home where your child's clothes, toys and books create clutter. Ask yourself if there is a way to limit the amount of clothes, toys and books. Reorganize the areas so they are readily accessible to your child. Where possible involve your child in making improvements to the care and storage of his clothes, toys and books.

■ **Accept help from your child**. Children like to be a part of adult work. Even though sometimes it seems easier and faster to do it by ourselves, look to ways in which you can include your child in the work of the home. Cooking is a favorite. Provide a place for the child to work and the child-size tools he will need to be successful. Demonstrate step by step what he needs to do to accomplish the task. Enjoy the result!

■ **Give your child a massage**. A tender touch is one of the most calming things we share with our children. As your child is going to bed, ask him if he would like you to rub his back to help him relax. If he is open to it, gently massage his neck, shoulders and back. Observe his responses.

Record what you observe.

CHAPTER 9

Creating the Mental Environment

Children are born with specific mental abilities based on heredity; however, the degree to which these abilities develop largely depends on what parents do in the home. While the schools do their part to educate children, parental influence makes the biggest difference in children's abilities to successfully make use of their minds. The mind's ability is far more than what shows up on an IQ score. It is not simply an accumulation of associations in the memory bank that can be brought up at the appropriate time. Rather, the mind is a complex system that determines our thinking processes, decision making, creativity, inner wisdom, understanding, attitudes and memory. With thoughtful attention, parents can support children's processes of creating strong mental habits that will bring success and fulfillment throughout their lives. Following are some suggestions:

Keep a Positive Attitude

Children thrive in an atmosphere of loving support and joy. As parents we can provide this by doing our best to maintain a positive attitude. Keeping a positive mind means that we make conscious choices to see events from the perspective of love instead of fear. Gerald Jampolsky, in his book, *Love is Letting Go of Fear*,[1] speaks clearly to the simple truth that our natural inner state is the spirit of love and that what keeps us from connecting to this source is fear. Every choice we make is either one of love or fear. When we become aware that we are disconnected from love and are coming from fear, it is an opportunity for us to see what we are thinking to bring us fear. We can then make a conscious choice to change how we see the situation.

Seeing your child in a positive light and expressing confidence in his abilities provides strong thought patterns in his subconscious mind that will serve him well throughout his lifetime. When he is discouraged, your words of encouragement and support go a long way to help him persevere and work through his challenges. Confidence building begins in infancy when parents encourage a child to attempt a new skill. When the child completes the task and naturally feels good about this, it is important that you share the joy of the child by reflecting back what you see, "I see how pleased you are with your accomplishment." Acknowledging your child's accomplishment is imperative; however, it is important how you do it. If you say such things as, "You did a good job!" you set yourself up as the judge. When your child perceives you as the judge he may begin doing things for your positive response rather than his own inner motivation. While it is important to acknowledge your child's accomplishments, it is also important that your enthusiasm doesn't replace his spontaneous inner joy and satisfaction.

The opposite of encouragement, is criticism, threat and judgment. If you succumb to these tactics, you undermine your child's confidence and plant poisonous seeds of doubt in his subconscious mind that can be a barrier throughout his life. Regularly acknowledging the positive actions of your child goes a long way towards building his self confidence and self-esteem. In this same light, it is important to create a habit of looking for the positive actions of your child and acknowledging them. Too often we have the automatic habit of looking for what is wrong and then point out the error by criticizing, threatening or judging. Some examples: "If you were paying attention you wouldn't have spilled your milk." or "If you spill again, you will go to your room." or "You are so clumsy!" Rather than resorting to these harmful responses, it is more effective to take a deep breath, remember who the child is, and speak to him in a respectful tone. An example might be: "Please get the clean up bucket and wipe up your spill." or "What can you do next time so you won't spill your milk?"

Keeping a sense of humor is a wonderful way to release tension and retain a positive attitude. When it feels like chaos has taken over look for the humor in the situation and laugh. Don't take things too seriously— this too will pass.

Foster Curiosity and a Love of Learning

Children are naturally curious and love to learn. They are filled with questions about life and it is vital that we help them discover what they are interested in at the time they are asking. Instead of immediately giving your child an answer, it is helpful to ask him what his thoughts are on it and build on that. When the situation calls for it, guide him to resources where he can discover answers for himself, with or without your help. Reading to and with your children is a most effective way to stimulate children's thinking and enthusiasm for knowledge. Engaging in conversation about what is being read and asking questions that stimulate your child's mind to think about what he is reading adds to his comprehension and critical thinking skills.

Another important aspect of nurturing children's love of learning is to provide ongoing activities that are of interest to them. In selecting these activities it is important that the correct level of difficulty be considered. If it is too easy the child will be bored, if too challenging the child will be discouraged. Research by Mihaly Csikszentmihaly, indicates that children learn more, engage more and remember more when the task of learning meets the skill level of the child—when they can be in the flow of learning.[2]

Enthusiasm is contagious! You are the best teacher of enthusiasm for your child. What you model directly affects his attitude and approach to life and learning. It is, therefore, important to keep your enthusiasm alive by engaging in those things that bring you happiness and joy. Keeping the love of learning and the sense of inquiry alive in your child will serve him well throughout his life.

Provide Space for Concentration and Quiet Time

As we know, a child needs to have periods of deep concentration so he can quiet his lower mind of sensorial stimulation, memory and ego to access his wise inner guide and bask in the glow of his Spirit. Your child needs both a physical space where he can be free of distraction and a mental space where he can be free of unnecessary interruption from others. He also needs personal quiet time at home to just be a child playing in the yard, climbing a tree, or finding creative activities in his room. In her book, *Whole Child—Whole Parent*, Polly Berends suggests that, "Our main role in our children's explorations is attentive non-interference. We can provide materials and opportunities while simultaneously getting out of the way to let be seen what will be revealed."[3]

Our lives can become very busy taking children to school, lessons, sport's practice, play dates and other outside activities. As parents we sometimes feel guilty if we are not providing a myriad of additional activities for our children. However, in his book, *The Hurried Child: Growing Up Too Fast Too Soon*, David Elkind laments that, "children… are all too often not permitted to be just children but are pushed to be mini-achievers."[4] While extracurricular activities are beneficial, it is important to evaluate how much is too much. By keeping a balance between "outer" time and "inner" time, your child will prosper and your life will be calmer.

Modeling concentration goes a long way as well. Mindfulness is the term often used to describe this state where we are able to completely focus our mind on the present moment, letting go of past and future thoughts. "Be here now!" is a popular term to describe this wonderful state of being. When we are successful in doing this, we experience a sense of well being and calm that our children absorb.

Set Reasonable Boundaries

While children come to us with the purity and innocence of their Spirit, they need healthy boundaries to be able to retain this authenticity.

They come to earth as divine beings and need to learn how to be human beings. Our responsibility as parents is to guide them in this process by allowing them freedom to develop within responsible limits. In our homes we need to find the balance between freedom and responsibility. In general, the more responsible a child can be, the more freedom he can enjoy.

Dr. Montessori frequently spoke about the importance of following the child. This has sometimes been misinterpreted to mean that we need to provide whatever a child asks for and allow him to do anything he desires. This is not what she meant. She meant that when a child is thoughtfully centered, following the promptings of his inner wisdom, we need to follow his interests and enthusiasm as much as possible. However, when a child is not centered and is acting primarily from sensory overload, ego or unhealthy habits formed in the subconscious mind, it is important for adults to redirect the activity to a more purposeful one. A helpful thought I hold is, "I trust you and will intervene only when I sense you are not being thoughtful or respectful." Of course, there are times when we must intervene because of time commitments and schedules.

Saying "no" to thoughtless or out of control behavior is absolutely necessary. Without this outer direction children fail to develop the ability to manage their impulsivity and come to expect instant gratification. Sometimes parents hesitate to say, "No" to children's requests and do their best to fulfill every desire. Children soon come to expect instant gratification and fail to develop patience. To help children develop patience parents need to say "no" to unnecessary demands. When children practice patience they connect to their Authentic Self rather than their impatient and often greedy ego self. One of the most valuable tools I have used over the years is to distinguish the difference between a child's "wants" and "needs." For example, a child may *need* food but *want* ice cream. Fulfilling the needs of our children is imperative, fulfilling their wants is not. Learning to discriminate between needs and wants helps us make wiser decisions and not be afraid to say "no" to unnecessary or unreasonable demands by the child. Of course, there times when fulfilling a want is the perfect thing to do.

Setting reasonable boundaries or ground rules in the home is essential for this is where children learn respect and responsible behavior. A very young children can begin to understand the limits of his behavior by telling him what you need him to do and why. "Please stop pulling the dog's hair because it hurts him and he might bite you." As soon as your child can communicate, you can involve him in the process of establishing the appropriate rules and roles in your home. I have found it helpful to talk about what kind of a home we would like to have by asking our children if they want a home that is: peaceful or violent, orderly or messy, quiet or noisy, etc. Once this is written down, begin the discussion of what needs to happen for the desired outcome to happen. For example, if you all want an orderly home, discuss what each family member needs to do to make the desired results happen. As a family you might decide that one agreed-upon behavior might be to put belongings away when people are finished with them. Again, write down the agreed-upon behaviors using positive language. Instead of saying or writing "We *will not* leave our belongings around the house." use "We *will* put our belongings away when we are finished with them." To get a desired result it is most effective to use positive language. Establishing healthy boundaries is discussed further in Chapter 15.

Nurture Children's Creativity and Imagination

Creativity is the ability to take what is and imagine new ways of expression. For children to engage in creative activities, they must feel emotionally safe and know it is all right to take risks. It is, therefore, important that we refrain from judging their work with such words as "good" and "bad" as this encourages them to do things that we will like rather than what is coming as an idea for them. When they come to us with a finished product it is helpful to respond with general descriptions such as, "The colors you used are bright" or open-ended probes such as, "Tell me about your picture," or general observations such as, "You seem pleased with this work." No matter the outcome of a creative *project*, be encouraging of their *process*. Discouraging words heard by a child early in life can affect his creative confidence throughout his life.

Children's dramatic, interactive play is an important venue for children to exercise their imaginations. Other activities such as dress up and music also spark the imagination. Often when our young daughter, Jeannie, came home from school, she would immediately go to the dress up box, try on various outfits and talk to herself and/or dance by the full length mirror. Having a variety of craft materials available for your children's creative projects also encourages them to follow their creative spark of spontaneity. It is helpful to have a place where children can comfortably do those projects that tend to be "messy." Providing an art smock or old shirt protects their clothes and a small bucket and sponge, encourages them to clean up after themselves.

Thinking creatively is a practice that can be nurtured by encouraging children to think out of the box. When reading to children, engage them in the process of guessing what they think the outcome of the story might be. In discussions, ask them their thoughts and opinions on the subject. Ask open ended questions as much as possible. Instead of saying, "Did you have a good day?" ask "What did you enjoy about your day?" As children get older ask them more probing questions such as: "What do you think would happen if you...?" " Why do you think this is happening?" "What other options do you have?" This process helps children develop the ability to more fully understand a situation, look at various solutions and eventually make a more informed decision. It also leads to the ability to see things from a variety of perspectives.

Young children have an amazing ability to imagine and create; however, too much time spent in the world of fantasy, at the expense of real life interaction, can be harmful. From birth to six children are engaged in the process of forming their conceptual framework of what the world is, and find it difficult to distinguish between what is real and what is fantasy. Also, if young children spend too much time in the world of fantasy their opportunities to ground themselves and develop their bodies and minds through concentrated constructive work within their environments are compromised. Once children become elementary age, they can distinguish between what is fantasy and what is real. They are now prepared to use their imaginations to learn and create from a more grounded space.

To inspire your child to be creative, it is helpful for you to model creativity in both your thinking and work. Your creative work can show up in a variety of ways such as art, crafts, music, decorating, landscaping and cooking. The joy you experience through your creativity will touch the heart and enthusiasm of your child.

Encourage Children to Think about Thinking

To be able to think about our process of thinking requires the ability to move into the position of the observer of our mind. It is the process of watching ourselves think and acting from the wisdom of our inner guide. The technical word for this process is "meta cognition." "Meta cognition means becoming increasingly aware of one's actions and the effect of those actions on others and on the environment...."[5] Around the age of twelve children's brains have matured enough to be able to experience meta cognition; however, there are some activities you can do with young children that plant the seeds of being aware of what they are thinking.

In my work with young children, I introduce the idea that the mind is a powerful tool that helps us to think, remember, imagine and make choices. Most of the time, it tells the truth that we are capable, strong and kind. We call this Positive Mind. Sometimes, however, the mind wants to play tricks on us and attempts to tell us that we are dumb, weak and mean. We call this Negative Mind. I reinforce that Positive Mind speaks to our loving Spirit and that Negative Mind likes to trick us. I emphasize that their inner guide gets to make the choice of whether to listen to Positive Mind or Negative Mind. I often hear children say, "My Positive Mind gave me the idea," or "My Negative Mind told me to do that."[6]

Helping children develop awareness of how their inner thinking affects themselves, others and the environment will support them throughout their lives. Learning to observe their thinking processes gives them the ability to reflect, evaluate, explore and make wise decisions about how they are thinking and what actions they may or may not want to take. This skill helps children consciously connect to their inner guide and be led by its deeper wisdom. Children can most easily participate in this observation/reflection process when they feel emotionally safe. For example, when a child has done something inappropriate, let him know he is *not in trouble*. This will help him move from a position of defensiveness to a willingness to engage in a discussion of what happened. To facilitate this discussion help your child reflect on 1) what happened (reflection), 2) the results (evaluation), 3) the possible actions that could be taken and what the results of each action might be (exploration), and 4) the final decision (decision).

Facilitate Choice Making

As discussed in the Phase of Engagement, the more we give children freedom of choice the more likely they are to engage in meaningful activity. As parents we need to be aware of their needs and desires to make choices and remember that making choices is a vital part of their unveiling process. For these reasons it is important that we help children to learn how to make thoughtful choices at an early age. One of the first conscious choices a child makes is to reach for one particular object when there are several objects to choose from. Young children need only a few alternatives as they can become overwhelmed by too many possibilities. It helps if we give them a choice of whether they want to go to the park or to the lake for an outing rather than asking them an open-ended question like "What would you like to do today?" As children mature, they can handle a greater variety of possibilities.

Choices are made daily by our children. Some are simple choices like what to eat first at breakfast and others are major choices like what should I do to make up with a friend. When your child is floundering with which choice to make, you can be of assistance by thoughtfully listening to him and engaging him in a discussion of possible choices. From this point help him reflect on what the result of each choice might be. Once he makes a choice and carries it out, follow up with the child to see how it worked out. This is a good time for further reflection on what worked or what would be another choice for the future.

Increase Memory Skills

To help children develop strong memory skills there are a variety of activities that can be used at home. For young children it is helpful to ask them to recall specific details of past events i.e., "Can you name all of the children who were at the party?" Create games that require the use of memory. One especially fun game for young children is to have a set of matched cards of objects they recognize. Turn the matched cards over so the pictures of the objects cannot be seen. Take turns turning over two cards to see if you can match them. If the two cards match, they are placed in front of the person who matched them. If the cards do not match, they are both turned back over and left in the same place. The point of this game is to remember where the cards are placed so they can be retrieved and matched at another turn.

Older children can increase their memory power by learning to visualize what they want to remember. One exercise is to ask your child to carry out a multi task. Encourage him to close his eyes and see himself doing each of the tasks as you describe what you want him to do. An example might be: "Go to your room and bring back your notepad, a pencil, a stapler and an eraser." Once they have successfully accomplished the request, add a level of difficulty by increasing the number of items to visualize and remember. Another memory skill is to suggest they visualize a connection between a new memory item and something they already know. For example, when meeting a new person, find something about that person that reminds you of something familiar. The other night I met a person with the name of Yodi—I immediately visualized him as Yoda from the movie *Star Wars*. I think I will definitely remember his name the next time I see him. In general, it is easier to remember things that are related and have meaning to us.

Limit and Monitor Media

Modern media is both a blessing as well as a challenge for children if we fail to monitor its use. As we know, young children automatically absorb everything within their environments, and television has the power to totally capture and absorb their attention. It can be so captivating that it robs children of their natural interest of involving themselves in constructive and creative work. The result of this is that, instead of children's brains forming the neurological patterns internally through children's interactions within the environment, television images are absorbed directly and begin to script their thinking externally. This type of absorption requires no thought, choice, evaluation, or creativity on the part of the child and can lead to passivity and the inability to concentrate. As we know it is through deep concentration that children contact their inner guide or wisdom. To decrease this contact through too much television or internet use is to put children at risk of being led by the thoughts of the media and others rather than developing their own inner knowing.

Another challenge is that young children are in the process of sorting out the real from the unreal and can't differentiate between what is a show and what is happening in reality. Without being aware of what our children are watching, they may be absorbing unhealthy images that remain in their subconscious and can potentially develop anxieties. In her recent book, *So Sexy So Soon*,[7] Diane Levin and Jean Kilbourne warn parents of the strong media/marketing messages that put subliminal images in the minds of young children that lead to the development of false self images. Girls and boys, as young as six years old are bombarded by unhealthy messages. Girls receive the image that to be popular is to be sexy. For young boys, the message is that to be popular one must be tough, macho and even violent. Obviously, too much of this input can add to the veil and make it more difficult for your child to unveil his Authentic Self.

The American Academy of Pediatrics recommends that children under the age of two do not watch television at all as this is such a sensitive time for the development of the mind and "an infant's visual system is not fully developed until the end of the second year."[8] Once they are old enough to begin viewing television, it is important to create guidelines in the home that provide appropriate limits. Some suggestions are:

- Do not use television as a babysitter.

- Limit children's television viewing time to a few hours per week.

- Monitor the commercials.

- Carefully select shows that will enhance children's knowledge and awareness.

- Join in the watching of uplifting shows so that family discussion can follow.

There is a great deal of pressure put on parents to start using computer technology with very young children to give them a head start. Lap ware is available for children as young as nine months to be used while sitting on the lap of an adult. For the same reasons that television viewing is harmful for infants, so is the use of lap ware. David Elkind clearly states that, "The first year of life is the time when an infant should concentrate on sensory integration...a too early concentration on the visual could impede the development of the other senses and the all-important process of sensory integration." He goes on to say "Although some exposure of children over the age of three to well-designed, age-appropriate programs may do no harm, it is unlikely that such exposure will have important or lasting benefits."[9]

As children get older and discover the internet and cell phones, additional precautions need to be taken. Namely, parents need to monitor the sites children use and limit the amount of time spent on the internet as well as calling and texting. Television, cell phones and the internet are helpful in many ways and need to be used in a thoughtful and balanced way.

Our responsibility as parents is to protect the mental environment in our home and do our best to eliminate any obstacles that might create false or negative beliefs about who our children think they are. We need to reinforce by our actions and thoughts the authentic nature of who they are and help them embrace this reality. Loving, focused thoughts will guide us in this mission.

Conclusion

The mental environment we provide for our children is crucial to their development. This is where their attitudes and basic approach to life are learned. As parents, we are the most prominent models in their lives. Life is what it is. What we make of it depends on how we see it and how we process what is happening. Our children absorb the mental environment we prepare as much as they absorb stimulation from the physical environment.

Suggestions for Follow Through

▪ **Practice mindfulness**. For one hour, do your best to breathe deeply and stay centered in the present moment. If you find yourself thinking about the past or future, gently bring your thoughts back to the present moment. Be aware of what your mind does during this time. Write about it in your journal.

▪ **Provide a place for solitude and concentration**. Is there a place where your child can find quiet and solitude in your home? This might be a special "hidden from view" place where he can be alone with his thoughts and imagination. It also means a special table or desk where he can concentrate on his work without distraction. Involve your child in creating special places of solitude in your home.

▪ **Establish agreed-upon boundaries**. Meet as a family and discuss how you would like your home to look and feel. Write down the joint vision you share. Follow this up with a discussion of what it will take for the vision to be a reality. Make positive statements such as: "Everyone needs to pick up their belongings." "We need to be ready to eat by 6:00." "We need to talk about our challenges." Write these down. When agreement is met, have each family member sign the paper. Use these ground rules to establish the expectations and boundaries of behavior in your home.

▪ **Help your child reflect on his behavior**. When your child's behavior is not acceptable calmly call him aside. Let him know that he is not in trouble, and that you need to talk with him. Tell him what you saw him do, how you felt about it and why it upset you. Ask him what he heard you say. Once he is able to let you know that he heard you, ask him to reflect on what happened (his original behavior), how he was feeling and what he needed. Once he expresses this, feed it back to him so he knows you heard him. At that point ask him if his actions got him what he wanted or if there might be a better way to handle the situation in the future. Ask him to think or reflect on other possible solutions. Continue the discussion until both you and your child have a sense of closure.

CHAPTER 10

Creating the
Emotional Environment

Daniel Goleman, the author of *Emotional Intelligence*, coined the phrase "Emotional Intelligence" and provided a framework and research to suggest that people with strong emotional intelligence quotient (EQ) do better in life than people with a high intelligence quotient (IQ). Of course, having both is optimal. He suggests that there are five primary competencies that result in high performance in adult life.[1]

- **Self-Awareness—Knowing one's internal states, preferences, resources and intuitions**: Self-awareness includes recognizing one's emotions and their effects on self and others, knowing one's strengths and limits and having a strong sense of one's self-worth and capabilities. As discussed previously, children whose authenticity is recognized and they are supported in their pursuit of self-actualization do discover their strengths and challenges. They also develop a sense of confidence and well being. In this chapter we discuss specific activities to help children recognize their inner emotional states and become aware of how their emotions affect themselves and others.

- **Self-Regulation or managing one's internal states, impulses, and resources**: Self-regulation includes the ability to keep disruptive emotions in control, maintaining standards of honesty and integrity, taking personal responsibility, adaptability and being comfortable with new ideas, approaches and information. When children feel comfortable with whom they are, they can adapt to new situations, accept personal responsibility and maintain integrity. Since they have a positive view of themselves they are less likely to feel a need to defend themselves and are able to welcome new thoughts and ideas. In this section we will share several ideas for helping children regulate or change undesirable emotions.

- **Motivation—Emotional tendencies that guide or facilitate reaching goals**: Motivation includes striving to meet a standard of excellence, an ability to align personal goals with group goals, ability to take initiative and persistence in pursuing goals despite obstacles and setbacks. As discussed earlier, children are naturally motivated when they are engaged in their Unveiling Cycles. The more children engage in these cycles the more likely it is that their internal sense of motivation will stay intact throughout their lives.

- **Empathy—Awareness of other's feelings, needs and concerns**: Empathy includes sensing others' feelings and perspectives and taking active interest in their concerns, sensing others' needs and bolstering their abilities, anticipating and meeting others' needs, cultivating opportunities in diverse situations, reading a group's emotional currents and power relationships. This skill develops naturally when children feel comfortable with their Authentic Self and have opportunities to live, play and work with other children as well as learn the interpersonal skills of sharing and helping others.

- **Social Skills—Adeptness at inducing desirable responses in others**: Social skills include the ability to influence or persuade others, good communication skills, conflict management skills, inspiring leadership skills, initiating and managing change, nurturing relationships, ability to collaborate and cooperate with others and the ability to create group synergy for collective goals. When children are engaged in the Unveiling Cycles, they naturally experience confidence in themselves and naturally reach out to others, work cooperatively and become dynamic leaders.

In reading these competencies, we are impressed with the similarity and congruency between these stated emotional competencies and the characteristics of a child who is moving through the Unveiling Cycles toward self-actualization. In other words, a child who is in the process of unveiling his Authentic Self displays the characteristics of self-awareness, self-regulation and spontaneous motivation. A child feeling comfortable and confident naturally reaches out in empathy toward others and is also able to be a sensitive leader. Of course, the degree to which children are able to manifest these skills is dependent on their age and maturation.

Following are a few ideas to encourage the further development of children's emotional intelligence.

Provide Emotionally Supportive Environments

In The Integration Phase chapter we discussed the need for children to be in an emotionally safe environment so they can learn and develop their capabilities. We described how the amygdala gland completely hijacks the learning process when emotional stress or fear is introduced. If the general climate in the home is one of threat, criticism, judgment and other fear-based emotions, you can be sure that your child is suffering.

The home is where your child's sense of well being is either nurtured or harmed. The feelings he experiences in relationship to his family determine, to a large degree, how he sees himself. If a child feels loved and supported, he will most likely hold a positive view of himself and have a healthy sense of well being. If, on the other hand, he feels ignored or unimportant, and he has to struggle to be seen, he will experience frustration and anger and his sense of well being will be threatened.

From birth babies receive impressions as to whether or not their parents are attuned to their feelings. The first years of life are when children need to experience bonding with their parents. Bonding occurs when children consistently experience deep feelings of love and well being when in the presence of parents. Children can tell how we see and experience them by the sound of our voice, the manner in which we pick them up, the words we say to express ourselves and the non verbal messages we demonstrate. Studies have found that children whose parents are attuned to their feelings demonstrate more affection, get along better and are more relaxed with their parents.[2]

The early years between birth and six years of age are the primary time when the impressions of well being or failure are established in the child's unconscious memory. This can make the difference between a child approaching life from a position of confidence or incompetence. If a child is having difficulty with self confidence, it makes it all the more important for us to see the child in his authenticity (even if it is not at that point manifesting itself) and reflect this back to him through our thoughts, words and actions. Encouragement and honest acknowledgement of his strengths help to change the negative thoughts in his subconscious mind to positive ones.

Build Positive Emotional Bank Accounts

Stephen R. Covey in his book, *The 7 Habits of Highly Effective People*, defines the term, "Emotional Bank Account" as: "a metaphor that describes the amount of trust that's been built up in a relationship. It's the feeling of safeness you have with another human being."[3] Building positive emotional bank accounts is about creating a surplus of trust between you and your children. This trust is created by the following guidelines: 1) understand and support the children's interests, 2) demonstrate kindness, thoughtfulness and respect, 3) keep our promises, 4) act with integrity, 5) sincerely apologize when we misjudge a situation or act improperly to our children, and 6) demonstrate unconditional love.

When we follow these six guidelines with our child, trust develops in our relationship. Each thoughtful act we do makes a positive deposit in our child's emotional bank account. When there is sufficient trust in his emotional bank account, he is more likely to listen and follow suggestions, share his thoughts and ideas, and engage in activities with us. As we experience the joy of this sharing between us, positive deposits are made to our emotional bank account as well. The more positive deposits in our account, the more we have to share with our

154

child. The goal is to consciously do those things that will increase our child's emotional bank account which, in turn, increases ours, thus creating a spiral of connectedness and trust between us.

The opposite happens when we fail to follow these suggested guidelines of respect for our child. For example, when we fail to take the time to understand our child's interests, become lax in doing thoughtful acts of kindness or fail to follow through on commitments, we actually withdraw trust from our child's emotional bank account. Instead of trust expanding in our relationship, distrust enters and our child's emotional bank account decreases. If there are too many withdrawals, the relationship between us breaks down and our child's behavior becomes less and less cooperative. The result of this is that our emotional bank account decreases and we begin to experience such feelings as frustration, exasperation or disappointment. The more our account is withdrawn, the less hope and patience we have. If the withdrawal from both of our emotional bank accounts gets too low, our relationship begins to spiral toward disconnectedness and distrust. To begin to rebuild this "emotional bankruptcy," it is essential that we make a concerted effort to pay greater attention to the six guidelines listed above.

Enjoy Family Meals Together

Enjoying one daily meal together as a family creates an emotional bond and connection in the family. This meal is frequently the evening meal and as such provides an excellent time to share the activities of the day with one another and communicate about what is coming up, what is needed, etc. Family mealtime is also an opportunity to share in the responsibilities of meal preparation, table setting and cleaning up which adds to the emotional bank accounts of the family members. A final touch of emotional uplift is lighting a candle and taking a moment to express gratitude for the meal and the family.

These are busy times with a lot of schedules to meet and family mealtime is often sacrificed for fast food fixes, individual grazing or television dinners complete with the television as the entertainment rather than family conversation. While it may be necessary to "eat on the run" some of the time, it is important for family meal time to be preserved as it not only offers better nutrition but healthy emotional sharing as well.

Have Fun Together

Think back on your childhood and remember some of the family activities you enjoyed as a child. When I do this, I remember all seven children in our family climbing into our station wagon and heading 2 ½ hours west to play in the Pacific Ocean for the day. This experience included walking into the ocean where the surf was breaking and laying stomach down on a rubber raft in the hopes of catching the rising surf to get an exciting ride to the shore. Of course, the day was spent laughing and playing with one another. These experiences are deeply embedded in my memory and in my emotional bank account as it relates to my family. In fact, the majority of my early family memories are about the fun things we did together as these were definitely emotionally bonding experiences.

When planning family outings, make sure the children are involved in visualizing, planning and implementing the activity. Taking the time to get their input will result in some new ideas and emotional buy-in for the experience. One such activity took on a life of its own with our grand children, Andy and Sera during one of their Summer Camp G & G (Grandpa and Grandma) visits. We have an outboard motor boat and wanted to take the children to one of the local lakes for a day outing. Before going, we talked to them about the possibility of looking for treasure on the island in the lake. This fantasy fascinated the children and they added their input. This included everyone pretending to be pirates. We all took names and used them throughout the day. Of course, they wanted to bring a couple of friends along which worked for this occasion. The enthusiasm for the trip grew as they anticipated the possibility of finding a treasure. Preparation for the trip went smoothly as the children spontaneously wanted to help. Once on the island the children began to look for treasure and lo and behold near the end of the trip, one of them enthusiastically ran to the campfire yelling that he had found a treasure. What he had found was a rock shaped as a heart. All agreed that what we had found on this adventure was love and joy—all symbolized by the heart-shaped rock.

Having fun creates emotions of happiness, enthusiasm and joy. These emotions are healing and provide significant deposits for all family members' emotional bank accounts. Being flooded with joy washes away a great deal of accumulated negativity. Look for opportunities to have fun, laugh and remember to smile.

Help Children Learn to Wait

A critical aspect of emotional competence is the ability to wait, to have impulse control. According to Daniel Goleman, "There is no psychological skill more fundamental than resisting impulse. It is the root of all emotional self-control...."[4] A 1960s study at Stanford University with four-year old preschool children showed that the children, who were able to control their impulse to eat a marshmallow until the researcher returned, showed greater skill when they were in high school to control their impulses than those children who could not resist eating the marshmallow. Those children able to wait for the marshmallow as four year olds were more personally effective, self-assertive and better able to cope with the frustrations of life in high school They also handled stress more easily, embraced challenges, were more self-reliant and dependable, and also received higher SAT scores.

Children who are actively engaged in the Unveiling Cycles develop the ability to control their impulses through the natural development of the will. At a very young age children, who are given the opportunity to follow their inner guide and engage themselves in meaningful work, naturally practice impulse control. They learn to ignore all unnecessary sensorial information so they can concentrate on the work that has drawn them. They want to persevere and complete their work. When finished, the satisfaction they experience naturally compels them to repeat this process over and over again. Through their inner work of self construction, their will is developed and they naturally learn to wait.

As parents we need to respect our child's unveiling process by encouraging his involvement in meaningful activity in the home. We need to do our best not to disturb the inner workings of his inner guide and the development of his will. It is important that we develop the ability to say "yes" to that which is a true need of our child and "no" to those things that are not necessary or potentially harmful to him. When we fear that our child might not like us if we say "no" or if we feel guilty if we don't give him everything he asks for, we take away his opportunity to learn patience or impulse control. By indulging his every wish, he comes to expect instant gratification and has a difficult time waiting. It is our responsibility to help our children learn to wait.

Help Children Understand Their Feelings

Parents have the unique role of establishing children's patterns of emotional expression. If we are uncomfortable with emotions we will most likely pass this discomfort on to our children. What do we do when our children express emotions? Do we usually ignore the feelings? If so, we are missing an important opportunity to help them develop emotional competence. Do we allow our children to express their feelings however they wish? If this is the case, we are keeping them from learning constructive ways of handling emotions. Do we refuse to deal with their emotions and even show irritation, anger or other violence toward them? This can leads to children feeling guilty, developing resentment toward us and learning that it is not alright to express emotions.

The best thing we can do when children are emotionally upset is to acknowledge their feelings and do our best to understand what is upsetting them. "Are you mad because I told you it is bedtime and you are not finished playing with your toy?" If this is the case, usually the child will show some sign that this is what is happening. This might be a sigh, a deep breath or a twitch of his head. Being emotionally understood is the first step toward helping children learn to calm down and then begin to deal with the difficulty. When a child feels understood by us, he is more open to discussing how to solve the issue. "I can see that you need a few more minutes to finish what you are doing. Would it work if we wait ten more minutes before getting ready for bed so you can finish playing the game?"

Children need a vocabulary of emotions before they can express what they are feeling. To young children it must be confusing to have a mixed variety of feelings rush through their bodies for no apparent reason. Initially, when we see a child experiencing an emotion, it is helpful to reflect it back to him by giving it a name. "It looks like you might be feeling mad right now." "You seem like you are feeling happy today." When working with young children I find it very helpful to only use the four basic emotions of happy, mad, sad and afraid. Most emotions experienced by a young child will fit within one of these categories. As a child develops more awareness of feelings, he can expand his vocabulary of emotions.

A further refinement of emotional awareness is to show your child a picture of a "happy face." Ask him to show you "happy" with his body. Once he demonstrates "happy," give him a mirror and ask him how his face looks (smile, open eyes), ask him if his muscles are relaxed or tense. Next, ask him if his breath is deep or shallows. Finally, ask him if his positive or negative mind is talking to him. Repeat this exercise with the other emotions of mad, sad and afraid. With each emotion ask the child to look in the mirror to see his facial expression and then inquire about what is happening with his muscles, breath, and mind. By helping the child be aware of these physical aspects of emotions, he develops the ability to recognize these emotions in others. Recognizing the physical signs of emotion is one of the first steps toward empathizing with others. Another benefit is that they learn how to move from one emotion to another.[5]

To help children learn to move from the emotions of mad, sad and afraid to being neutral or happy, suggest the following:

- Ask the child to be aware of what his body is doing (especially his breath and muscles). If the breath is shallow suggest he take several deep breaths, if the muscles are tense, ask him to send a message to his muscles to relax.

- Ask the child whether negative or positive mind is talking. If he says negative mind, ask him if he would like to talk about it to someone. Or, if it is helpful, as in the case of being afraid or sad, suggest he think of something nice.[6]

As children develop awareness of their emotional states and learn to manage them in thoughtful ways, they free themselves from the slavery of emotional overload and experience a new sense of empowerment and control over their lives. Helping children learn how to express their emotions effectively and problem solve is covered in Chapter 14.

Examine Our Emotions

What we feel is directly linked to our thinking process. Sometimes we are consciously aware of what we are thinking, but most of the time, our emotions spring from thoughts planted deep within our subconscious mind. In the recesses of our subconscious mind lay all the mind sets and attitudes we have accumulated throughout our lifetime. For example, if we were brought up in a home where our parents assumed an authoritarian attitude that implied that they knew best and were always right, this mindset has also embedded itself in us. Have you ever heard yourself saying something to your child that you despised hearing from your parents? This is an example of those hidden thought patterns that need to be recognized and replaced by thoughts based on the true nature of things. In other words, instead of holding the thought that "My child needs me to tell him what to do," we can change the thought to "I trust my child's inner guide."

When we find ourselves in the clutches of negative emotions, it is important to recognize this and remove ourselves from the situation that is triggering our emotional outbreak. By finding a neutral place (to stop the amygdala phenomenon) and doing some deep breathing (to sooth our thinking) our emotions will calm down. From this more centered state of observer, we can begin to think about our thinking (meta-cognition). Gradually we will discover patterns of thought that are not healthy and are not based on the true reality. As we have these insightful moments, we can begin to consciously replace the untrue thoughts with those that are authentic. When we find ourselves emotionally upset, it is a red light letting us know that we have some internal work to do to further our process of cleansing our lens of perception. Montessori recognized this. "We must believe in all the good that lies hidden in the child and prepare ourselves to recognize it with loving concern; only in this fashion will we gradually begin to assess the child correctly."[7]

Walk in Humility

Montessori spoke passionately about the benefits of being in a state of humility so that we can enjoy the blossoming of our children. She says that if adults "can really enter into the joy of seeing things being born and growing under his own eyes, and can clothe himself in the garment of humility, many delights are reserved for him that are denied to those who assume infallibility and authority..."[8] When we free ourselves from our ego thinking that says "I am always right" (infallible) and "I must be in control" (authority), we experience our authentic state of humility. Being humble allows us to observe what is happening and be open to the joy of being present for our child. In this sacred presence the child feels safe, affirmed and able to reveal his authenticity.

Conclusion

The emotional environment we offer our child is central to his sense of well being and self-confidence. As we reflect back to Maslow's Hierarchy of Needs, we see that the second level of Safety Needs relies on having both his physical as well as his emotional safety needs met. If his needs for safety are not met, he will have difficulty moving up the pyramid ladder to the Love and Belonging Needs, the Esteem Needs and the Self-Actualization Needs. A child's basic emotional nature is nourished in the home and as parents we are responsible for providing a positive emotional climate and reflecting our child's authentic nature back to him through our thoughts, words and actions.

Suggestions for Follow Through

▪ **Observe the connection between thinking and emotion**. When you find yourself experiencing an unpleasant emotion, remove yourself from the situation; calm your body and mind by breathing deeply. Once you have reached a place of neutrality, reflect on what thoughts you were having prior to and during the emotional eruption. Write about the experience in your journal.

▪ **Play together**. As a family plan and implement a fun family outing. Establish the general guidelines such as the day and amount of time available. Encourage each member of the family to share what he would like to see happen. Cooperatively work together to create a day that all will enjoy. Once the itinerary is decided, create a list of what needs to be done to prepare for the outing. Have each person agree to specific responsibilities to carry it out.

▪ **Make a deposit in your child's emotional bank account**. Make a conscientious effort to listen to your child discuss something that he seems particularly interested in. Ask him leading questions about his interest so he feels comfortable to share even more information with you. Look for opportunities to share this interest with him in the future.

▪ **Distinguish between wants and needs**. Make a list of what you consider "wants" and what you consider "needs" for your child. When your child asks for something, make a conscious effort to determine if what he is asking for is a want or an authentic need. From this knowledge make a decision about whether or not to grant his wish. Whatever you say, say it with confidence. Observe how you feel and how your child reacts. Record it in your journal.

CHAPTER 11

Creating the Spiritual Environment

"We must open the way for his spiritual development.
We must, from the very first day, respect the impulses of his spirit
and know how to support him."[1]

—MARIA MONTESSORI

Trust is the cornerstone of love and love is the key to providing a nurturing spiritual environment. A nurturing spiritual environment provides a safe climate so a child can feel secure enough to reveal his Authentic Self. The more we trust in the child's authentic nature and natural unveiling process, the easier it is for us to create a warm spiritual environment for our child.

Following are a few thoughts about creating a spiritual environment in the home where children experience affirmation and have enough trust to unveil their authenticity.

Understand the Power of Love

Being surrounded and bathed in love is both a healing and inspiring experience. Love is the connecting link to all aspects of creation and when we can actually feel its comfort and inspiration in our hearts, we are renewed and affirmed. Children, who are already so close to their Spirit, are naturally drawn to people who exude love. They want to be with them because they feel comfortable enough to express their authenticity.

Our consciousness is the primary spiritual environment for our children. When we hold a consciousness of love and trust, our children flourish. When we begin to let fear appear in the form of worry about "what if…." or when our ego steps forward and wants to control the child, the flow of consciousness is interrupted and the child's spiritual environment is compromised. Our power of love allows us to see the glorious light of love within our children.

The secret of the child is his Authentic Self. For us to see and understand our child's Spirit of light and love, we must do our best to stay in touch with our Authentic Self. In order to let our light and love shine forth, requires that we make a genuine effort towards transformation. This transformation requires a gradual process of burning our ego attachments and trusting in our own inner guidance—the intuitive wisdom of our heart. I have found it helpful to see apparent difficulties as opportunities to let go of something within me that is blocking the expression of my Authentic Self. Difficulties are the sandpaper that brings greater smoothness and shine to our lives. Because we love our children so much, we willing go through this transformational process of moving from a caterpillar to a butterfly. As we are cleansed of our faulty thinking and corresponding emotional reactions, we become more and more sensitive to the amazing beauty and love dwelling within the heart of our children. The more love we see in our children, the more they manifest loving behavior. The more love they manifest, the more love we feel. The more love we feel, the more love we share with our children. The more they feel seen in their love, the more they manifest it: This is the power of love.

Demonstrate Unconditional Love

To love unconditionally means that our children know that, no matter what they do, we will always love them. Our love must not be dependent on who they are or what they say or do. They need to know that our love is with them, even if their behavior is inappropriate. Children thrive on knowing that they are surrounded by our arms of love. If this love is threatened, it can have a devastating effect on their self worth and confidence. Removing love from our children is like taking oxygen from a fire—it lessens their flame of love. Our children need to know that they will be supported forever by our love and understanding.

To love our children unconditionally does not mean that we ignore their misbehavior. On the contrary, when children know that we love them unconditionally, it is easier to approach them about their misbehavior because they feel less need to be defensive. Instead of saying, "You really messed up so I am not going to take you to the game." (a threat of losing love from the parent); we can say, "I love you, and I want to talk with you about what just happened." (a statement of reassurance and an opportunity to bring clarity to the issue) Understanding children's behavior will be covered in more depth in Chapter 16.

Reflect the Light of the Child

If we could hear the heart song of a child, I think we might hear him say:

I am a child with a vision to share,
Of a world of peace and a world of care.
I so recently came to planet earth,
That I remember the peace I had at birth.
Please see my Love and nurture me,
To make peace on earth a reality.

How empowering it is for a child to have us look into his eyes, see his Spirit shining through, and say to him, "I see your love!" When I was teaching in the classroom I told the children that they each had a beautiful light of love inside them. I went on to say that I could see their love shining by the twinkles in their eyes and the smiles on their faces. For months afterward, children came up to me with eyes blinking and big smiles on their faces because they wanted me to tell them "I see your love!"

When a child is recognized as a divine, loving being he begins to relate and define himself accordingly. He learns that his Authentic Self is a reliable inner guide and he learns to trust its promptings. When he engages in meaningful activity using the VEIL Model, he experiences the joy and satisfaction of learning, growing and blossoming. He wants to repeat this satisfying process again and again at higher and higher levels creating the Unveiling Spiral. The more successes a child experiences through this unveiling process, the more likely it is that he will be a lifelong learner guided by his native inner wisdom.

On the other hand, if a child is seen as anything but a spiritual being he begins to accept our feedback as the definition of his self image. Whether these definitions are positive judgments such as "You are the best!" or negative judgments such as "You are stupid!" they feed the child's ego rather than his Spirit. If the ego is reinforced too frequently, at the expense of nurturing the authenticity of the child, he will suffer because he holds a false identity of who he really is. Instead of making decisions from his wise inner guide, he makes choices according to the false views he holds of himself. Identifying with false self images, rather than authentic self images, is the basis of addiction. The root cause of addiction is losing contact with our "Inner Child" or Authentic Self and substituting outside substances, objects, relationships or activities for our self-identity. For example, a person who has learned to do things primarily to please his parents (ego need), will most likely continue, as an adult, to make decisions based on whether or not he will please others. Deeply buried in his subconscious is a mindset that keeps reminding him that, "My happiness depends on pleasing others."

Foster Awe and Wonder

Watching a young child immerse himself in nature is a sight to behold. They are completely entranced by the smallest creatures, the beautiful flowers, the birds and even the dirt. Because nature is love manifesting itself and childhood is also love manifesting itself, they are a wonderful match. Taking children into nature frequently helps his love to flourish. Bringing nature into the home fosters awe and wonder as children watch a puppy grow, a flower bloom or a fish eat its food. When they are empowered to water the plants, wash the leaves and plant a seed, their sense of awe and wonder is further increased. In addition to providing opportunities for children to be in nature we can inspire awe and wonder by providing opportunities for them to enjoy pleasing music, see beautiful art work, watch graceful dancing, hear inspiring stories and poetry. All of these opportunities promote children's ability to access the joy of being in a state of awe and wonder about life. An added benefit is that sharing this time with our children, gifts us with the joy of awe and wonder as well.

Provide Times for Silence and Gratitude

Life in the 21ˢᵗ century is fast moving and externally stimulating. Without conscious planning, this fast pace can have a negative effect on our children and on us. When we have too many things calling for our attention, we can easily become overwhelmed, overstressed and distracted. In these states, it is difficult to remain connected to our inner guide and spirit of love. Learning to balance our active times with our quiet times is essential if we want to be present for our children, other people and ourselves.

Personally, I have found it extremely helpful to give myself the first hour of each day to do yoga stretches and make silence. During the silent time, I close my eyes, breathe deeply and become aware of those people who bless my life. I hold an attitude of gratitude and send them love energy. I become aware of the many physical gifts and opportunities I enjoy and express gratitude. Holding an attitude of gratitude opens my heart and helps me release negative energy thoughts coming from my lower mind of ego and memory. Taking conscious deep breaths, I do my best to sit in silence to feel my Spirit and listen to the silent promptings of my inner guide or wisdom. This is a time of renewal and refreshment that helps me throughout the day.

We can encourage our children to enjoy times of silence and gratitude as well. Taking time before a meal to pause and in some way express appreciation for the food to be eaten is a healthy pattern to establish.

Engaging children in conversations about what it took to get the food to the table can be both fun and educational. Some leading questions that can be asked are: Where did the bananas come from? Who planted and cared for the plants and harvested the bananas? How did the bananas get to the market? Who took care of them in the market? Who brought them home? Who prepared them to eat?

Bedtime is another special time to sit calmly with children and make silence for a few minutes. It is wonderful for a child to have a special quiet spot in his bedroom that can be used for the nightly silence time as well as any time he wants to have a place to go on his own to calm down. I have found that the following words help children center their bodies, calm their minds and emotions and make silence.

I cross my legs,
I put my hands on my knees,
I make my back very straight,
I tell my body to be still,
I tell my mouth to be quiet,
I take a deep breath and
I close my eyes to make silence and feel my love.[2]

Making silence is a time when children can experience the warmth of their Spirit—their Authentic Self. Just as feeling the love of other people is comforting to children, so is the ability to feel their own center of love. For them to know they can connect to their authenticity independently is most empowering. Providing the opportunity to make silence together on a daily basis is an excellent way to remind children how much we appreciate them and honor their light of love.

Conclusion

Parents can create a lovely physical environment for their children complete with the latest objects or toys of interest. They can attempt to interest them in becoming involved with some of the practical life activities in the home; but, without the presence of love, the child's Spirit will not be touched. He may engage himself on the surface, but will find it difficult to relate to the physical activities from the deeper level of his Authentic Self. On the other hand, when we are present and our heart is filled with love, the flood gates of enthusiasm open for the child. Spirit touches Spirit.

Whether we are creating the physical, mental, emotional or spiritual environments for our children, we will be most successful when we implement our actions from our Authentic Self—our pure place of love. Polly Berends sums it up beautifully. "Our children can go anywhere, sleep on anything, do with nothing, and still be happy and grow beautifully if their earthly dwelling place, the mind of the parent, is love-filled."[3]

Suggestions for Follow Through

■ **Practice silence**. Create a space somewhere in the home where you can relax and make silence. For one week wake up 20 minutes earlier than usual and sit quietly in silence watching your breath move in and out of your body. If thoughts come to you during this time just say, "thinking" and go back to watching your breath. Be aware of what affect this has on you during the week. Record it in your journal.

■ **Help your child center**. When your child is upset, touch or hold him gently and breathe deeply. Reassure him of your love and suggest that he take some deep breaths with you. Observe what happens and record it in your journal.

■ **Acknowledge your child's light of love**. Just as in the popular movie "Avatar" where the key phrase when greeting someone is, "I see you!" and in India where people greet one another with "Namaste," we can similarly honor our children by frequently saying, "I see your love!" For one week share this phrase with your child when you honestly feel love in your heart for him. Observe how saying this feels to you and how your child receives it. Record your observations in your journal.

■ **Make silence with your child**. For one week make silence at bedtime with your child. This can be done by both of you sitting on the bed, on the floor or a special quiet space. Use the words suggested above to help him center his body, calm his mind and emotion so he can enjoy silence. Record your observations in your journal.

PART IV

Being an Authentic Parent

PART IV

Being an
Authentic Parent

*"Nature always sees to it that the child is protected.
He is born of love, and love is his natural origin....Nature inspires
both parents with love for their little ones, and this love
is not something artificial...In the depth of their love, all parents
renounce their own lives to dedicate them to their children.
And this devotion is natural to them."[1]*

—MARIA MONTESSORI

In the previous chapters we focused on the authentic nature of the child and how to create nurturing environments that support the unveiling process within the child. We will now turn our attention to the authentic nature of the most significant adults in the life of the child—the parents. Just as the child comes to earth from the Divine Source of love and has a Spirit of love as his essential nature, we, as parents, also bring a Spirit of love with us as our Authentic Self. Like the children, our task is to remember our true nature and use it as a guide and compass in our lives. The more we can accomplish this, the greater is our joy, success and fulfillment in life.

It is interesting to note that a married couple may be willing to leave one another through divorce, but seldom will either of them want to leave the relationship they have with their children. The bond of love between parent and child is the strongest human connection. Because we are so devoted to our children, we naturally let go selfishness and willingly make sacrifices for the good of our children. It is this love we have for our children that inspires us to begin a conscious process of self transformation. Polly Berends describes it this way:

> *Parenthood is a time when we are pushed to discover the nature of the whole and our oneness with it. It is a time when both our mistaken ideas about who we are and truer ones are brought to light. There is so much that is beautiful and good to wake up to. Our children drive us toward this awakening.[2]*

To enter into a truly nurturing and helpful relationship with the child, we must see him as a spiritual being having magnificent potential and value. We must trust that within the spiritual embryo of each child there is an inner guide and vital force that yearn to guide him to construct a personality of glorious worth. We must remember that the child is a spiritual being living in a material world striving to fulfill his divine potentials.

Part IV includes five chapters. Chapter 12 provides a variety of skills to help us to center and recover our authenticity so that we can more clearly see the authentic nature of our children. Chapter 13 discusses ways to reflect authenticity to the child, various parenting styles and how our thoughts make a significant difference in our ability to be authentic parents. Chapter 14 discusses communication blocks, compassionate expression, roadblocks to listening, empathetic understanding and problem solving. Chapter 15 covers children's intrinsic desire to cooperate, rewards and punishment, healthy boundary setting and the application of consequences for behavior. Chapter 16 promotes understanding of the root causes of children's misbehavior and what can be done to encourage positive behavior instead.

CHAPTER 12

Centering Skills
for Adults

Children flourish and are much more likely to retain connection with their authenticity and move through their Unveiling Cycles if we are consciously doing our best to manifest our authenticity as well. Montessori parenting is a balanced partnership model that meets the unfolding physical, mental, emotional and spiritual needs of the children and allows us, as parents, to meet our needs and flourish as well. Being an authentic parent requires that we learn to observe ourselves, be willing to let go harmful patterns, and enter into a process of self-reflection and transformation. The more we work on this the easier it will be to be inspired by our inner guide and Spirit. Montessori recognized this truth and said,

> *The first essential is that the teacher (parent) should go through an inner, spiritual preparation.... She must study how to purify her heart and render it burning with charity towards the child. She must 'put on humility,' and above all, learn how to serve. She must learn how to appreciate and gather in all those tiny and delicate manifestations of the opening life in the child's soul. Ability to do this can only be attained through a genuine effort towards self-perfection.[1]*

Our ability to call forth the authentic spiritual nature of our children expands as we focus awareness on our own spiritual center of love, our Authentic Self. The more we come in touch with our authenticity the easier it is to appreciate and respect the authentic nature of our children. The task of becoming more aware of our Spirit, staying connected to it, listening to the prompting of our inner wisdom, and thoughtfully interacting with our children, is a continual process that continues throughout life. Because we love our children so deeply, we willing go through what it takes to give them what they need to flourish.

This transformation of self involves a process of clearing our lens of faulty perceptions so that we can better reflect the spiritual nature of our child. In other words, instead of seeing our child through our limited vision of lower mind (ego, memory and sensory input), we learn to see him through the eyes of our higher mind of wisdom. As we see his Authentic Self and mirror it back to him, he flourishes. What the significant adults in a child's life mirror back to a child in the first six years of his life, greatly affects how he will see himself for the remainder of his life. Being "seen" by another is one of the most important, powerful and lasting gifts a child can receive.

To better understand this process of self transformation, we are presenting a holistic model that includes the four major aspects of ourselves: Body, Mind, Emotions and Spirit. Through awareness and practice of specific skills, we can enhance the harmonious functioning of our body, mind and emotions so that our Spirit can more easily guide and direct our actions. As we become aware of how each aspect operates independently, and how each functions in relationship to one another,

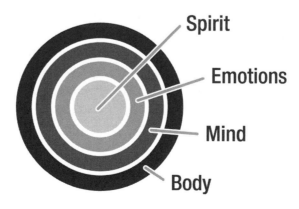

we enhance our ability to systematically work on clearing our lens of perception. Clearing our lens of perception is a continual process of observing ourselves, understanding the source of our disturbances, and removing the seed causes of these disturbances. The more we practice this, the greater ability we will have to tune into our Spirit and follow the lead of our inner guide as we nurture our children.[2]

When we express our authenticity we open the door for our child to express his authenticity. It is our Spirit that sees the Spirit of the child and motivates us to express unconditional love. When we are in tune with this aspect of ourselves we are calm, centered and effective.

Of course, there are many times when we do not feel at one with our Spirit. We feel cut off, blocked or otherwise out of touch. Generally it means that we have an unresolved issue on our mind that is creating disturbances in our body and emotions. When we are disturbed in this way, it is difficult for us to stay centered. By calming our body, mind and emotions we can reconnect with our Spirit's inner guide and observe what thought pattern is emerging from our subconscious mind. Once we are aware of a fearful thought pattern, we can consciously begin to replace it with a different thought that is based on the reality of love. Montessori described this process by saying that an adult must "purge herself of these defects of tyranny with which her character is unconsciously encrusted."[3]

This process of realizing the false concepts we hold and replacing them with concepts based on thoughts that coincide more closely with the true spiritual nature of life is the basis of clearing our lens and experiencing transformation. Montessori goes on to say that,

> *To see the child as he is, is made difficult for us as adults on account of our own defects....Because of this defective vision the adult is generally too much occupied in looking for defective tendencies also in the child and seeking to correct them. We must first remove the beam from our own eyes, and then we shall see more clearly how to remove the mote in the child's. In the 'removing the beam from her own eyes' consists the spiritual training of the teacher (parent).[4]*

When we are in touch with our Authentic Self we have the ability to receive wisdom from our inner guide in our parenting and all other aspects of our lives. Having this realization is a comfort that helps us let go of our fearful subconscious thoughts and replace them with trust in ourselves, our children, and others. Understanding how our body, mind, emotions and Spirit interact, and how to manage each, is an excellent tool to keep us centered in trust and love.

Body

Our body is the most visible and most directly experienced part of ourselves. When it is healthy and full of energy, we think clearly, feel positive, and can more easily connect to our Spirit. On the contrary, when we are sick, stressed or otherwise out-of-sorts physically, we are much more likely to have muddled thoughts, manifest negative emotions and be short of temper. Research has shown a direct correlation between stress and physical disease. When our body is in a state of stress, our nervous system is affected and this, in turn, affects the functioning of various organs of our body. Over a prolonged period of time, this can lead to actual disease. By being aware of our body and conscientiously caring for it, we will have a much better chance of being healthy and staying centered in our Spirit. Following are a few reminders of what we can do to support this goal.

DIET

What we eat affects how our body, mind and emotions function. When we fail to eat balanced meals and regular meals, our body suffers from fatigue, our mind has difficulty concentrating, and our emotions vacillate randomly making it difficult for us to experience our spiritual center of peace and tranquility. In addition to eating healthy foods, it is important to consider how we actually eat the foods. Do we frequently eat "on the run"? Taking time to prepare and enjoy the meal helps our food to digest properly and for us to enjoy the gift of eating delicious food.

WATER

Our bodies are made up of approximately 70 % water and must be "refilled" regularly to keep the body and mind functioning smoothly.

When we become dehydrated, it is difficult for the right and left hemispheres of the brain to contact one another and our thinking is negatively impacted. Drinking a glass of water affects our ability to bring our thinking back into focus and keeps our body vibrant.

REST AND RELAXATION

While it is important to be conscientious parents and take care of our responsibilities, it is also important to know when our body needs a rest. Learning to take time to relax throughout the day helps us to be more centered and effective in the work we do.

EXERCISE

Both aerobic and stretching exercises benefit the body in a number of ways. Aerobic exercise strengthens the heart, facilitates muscle tone, increases blood circulation and the lungs' capacity to distribute oxygen to the body. Stretching exercises help the body release tension, relax muscles and rejuvenate our energy. Treating our body to exercise on a daily basis will help us to, not only to be healthy, but also centered and balanced as well.

BREATHING

If there is one friend that benefits our work of transformation and centering, it is our breath. It is the link between our life and death and the key to balancing the workings of our body, mind, emotions and Spirit. When we find ourselves disconnected and "out of sorts," it can usually be traced to uncomfortable subconscious thoughts that are seeping into our consciousness. These unpleasant thoughts directly trigger our emotions and our loaded emotions trigger a stress reaction in our body. To reverse this process we can effectively use deep diaphragmatic breathing as described in Chapter 8.

Through the use of bio-feedback machines, researchers discovered that when a person has a disturbing thought in his mind, his brain waves register as irregular peaked lines. They also found that as the person consciously breathes deeply for a period of time, the irregular brain waves begin to smooth out. As this happens the disturbing thought recedes and the emotions that have been triggered by the thought mellow out. In addition the additional oxygen from the deep breathing soothes the nervous system. As the emotional reactions in our body disappear, and the additional oxygen enters our blood stream, our body begins to relax and let go the triggered stress. From this calmer place we can access our inner guide and observe what has been happening within our lower mind. We can then decide what we need to do to transform the disturbing thought pattern. Breath is the vital tool to help us maintain a positive connection between our body, mind, emotions and Spirit.

Mind

Our mind is the instrument that allows us to think, observe, reflect, imagine and create. Without the power of mind, it would be impossible for us to function on this physical plane of existence. In fact mind's power is so great that it can destroy us or bring us great joy in life. It can be compared to the power of the river. When the water of the river is flowing within its banks, the power it possesses can be used for great good; however, when the river's water overflows its banks and floods the lands around it, it can create much chaos and harm. How important it is that we learn how mind operates and how to channel its energy in constructive ways!

Learning to harness the power of mind through concentration is the equivalent of keeping the water within the river's banks. When we successfully concentrate the power of our mind we increase our ability to think, reflect and create. One daily practice is to do our best to live in the present moment rather than in the past or future. How easy it is to let our mind wander to what happened yesterday or to what we must accomplish tomorrow. Learning to live one day at a time and one moment at a time is powerful and exhilarating. Thich Nhat Hanh, a Vietnamese Buddhist Monk, sums it up by saying: "Peace is every step."[5] When we bring our full attention to the present moment, breathe deeply, and pay attention to what our physical body is doing, our lower mind becomes still and we experience the peace and calm of our Authentic Self. He calls this state of being, "mindfulness."

Eric Tolle, in his two books, *The Power of Now* and *A New Earth— Awakening to Your Life's Purpose*, goes into great detail on how to center our mind in the "Now." He talks about letting go of our lower mind attachments, and their resulting pain, so we can experience the joy of connecting with our Authentic Self. He said it clearly in this way. "Seeing beauty in a flower could awaken humans, however briefly, to the beauty that is an essential part of their own innermost being, their true nature."[6]

Another benefit of concentrating the power of our mind is that it enhances our ability to imagine and visualize. In his book, *The Power of Intention*, Wayne Dyer points out that when we combine our ability to imagine with our "universal mind" (Spirit) we have the power to create what we visualize. He discusses the difference between using ego's willpower and using imagination in connection with our Spirit.

> *Your willpower is so much less effective than your imagination, which is your link to the power of intention. Imagination is the movement of the universal mind within you. Your imagination creates the inner picture that allows you to participate in the act of creation. It's the invisible connecting link to manifesting your own destiny.*[7]

In Chapter 3 we discussed in detail the various functions of mind as it relates to the child. For ready reference we are including the same visual in this chapter as we discuss how the various aspects of mind affect our ability to be centered in love as we relate to our children.

The Map of Mind and Spirit

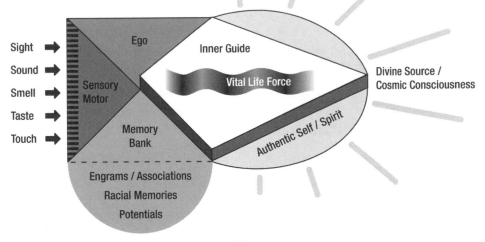

SENSORY MOTOR

The amount of sensory stimulation that bombards us on a daily basis can be overwhelming—particularly when we are juggling home and career, caring for young children, and managing the many activities of the family. The demands for attention from the sensory stimulation in our lives can keep us scattered and disconnected from our center as we dash here and there to get everything accomplished. When we become aware of being in this overwhelmed state, it is a good time to step back, take a break and do some deep breathing. From this point, we can reconnect to our Authentic Self, be present in the moment and more calmly go about what needs to be done. We can also look at all the commitments we are making and decide if there are some things that can simply be put aside for another time or eliminated all together.

MEMORY BANK

Embedded deep within our subconscious mind are all of the impressions (engrams and associations) we have accumulated in our lifetime. Over the years these impressions formed thought patterns or mindsets in our storehouse of memory. The seeds of these mindsets were planted by the people and environmental experiences of our life and now form the basis for how we view life.

Included in these mindsets or paradigms are both positive and negative ways of seeing ourselves and others. For example, if a significant adult in our lives told us we couldn't sing, we may now feel very uncomfortable when asked to join in singing a song. On a positive note, if a significant adult told us we have a lovely voice, we may love to sing now. To go a step deeper, how we see our children is based on what is stored in our memory bank from our past experiences. If our parents expected perfection from us, we will most likely expect perfection from our children. If our parents saw us as weak, we often pass that self image onto our children. It is these buried thoughts that unconsciously affect how we interact with our children.

The way to clear our lens of faulty perceptions is to recognize when our behavior is ineffective and begin the process of going within to reflect on the root causes or paradigms that prompted our actions. Once we see the faulty thought behind our action, we can consciously choose to let go of it and replace it with a more authentic thought. As we gradually change our thoughts, our emotions and behavior will naturally change. As our behavior changes, so will the behavior of our children change.

I witnessed this phenomenon a number of times in my classroom when working with a child whose behavior challenged me. Initially I did my best to reach the child, but normal attempts didn't seem to make a difference. Being frustrated, I began to see the child as a "disturbance to my classroom." The more I saw the child as a "disturbance," the more I lost my patience, and the more the child's negative behavior escalated. When I finally came to the point of exasperation and shared my feelings and thoughts with a trusted colleague, a transformation began to take place within me. Because I was able to express my emotional frustration in a safe setting my mind and body began to calm down and my breathing became deeper. I was then able to access my deeper state of wisdom and realize that I needed to change how I was "seeing the child." Rather than seeing him as a "disturbance" I saw him as a "beautiful child struggling to be seen." The next day when the child came to school his attitude and behavior reflected my new vision of him and, remarkably, his behavior improved as well.

Our mindsets are deeply embedded in the basement of our subconscious mind and it may take several repeat experiences to successfully change our habitual negative thought patterns. However, through conscious observation, examination and restructuring of the paradigms we hold, we gradually free ourselves of our unhealthy mindsets and replace them with healthy paradigms that are in line with our child's and our own authenticity.

EGO

Ego is that part of mind that sees itself as separate from, rather than related to, and sees itself as the owner with a right to possess the best. From the ego's point of view, our identity is based on such things as who we are, what we believe, and what we own. We become emotionally invested in the preservation of these ideas or objects and when any of them are threatened, we become emotionally upset because our identity is in question. The problem here is that from this perspective we are identifying with that which is impermanent and fail to identify with our authenticity which is infinite.

One of my most vivid lessons about the power of ego came when I was a new parent, a new teacher and a new owner of a school. Because our three year old son was ready for a Montessori school and there was not one in the town, we decided to start one. In my subconscious mind I held two thoughts: "It is important that the school be viewed in a positive way by those who come to observe it," and "My son should be a shining example of a centered Montessori student." On this particular day, an important visitor saw my son acting silly rather than being engaged in thoughtful work. All of a sudden, my fear that the visitor would not get a good impression kicked in and I grabbed my son's hand and took him out of the classroom. At that point, I proceeded to scold him for his behavior. All of a sudden, it dawned on me that I was treating him differently than I would ever treat any other child in the classroom. What was the difference between him and the other children? My ego had attached a wrongful expectation on my son (that he should always be an outstanding example of my school) and as a result I was treating him differently. From that time on, I did my best to treat him both at home and at school in the same respectful way I did all other children.

When we embrace the ego attitude of possession we become attached to the object because we identify with it. Therefore, when we lose the object, we experience pain. The more we can have the attitude that all things are here for our temporary enjoyment and that nothing belongs to us on a permanent basis, the more we will be able to appreciate our gifts and eliminate the pain when they are no longer ours. Detachment is not uncaring—it is caring from the truest sense—honoring and appreciating the independent existence of all things—including our children. Kahlil Gibran reminds us of this truth in his poem.

Your children are not your children,
They are sons and daughters of life's longing for itself.
They come through you but not from you.
And though they are with you yet they belong not to you.

You may give them your love but not your thoughts,
For they have their own thoughts.
You may house their bodies but not their souls,
For their souls dwell in the house of tomorrow,
which you cannot visit, not even in your dreams.
You may strive to be like them, but seek not to make them like you.
For life goes not backward, nor tarries with yesterday.

You are bows from which your children as living arrows are sent forth.
The archer sees the mark upon the path of the infinite,
and He bends you with His might that his arrows may go swift and far.
Let our bending in the archer's hand be for gladness;
For even as He loves the arrow that flies,
So He loves also the bow that is stable.[8]

INNER GUIDE

As we have discussed the inner guide is our personal link to wisdom and consciousness. It is a special kind of intelligence that provides us with internal control, judgment and discrimination as it interacts with our sensory-motor, ego and memory bank to provide organization and meaning to our mental functioning. The inner guide also provides a place where we can observe what is taking place in our lower mind and make conscious decisions about what action to take. As we refine our ability to voluntarily take the seat of the observer, watch what is showing up and listen to the promptings of our inner guide, our life becomes less complicated. As we align ourselves with our inner guide we experience peace and joy in our lives. It is not what we "see" that matters; it is what we "see with" that helps us fulfill life's purpose.

As you will note on the above diagram, the inner guide function begins within close proximity to the sensory motor, ego and memory bank and then expands as it moves closer to our Authentic Self where it becomes more and more refined. This symbolizes that the inner guide makes simple decisions such as: "Should I buy the green one or the red one?" to more complex ones such as: "What should I do with my life?" Our inner guide has the capacity to move from simple decisions along a continuum to the most complex decisions. The deeper we go into our thinking process the more wisdom we bring to our decision-making process. The more we quiet the "voices" of lower mind, the clearer we hear the voice of our Authentic Self and avoid unnecessary complications.

All too often stimuli enters our mind and triggers our unconscious thoughts which in turn signal our emotions and causes us to react without using the conscious discrimination of our inner guide. We call this a "knee-jerk" reaction and often regret what we have said or done. This reactive behavior can be illustrated this way.

Reactive Behavior

Stimulus ➡ Response

An alternative to reactive behavior is responsive behavior. In responsive behavior, we separate the stimuli from the response with several conscious steps: 1) Breathe deeply to connect to our inner guide, 2) Observe and analyze the stimuli entering our awareness, 3) Create alternative behavioral actions, 4) Choose the best action, 5) Engage our intention or will 6) Breathe deeply and respond. This responsive behavior can be illustrated this way.

Responsive Behavior

While it might seem impossible to go through the processes of: observe, create, choose and will before responding to a situation, it can all happen rapidly if we use the key of breathing to unlock the wisdom of our inner guide. It may be that the best choice in some matters is to approach our child in a calm manner, take a deep breath, look into his eyes, see his Spirit and firmly say, "Stop!" Wait a few seconds and then say what you want to say to the child. By taking the time to stay centered, the child has less of a need to react from the defensive posture of his ego. As we become more proficient at being responsive rather than reactive, we find that our life flows more smoothly and we experience fewer out of control emotional situations.

Emotions

Our emotions are continually fluctuating and we often use our emotions to identify who we are. For example we say, "I am angry!" rather than "I feel angry." Since emotions are so unpredictable and unstable, it is not safe to use them as a foundation for our self image. Emotions indicate how we feel at a certain point in time, but do not determine who we are. They are extremely powerful, and without proper understanding of them, they can take control of the body and mind, and overshadow our Spirit. Learning to be aware of our emotions and work effectively with them increases our ability to stay centered in our authenticity.

EMOTIONAL AWARENESS

The first step in working effectively with our emotions is to recognize that we have feelings and that it is healthy to express them in an appropriate manner. Some of us were encouraged to suppress or otherwise ignore our emotions when we heard our parents say, "Big boys don't cry," or "Don't be so emotional." If we do not have a healthy outlet to express our feelings we end up stockpiling our emotions and, when we least expect it, we have an emotional explosion that results in hurting others and ourselves. Once this happens we often regret our behavior and end up making amends and asking for forgiveness of our insensitivity. By recognizing, acknowledging and learning to express our emotions appropriately we avoid these unwanted and often embarrassing explosions of emotion.

EXPRESSING EMOTIONS

When we are disturbed by a child's or another's behavior, it is important to let them know what we are feeling in a way that is non-threatening. If we take the stance that the other person is to blame for our emotional upset and say, "You made me angry," we can expect a defensive reaction such as "No I didn't." In expressing our emotions it is important to take full responsibility for what we are feeling and tell the person 1) what happened, 2) how we feel, 3) what our need is, and 4) what we would like from them. This pattern of expression is called an, "I" Message. The former expression that doesn't work well is a "You" Message. This process of expressing our emotions is covered in more detail in Chapter 14.

EMOTIONS CONNECTED TO OUR THOUGHT

Emotions are the colors in the fabric of our lives and overlay what we think, say and do. Without them life would be dull and uninteresting; however, with them life can at times seem out of control and unmanageable. As stated earlier, our emotions are connected to our conscious and unconscious thoughts. When stimulus enters our mind, we interpret it according to the unconscious paradigms that arise without our conscious awareness. For example, we might meet a new person and immediately feel uncomfortable about him for no conscious reason. Most likely we are reacting to a previous negative experience with someone else who reminds us of this new acquaintance. If we fail to observe our emotional reactions and ignore the root cause of our disturbance (old paradigm), we may lose the opportunity to see this new acquaintance for whom he truly is. When we experience unsettling emotions, it is a good indicator that we need to do some self study to determine what subconscious or conscious thoughts we need to alter, let go or replace all together.

HIJACKED EMOTIONS

In Chapter 6 under "Emotional Safety" there is an in-depth description of what happens when sensory stimulus connects with an unconscious negative mindset and automatically triggers strong emotions of fear. Instead of the entering stimulus going to both the amygdala glands (centers of passion) and the neo cortex (thinking brain) to be dealt with thoughtfully, it can be hi-jacked by the amygdala glands. In this scenario the glands register the need to "fight" or "flee," emit strong chemicals into the body and by pass the thinking brain. Suddenly we find ourselves caught up in irrational thinking and behavior.

We can see this happen when we get into power struggles with our children or other adults. When we feel our power being challenged, our ego wants to step in and take charge of the situation. With the promptings of ego, we take a defensive posture and see the other person as "enemy." If he also goes into a defense mode, the stage is set for a major emotional hi-jacking for both parties. Each of us takes our stand and defends our position at all costs. As the emotional tension escalates, so does our irrationality. We watch ourselves saying things we would normally never say because our emotions are taking us on a ride with no driver at the controls.

When this happens, the best thing we can do is to recognize that we are in a useless power struggle, leave the situation so that the sensorial stimulation is no longer present and do deep breathing until we can calm our lower mind and regain touch with our inner guide. Once this happens, we can look at the situation from our rational mind and determine what action to take.

CONGRUENCY

Congruency is to live in harmony with our Authentic Self and core principles. When we are able to do this our emotions remain in a tranquil state. However, when we do things that are not in alignment with our authenticity and principles, we set up dissonance in our thinking process. This dissonance causes us to feel uneasy, frustrated, angry or guilty. Miguel Ruiz, in his book *The Four Agreements* describes four basic principles that, if followed, will bring us congruency and contentment in our life. The four agreements are:[9]

189

1. Speak your truth
2. Take nothing personally
3. Make no assumptions
4. Always do your best

As we align ourselves with our authenticity we begin to notice a calming of our negative emotional reactions and see them being replaced by more positive and supportive ones such as joy, happiness and contentment.

Spirit

Our Spirit is the essence of who we are—our Authentic Self. It is reliable and unchanging because it is directly connected to the Divine Source of Love. As we connect with our Spirit we automatically connect with the infinite energy and wisdom of Cosmic Consciousness. Because this connection is constant and the well spring of happiness and bliss, we can trust our Spirit to guide us at all times. In fact the more we trust in our Authentic Self, the easier it is to let go of our ego's incessant need to run our lives. Following are some ideas to help us nurture our Spirit and bring our body, mind and emotions into alignment with it.

AFFIRMATION

When we look in the mirror each morning, what do we see? Do we see someone that we like or do we look away with feelings of embarrassment or shame? How we define our self now is based on the paradigms embedded in our unconscious mind. If the embedded self images are primarily negative, we most likely reflect this negativity in our attitudes and behaviors. *"You are not capable."* On the other hand if our embedded self images are primarily positive, our attitudes and behaviors are generally of a more positive nature. *"You can do it!"* The question arises: Are we stuck with what we received as a child? The answer is a resounding, *no!* We have a choice.

This is where the power of observation and self study come in. Once we become aware that we have unhealthy paradigms about our identity buried in our unconscious mind, we can begin to consciously replace these paradigms with healthy thoughts that reflect our true nature. Instead of holding the thought: *"I am a helpless victim of life and have little to share,"* we can release that thought and replace it with the truth of who we are. We can affirm that: *"I am a loving being with many gifts to share!"* As we become aware of our self-defeating thoughts rising from our subconscious mind, we can examine them to see if they are true or false. If we determine that the thought is not a true reflection of our authentic nature, we can release the old thought and replace it with a thought that reflects the authentic qualities of our Spirit such as love, compassion, joy, kindness, patience, courage and creativity.

In order to reinforce this process of replacing negative self paradigms with positive ones, it is important to love our self unconditionally and to nurture our self on a daily basis. It is good to look in the mirror, see deep into our eyes and say, *"I am love!"* When we observe ourselves being foolish, rather than getting angry, it is more helpful to see the experience as a lesson to be learned, be grateful for the new insight and forgive ourselves. Holding an attitude of gratitude for the small, as well as the big things in our lives, keeps our hearts open to the love emanating from our Spirit. One of our favorite activities in the summer is to walk slowly through our garden to discover and appreciate the beautiful flowers and cheer on the new buds that are about to open and share in their splendor.

LETTING GO

Ego is the part of mind that keeps us from completely embracing our spiritual nature. Its natural tendency is to hold onto the reigns and attempt to direct the flow of our lives so that all outcomes will be beneficial to us. Ego's thoughts are based on the fear that we may not get our fair share and must look out for our self first of all. If we respond to this thinking, we find our self contracting and holding back natural love and compassion. The result of this is that we actually prevent the natural flow of goodness from reaching us. The way the universe works is that the more we let go of our ego's control and allow the Spirit of the universe to lead the way, the greater will be our gifts.

Being willing to give away, share, cooperate and celebrate the accomplishments of others increases our joy and nourishes our Spirit.

The more we give away, the more we receive. This idea can be expressed by a simple chant: "To love is to give, to give is to have, to have is to give love."[10]

RENEWAL OF SPIRIT

Just like we must nurture our body each day to keep it vibrant and healthy, we must also nurture our Authentic Self on a daily basis. Each of us has those special things we do that make our Spirit sing. This might be listening to beautiful music, reading inspiring words, walking in nature, taking a candle-light bath, singing joyful songs, sharing with a friend, caring for someone in need, or sitting quietly in silence to renew our Spirit. Each of these activities helps us release the physical stress of the day, calm our minds and emotions, and align ourselves with pure love and joy.

Whatever activity works best for us, it is important to give ourselves quality time to be with our Authentic Self so that we become more and more comfortable with the amazing gifts it offers us. What a joy it is to experience unconditional love, wisdom, compassion, happiness and peace which are just a few of our Spirit's numerous gifts. The more we remember our authentic nature the more confident and successful we will be. Our Spirit is our best friend!

Conclusion

The essential nature of all human beings is Spirit. It is the part of us that is constant and the ultimate source of life and love. Our body, mind and emotions are outer manifestations of us and change continuously. When we are able to recognize and identify with our Spirit, we feel centered, present and peaceful because we have a reliable fulcrum from which to make decisions and act. In this state we experience our authenticity. On the other hand, when we identify with our physical, mental or emotional body we experience uncertainty because we allow ourselves to be victims at the mercy of our fluctuating physical, mental and emotional states.

While most of us move in and out of being centered in our authenticity, we all recognize the joy and satisfaction that comes when we are in alignment. The more we consciously identify with our Authentic Self, the more peace we experience. It is important to be patient with ourselves and, like the children, see our life's work as a continual process of learning and refining ourselves.

In the meantime, we have the amazing gift and responsibility of nurturing our children in a way that they can recognize and maintain connection to their Authentic Self throughout their lives. Having so recently come to planet earth, they are directly connected to their Spirit in ways adults are not.

Our role as parents and teachers is to help children recognize their authenticity and retain connection to it throughout life as they participate in the physical, mental and emotional worlds surrounding them. This is an awesome task, and the good news is we don't need to do it "all by our self" because our children come equipped with the tools and abilities to fulfill their potentials. Montessori reminds us of this truth.

> *Only the voice of life can choose the work that the child truly needs. Therefore, it is enough that the teacher respects this mysterious process and knows to wait with faith… Instead of frustrating the child's development, our task is precisely to set him upon the road to his inner being.*[11]

To understand the special language of the child's Spirit requires that we stay aware of our own spiritual nature and trust in the guidance of our inner teacher to lead us on the path of being an authentic parent. Polly Berends describes this journey well. "Parenthood is just the world's most intensive course in love. We are not parents merely to give or get love, but to discover love as the fundamental fact of life and the truth of our being and thus bring it into expression."[12]

Suggestions for Follow Through

■ Observe yourself in action. Practice observing yourself working, talking, interacting and even thinking. Become conscious of your breath, breathe deeply and assume the seat of observer located within your Authentic Self. Reflect and record your insights.

■ When you notice yourself becoming emotionally upset, remember to breathe deeply and find a place where you can be undisturbed. Reflect on what thought you were holding that created the emotional disturbance. Determine if the thought is based on fear and thus inaccurate. Reflect on what the truth of the situation is and replace the false thought with an authentic thought based on love. Record it in your journal.

■ Practice mindfulness by consciously being present in your actions. If you find yourself distracted, just bring your awareness back to the present moment. Be aware of how you feel when you are able to bring your full attention to the here and now. Record it in your journal.

■ Take at least ½ hour each day to nurture your Spirit. Be aware of what you discover and record it in your journal.

CHAPTER 13

Parenting Styles
and Practices

How wonderful it would be if the moment we become a parent we automatically receive the wisdom and insight about how to be an authentic parent. The truth is that none of us come so equipped. Most of us come with the memories implanted in our subconscious mind of how we were parented, and if that was not too offensive, we repeat these patterns with our own children. If we strongly disliked our parent's style of parenting, we may move to the extreme and seek parenting techniques that are opposite those we encountered as a child. For example, if our parents were very controlling and autocratic, we may find ourselves being more lenient and permissive. If they were very permissive, we may find ourselves leaning toward a more authoritarian manner of parenting our own children. The challenge with this is that, in either case, we are perpetuating domineering relationship patterns that can be harmful to the natural development of our children.

To change our harmful domineering patterns of parenting requires that we make conscious decisions to replace them with supportive partnership relationship patterns. This begins by acknowledging children's authentic nature and acting in accordance with their natural processes of development. Michael Gurian speaks to this, "The thrill in parenting comes from looking so deeply into the eyes of your child that you can see what is there, what you are really working with, and work specifically with that."[1]

Our children cry out to be seen by the significant adults in their lives. Think back on your life growing up. Did you have a parent, teacher or other significant adult that saw your authentic nature? Was there a person who recognized your uniqueness, talents and gifts? Was there someone who had faith in you and encouraged you to do your best and accept challenges? Was there a person who loved you unconditionally? How did it feel? How did it influence you and who you are today?

In 1932 Maria Montessori delivered an address to the International Office of Education in Geneva, Switzerland calling for a new understanding of how children learn and develop their potentials. One of her key points was to illustrate the value of recognizing the authentic nature of the child. She indicated that, "If education recognizes the intrinsic value of the child's personality and provides an environment suited to spiritual growth, we have the revelation of an entirely new child, whose astonishing characteristics can eventually contribute to the betterment of the world."[2]

When a child is recognized by adults as a loving being, he begins to relate and define himself accordingly. He learns that his Spirit is a reliable inner guide and learns to trust its promptings. As the child repeatedly experiences the joy and satisfaction of learning and blossoming, he develops positive habit patterns in his personality. Encouragement and reinforcement from his parents and teachers greatly supports this process.

Montessori went on to describe what happens when the child's authentic nature is ignored. "This inner-directed life of the child has its own characteristics and ends, different from those of the adult. When the adult interprets these as being errors in the child that must be immediately corrected, a struggle arises between the strong and the weak. This struggle can devastate the human race."[3]

When the adults in a child's life fail to see his Authentic Self and, knowingly or unknowingly, block his natural path of unveiling his authenticity, the child must struggle to be himself. This struggle brings out behaviors based on frustration, defensiveness, anger and rebellion.

As a result, the child begins to see the world as unfair, hostile and unsupportive. The seeds of violence are thus planted in his personality. This struggle makes it difficult for the child to relate to his inner guide and engage in the natural laws of development. As a result, he risks becoming a victim to alienation and outer authority because he has not been able to experience the comfort and assurance of his inner guide.

Reflecting Children's Authenticity Back to Them

To recognize the authentic nature of our child and provide optimal support for his growth and development, it is our responsibility to develop a nurturing relationship where he feels respected and honored for who he is, unconditionally loved and understood. After many years of practice as a psychologist, Carl Rogers[4] discovered three qualities that must be present in nurturing relationships. These qualities are:

1. Authenticity
2. Acceptance
3. Understanding

Studies validate that regardless of the philosophy or method teachers or parents use, if these three qualities are absent, the work they do will be minimally successful. The following Triad of Nurturing Relationships describes these qualities and how each impacts the child's ability to reveal his Authentic Self.

The Triad of Nurturing Relationships

Authenticity

Acceptance   **Understanding**

AUTHENTICITY

The principle of authenticity refers to the need to be genuine and authentic when interacting with others, to be free of acting from a façade—of feeling one way on the inside and acting another way on the surface. Children have a keen ability to know when a person is not honestly representing himself and, in that person's presence, they often feel a need to have a defensive posture. When we are authentic, children recognize it and more easily reveal their authenticity in our presence. To see the children's authenticity, we must do our best to be centered in our own. Rogers says it this way, "It is only by providing the genuine reality which is in me, that the other person can successfully seek for the reality in him."[5]

ACCEPTANCE

Another word for acceptance is unconditional positive regard for another. This means that we approach others free of prejudice or judgment and hold a warm feeling of unconditional positive regard. Children need to know that no matter what they feel, do or say we will love them unconditionally. We may let them know that we do not like their behaviors, but at the same time, we need to let them know we love them unconditionally. To threaten the withdrawal of love from children negatively impacts their positive upward motion of self construction because their emotional safety is threatened. Acceptance also calls for us to accept our own shortcomings, to walk with humility, and to make changes in our own lives when it is beneficial to all concerned.

UNDERSTANDING

The third element of nurturing relationships is empathy and understanding. Research shows that the healthy development of a child's brain and emotional capacity is directly connected to the amount of empathy and caring he receives. Empathy and understanding come from doing our best to see from another's perspective. This can be challenging because, while another is talking to us, we are often thinking about what we intend to say when the person is finished. Empathetic understanding requires that we quiet our own mind and receive, with both our heart and mind, what another is communicating or feeling. In other words, we do our best to walk in another's shoes—to absorb another's beingness—to "get it." When we are successful in doing this for others, including our children, they feel comfortable enough to honestly share their authenticity and explore the hidden aspects of themselves.

Carl Rogers recognized the intrinsic goodness within people and, through his work and research, determined that safe psychological environments are essential to our being able to support and encourage people in the manifestation of their potentials and authenticity: "the individual has within himself the capacity and the tendency, latent if not evident, to move forward toward maturity. In a suitable psychological climate this tendency is released and becomes actual rather than potential."[6]

Parenting Styles

Parenting styles come in a variety of shapes and sizes ranging from extremely authoritarian to extremely permissive. In between the two extremes is a balanced approach that we are calling Montessori Parenting. This can be illustrated in the following way:

Extreme   Extreme

Autocratic Parenting   **Montessori Parenting**   **Permissive Parenting**

Each style is discussed below.

MONTESSORI PARENTING

Montessori Parenting is based on the philosophy, principles and practices of Dr. Maria Montessori that have been discussed. This style is based on respect and recognition of the child's true nature. When we can do this we naturally express the three qualities of authenticity, acceptance, and understanding. In this state we are free from the distractions and demands of our ego and are able to experience love blooming forth from our center and, like the children, we are propelled by our vital life force and directed by our inner guide. The more we trust in this reality, the easier it will be to access the wisdom and strength we need to be an authentic parent.

When we act from authenticity, we naturally respect both our self and our child. We seek to create harmonious relationships, offer encouragement, establish healthy limits and find win/win solutions when difficulties arise. We see our self as a guide for the child and refrain from being overly controlling or permissive. We seek a balanced approach that allows our child freedom to follow his inner direction and engage in his Unveiling Cycles. At the same time we provide wisdom and guidance to help our child be responsible and accept healthy boundaries for his behavior. Montessori Parenting creates a healthy balance between freedom and self-discipline.

Riane Eisler, in her insightful book, *The Real Wealth of Nations*, discusses the need to create family relationships of partnership, rather than domination, with our children. She says, "partnership families are of particular importance in determining whether the institutions of a society are authoritarian and inequitable or democratic and equitable.... from the start, children are respected in partnership family structures, and their caregivers are attuned to their needs and wants."[7]

Montessori Parenting is a partnership model of mutual respect, and as such prepares children to be cooperative, responsible, enthusiastic, courageous, creative, concentrated and self disciplined. Montessori Parenting is based on and motivated through the power of love. In contrast, the following two models: Autocratic Parenting and Permissive Parenting are based on and motivated by fear and fall under the domination model. They are considered domination models because either the child or the parent is being dominated or controlled by the other. Eisler sums up the domination model by saying, "In the domination system, there is no partnership alternative. There are only two perceived choices: you dominate or you're dominated."[8]

AUTOCRATIC PARENTING

The autocratic style of parenting is based on fear rather than love. Fear is the opposite of love and brings with it a different set of attitudes and beliefs. Fear is a natural emotion and at times a necessary protection for us when we are in danger. When we anticipate or are aware of danger, we automatically move into a flight or fright mode and respond physically as well as mentally to protect and defend ourselves. If we experienced such things as consistent insensitivity, ignorance, violence, trauma, etc. in our childhood, we may suffer from an underlying energy of fear in our personality that makes it difficult to trust others and often influences our thoughts and actions. A major thought that often develops for many of us is, "I do not trust life and, therefore, I must control what happens to me and others."

The Autocratic Parenting style grows out of this need to control and is considered a domination model rather than a partnership model of relationship. As parents we feel a need to control not only our self, but our child as well. We expect obedience and react negatively when we see our child challenge our authority. In addition, we think that if our child has a healthy fear of us, they will be more likely to follow our direction. We keep this fear alive in our child by threats, punishment, name calling, demands, chastisement, judgments, etc. We often find ourselves frustrated, angry, harsh, and critical of our child. The result of this approach is that our child will begin to retreat from his loving Authentic Self to defend himself with his own ego and defensive behaviors. When threatened, it is natural for him to take a defensive posture which will bring with it behaviors such as frustration, anger, defiance, revenge, and distrust.

When autocratic behavior is the major parenting style in the home, a child has a difficult time staying in touch and identifying with his authenticity, trusting anyone (let alone his inner guide), following his intrinsic interests and entering naturally into his creative process of unveiling his authenticity. Authoritarian behavior interrupts the natural flow of child development and thoughtful self-discipline. The child becomes dependent on what others (parents, teachers, and peers) tell him rather than learn to make sound decisions through listening to his inner wisdom. This leads to the child being outer-directed rather than inner-directed. He does not identify with his Authentic Self, but with fake selves he thinks others want to see. He then grows up doing things for the wrong reasons—seeking love and acceptance by following what he thinks others want of him. This false identification and search for love often creates a "hole in the soul" that may result in future addictive behavior.

PERMISSIVE PARENTING

Permissive Parenting often comes from positive thoughts such as, "My child is capable of self-regulation and has an abundance of potential waiting to be manifest." However, it is also based on the fear thought that, "If I interfere with my child's desires, I might harm his development." With this thought, our main objective is to keep our child happy by allowing him maximum freedom so he can develop his potential. The net result of this attitude is that we hesitate to do anything that might upset our child and, thereby, hesitate to set guidelines and limits on his behavior. The Autocratic Parenting style gives parents the power to dominate their child. The Permissive Parenting style gives the child the power to dominate his parents.

When we use the permissive paradigm as our model for parenting, there is a danger that we will do too much for our child and ask very little from him in return. Doing for our child what he can do for himself, creates feelings of inadequacy within him and slows his natural quest for independence. He becomes dependent on us to fill his needs and when we aren't able to do this to his satisfaction, his ego feels threatened and the resulting behaviors we may observe are: non cooperation, screaming, stomping feet and/or temper tantrums. This over dependence on us, rather than his inner guide, prevents our child from naturally developing responsible behavior. A side effect of this over indulgence is that the child comes to expect instant gratification and we become a slave to his every desire.

Another hazard we encounter using a permissive style of parenting is that we hesitate to say "no" or set reasonable limits. Children respond well when they know their parents believe in them but this alone is incomplete. A child needs to know what behavior is appropriate and what behavior is harmful to him and to others. It is up to us as parents to guide our child and create reasonable boundaries for him. When left without limits, a child experiences insecurity and often manifests behaviors such as selfishness, self-centeredness, and a general lack of discipline. When this happens, as parents we often resort to pleading with him, offering rewards for good behavior, and giving in to his wishes. While these helping behaviors may seem supportive to our child, ultimately they keep him from identifying with his Authentic Self and engaging in the natural learning path of self construction.

As you read the above descriptions of three distinct parenting styles, you probably saw yourself to one degree or another in each of them. This is because we are all evolving in our maturity and parenting skills. It is natural for us to watch ourselves being calm, patient and joyful with our child (Montessori Parenting) and then find ourselves losing that serenity and resorting to threats or demands (Autocratic Parenting). Then after a time, we find ourselves feeling guilty that we might have overreacted to the situation and move to the other extreme of over indulging our child (Permissive Parenting). While this movement is quite normal, it can send inconsistent messages to our children.

Montessori Parenting is a balanced approach that is responsive to the natural inner life and development of the child; however, because we are parents in process, we may find ourselves moving toward an autocratic or permissive style of parenting depending on the situation we face. This vacillation is normal and correctable. When we become aware that we have moved too far to either side of the center we can make conscious corrections by observing our thinking processes and embracing new ways of thinking. Since our actions are rooted in our unconscious thoughts, we can begin to refine our behavior by changing how we see the situation.

Good vs. Responsible Parenting

If our subconscious thoughts are based on false images of who the child is and how we see our role as parent, we often act in ways that we think are "good" for the child, but in reality are harmful to his development. These false images, or adultisms, are motivated by our fears. When we make decisions from ego they often come from our need to control, our sense of superiority, our desires to appear perfect or from our feelings of inadequacy. Following are a few examples of inaccurate and harmful thinking.

GOOD PARENT—HARMFUL THOUGHTS

- **"My child is incapable of controlling himself; therefore, I must control him."** When we hold this subconscious thought we make demands, threaten, punish and use rewards to get him to do what we think is "good." How often have we heard ourselves or others say, "I am doing this for your own good." Rather than being good for the child, it more often than not results in the child feeling insecure, angry or even rebellious. In this emotional state the child has a difficult time connecting with his Authentic Self.

- **"I am superior and my child is weak."** When we hold this thought we think that the "good" thing to do is take responsibility for our child by making his decisions, telling him what to do, over indulging and over protecting him. It often leads to our feeling a need to solve his problems, do his homework and arrange his life. The contemporary name for this is "Helicopter Parenting" These over-indulging behaviors actually do harm to our child because he soon assumes the persona of helplessness and tends to blame others for his difficulties. The child becomes disempowered and out of touch with the inner strength and vitality of his Authentic Self.

- **"I need to be perfect and my child should be perfect as well."** This type of thinking is based on our ego's need to be the best. We see our child as a direct reflection of us; therefore, it is "good" for him to be perfect at all times. This type of thinking is based on our own insecurity and need to seek approval of others. It leads to our continuously finding fault, being critical and being overbearing with our child. The result for the child is that he begins to feel inadequate, unworthy and discouraged. He can become extremely dependent on what others think of him and be overly concerned about pleasing others at his own expense. Lacking in self confidence and self-esteem, the child suffers and remains out of touch with the power and wisdom of his Authentic Self.

- **"I am not as important as my child."** This thought leads to our thinking that the "good" thing to do is recognize the superiority of the child and give him whatever he wants. Because we see the child as better than ourselves, we resist setting limits or saying, "no" to the child. This attitude leads to over-indulgence and gives him a false sense of entitlement. This, in turn, breeds selfishness and a lack of respect for others because he has not learned to see himself in relationships of mutual respect. Again, the child suffers from a false identification with ego and is unable to enjoy the experience of being connected to his Authentic Self.

In reflecting on four common subconscious thought patterns of parents, we can see that they are all based on fear: fear of chaos, fear of danger, fear of failure and fear of inadequacy. When our thoughts are based on fear we can be confident that they are not originating from our authenticity; therefore, we will be ineffective in helping our children identify with their authenticity. Maria Montessori observed the above patterns in the parents and teachers of her time and saw how they negatively impacted the inner life of the child.

Evidently, our students' natural spontaneity, which derives mysteriously from the child's inner life, had long been suppressed by the energetic and inopportune intervention of adults, who believe they can do everything better than children, substituting their own activities for those of the children and forcing them to submit their will and initiative to adult control.[9]

Montessori saw that parents' well intentioned "good" behaviors were based on a misunderstanding of the inner spiritual life of the child.

Perhaps many doubt that an inner life exists in the very young child. Certainly, these people must learn to understand the special language of the spirit if they would understand the needs of these tiny beings and be persuaded to the importance of these needs for the life that is developing. Respect for the liberty of the child consists of helping these powers to grow.[10]

The partnership model of Montessori Parenting is based on meeting the genuine needs of children and is centered in love rather than fear. In this model parents seek to be authentic and honor children's authenticity. Rather than holding thoughts of control, superiority, perfection or inadequacy, we seek to hold thoughts of trust, mutual respect and patience both for the child as well as ourselves. Following are three examples of truth-based thoughts that motivate responsible behavior toward our children.

RESPONSIBLE PARENT—TRUTH-BASED THOUGHTS

- **"I know the authentic nature of my child and trust in his ability to engage meaningfully in his Unveiling Cycle."** The foundation of responsible behavior is to be able to trust the child. When we hold this thought our fears and need to control are replaced by the love and joy we experience as we see the child discover life and share it with us. We demonstrate trust by allowing children time to discover for themselves, assume appropriate responsibility, and make decisions they are ready to make. When children feel trusted they develop self confidence, creativity and the courage to follow their inner guidance. They have a sense of well being and happiness most of the time.

- **"I am equal to, and not better or less than, my child."** Mutual respect comes from this thought. When we consciously act from it we naturally believe in children's capabilities, prepare nurturing environments for their exploration, and encourage their independence. We give them responsibilities and seek their input and contribution to the family. We communicate respectfully and use effective means for solving problems. We also realize that mutual respect means that we respect ourselves and do not hesitate to say "no" or set responsible boundaries for the children. We speak and act with respect and expect the same of our children. When they experience mutual respect, they are able to naturally engage in their creative Unveiling Cycles and develop the maturing fruits of self reliance, responsibility, independence, cooperation, and the joy of self-actualization.

- **"My child and I are in the process of living and learning and this is the purpose of life."** Patience comes from understanding that life is a process, not a finished product. When we hold the above thought, we free ourselves from guilt or blame of others and develop patience within ourselves and our children. We are better able to let go blame and shame and see the imperfections of life as natural lessons to be learned. We are able to step back, reflect and learn from our experiences. Children respond beautifully to this approach because it allows them to take a look at themselves without fear of punishment or shame. This attitude also develops tolerance and understanding in the child as well as in us.

Conclusion

Accepting the responsibility of being a parent is probably the most important decision we will ever make in our lives. However, in carrying out the parental responsibilities, there is danger that we might lose touch with our authenticity and define ourselves in the role as "parent." Eric Tolle suggests that, "When being a parent becomes an identity, however, when your sense of self is entirely or largely derived from it, the function easily becomes overemphasized, exaggerated and takes you over...."[11]

When we exchange our authentic identity with our role as parent we become vulnerable to the clutches of our ego. Our actions and reactions become driven by our ego's need to be right and this makes authentic interaction with our child difficult. We easily become driven by the need to look good as a parent and when our child acts in ways that do not reflect our "good" parenting we become stressed and emotionally upset. It is quite common for us to want to use our child to fulfill our unfulfilled needs. In doing so, we put heavy expectations on him that interfere with his natural process of unveiling his authenticity. Our child gets the message that in order for him to gain our approval or love he must please us. When this attitude is repeated frequently the child replaces his authentic identity with a false identity that says he is only important when he is pleasing us. The important question is whether or not we can be an authentic "responsible" parent without letting the role of being a "good" parent take over.

This process of being an authentic responsible parent requires that we replace our faulty thinking with truth-based thinking in our subconscious mind. This clearing of the mind is equivalent on a physical plane to cleaning the basement or storage area in our homes where we collect stuff and more stuff that we will "take care of later." For some of us that "later" may be 40 years later. When the cleaning and sorting has been completed and some order has been brought to the situation, there is a feeling of relief and exhilaration. Similarly, when we are able to let go our ineffective patterns of thinking and replace them with fresh effective ones, we experience a sense of freedom and joy as we experience the positive results of our changed behavior due to our changed thinking.

Suggestions for Follow Through

▦ Write down each of the four "harmful thoughts" in your journal. Examine them and see if they or other similar thoughts are how you view your role as parent. Reflect on the possible root causes in your own life as a young child.

▦ When you have a stressful interaction with your child, take time to calm yourself by removing yourself from the sensorial stimulation and doing deep breathing. Reflect in your journal on what just happened between you and your child. Particularly examine the thoughts you were thinking at the time of the incident. How were you seeing your role as parent?

▦ Write down each of the three "truth-based thoughts." Examine them and see if they or similar thoughts are how you view your role as parent. Reflect on the possible root causes in your own life as a young child.

▦ When you have a particularly satisfying interaction with your child, take time to take it in and enjoy the moment. Reflect in your journal on what just happened between you and your child. Particularly examine the thoughts you were thinking at the time. How were you seeing your role as parent?

CHAPTER 14

Communicating with Compassion

For a moment let's go back to a time when there was no means of verbal communication among our earliest ancestors. Imagine what it would be like to be unable to reach out to another person and share thoughts. It seems that it would be a lonely and frightening world to live in. Language was born from a basic human need to communicate with others.

This process of acquiring language most likely began by people giving objects a specific sound or name that the entire group agreed to adopt. This would have been the beginning of what we now call nouns. Perhaps descriptive words such as "big" and "two" may have helped clarify the communication. It would make sense that action words such as "walk" and "run" would have come next and then be followed by adjectives such as "quickly" and "slowly" to further describe the verbs. For thousands of years hundreds of groups of people have developed hundreds of different languages. While each language has its own unique sounds and meanings, they all share a universal core purpose—to have the ability to communicate with others.

Now let's come back to our current time and reflect on our ability to communicate with others. It is phenomenal! We not only have the ability to verbally communicate with people living near us, we can now instantly communicate with others around the globe. There is literally a communication explosion via the technological advances of satellites, television, computer, electronic messaging and cell phones. With all this advancement, however, there is an important component that is lagging behind. That component is the ability to communicate with compassion. To quote Marshall Rosenberg the current voice of compassionate communication, "What I want in my life is compassion, a flow between myself and others based on a mutual giving from the heart."[1] Most of us have grown up using language to share and acquire information, but few of us have had the opportunities to learn how to express ourselves from the heart—the seat of compassion.

The first communication our children experience is in our homes. This is where they acquire the ability to speak and, with our help, acquire the ability to communicate compassionately from their Spirit of love and compassion. Our ability to speak to them from our heart automatically touches their heart. When children experience the warmth of our compassionate communication, they feel safe enough to reveal their authenticity. This chapter focuses on communication blocks, compassionate expression, roadblocks to listening, empathetic understanding and problem solving.

Communication Blocks

Children naturally want to learn from us and for the first six years of life absorb almost everything in their environments. This includes both our verbal as well as our nonverbal language. A child quickly picks up the messages we are sending him and embeds these images in his subconscious mind. The most important message he incarnates is whether or not he is loved and respected by his parents. A child unconsciously holds the question of whether or not we recognize his authenticity. If he experiences a sense of compassion in how we speak and physically relate to him, his Authentic Self is touched and he will be able to relate to us from the wisdom of his inner guide. Some specific ways to nonverbally reinforce our respect for our child is to give him our full attention when he wishes to talk to us, get down to his level and look into his eyes. By taking the time to do this, we say to the child—

"You are important and I want to hear what you have to say," and we are most likely to open the door to heart to heart communication.

Conversely, if the child interprets our messages as a threat to his authenticity, his ego will take over to defend him and likely initiate negative behavior. Following are some of the statements that block the flow of compassionate communication and our connection to our child's authentic nature.

- **Blaming Statements**: Blaming statements have their roots in our ego thought that "I am right and if something goes wrong, it is someone else's fault." When we respond to our child or others by blaming, we are refusing to take responsibility for our own thoughts, feelings and actions. A couple of examples are: "You made me do it," or "It is your fault we are late." Blaming statements are often called, "You Messages." We may feel good temporarily when we blame another, but we are actually relegating ourselves to the role of being a victim by becoming dependent on others for our happiness. When we blame our child we actually engage the indignation of his ego and block the possibility of heart to heart communication.

- **Judging Statements**: Judging statements have their roots in our ego thought that, "I know what is right and wrong and I expect you to do what I say." When we sit as a judge and tell our child that, "You were wrong to do that," we undermine his confidence and ability to make thoughtful choices from his inner wisdom. Rather than opening up a dialogue to help our child determine what happened and how it might be better in the future, we automatically engage the wrath of his ego and his corresponding defensive behavior.

- **Criticizing Statements**: Criticizing statements have their roots in our ego thought that, "I am smart and you are not as smart." Closely related to judging statements are those that criticize our child. "You are always so slow to finish eating. Why can't you just eat your dinner?" Again, by making such a statement, we block the possibility of connecting compassionately with our child. Instead, we engage his ego and trigger hurtful feelings such as shame, guilt, resentment and anger.

- **Insulting Statements**: Insulting statements have their roots in our ego thought that, "I am better than you." When we engage in statements that put our child down by saying such things as, "How can you be so dumb?" we deeply cut into our child's sense of well being and confidence. We again engage the child's ego rather than his authenticity.

- **Comparing Statements**: Comparing statements have their roots in our ego thought that, "One person is better than another." When we have more than one child it is easy to fall into the trap of comparing one child to another. We may find ourselves saying, "Why can't you be as smart as your sister?" This also cuts deep into the heart of the child's confidence and blocks the natural flow of compassion. His ego is most likely going to send defensive messages to his subconscious mind that he is better than his sister in many ways and that it is unfair for us to make such a comparison. This can gradually turn into feelings of resentment within him. Making such comparisons with our child blocks the possibility of spontaneous communication.

- **Demanding Statements**: Demanding statements have their roots in our ego thought that, "I am in control here and you need to do what I say." Demands imply that we expect immediate obedience or else punishment will follow. When we make demands such as, "You must stop doing that right now!" children automatically have a strong ego reaction of defiance that can accelerate into revenge. The effect of this is that we create unnecessary blocks to the flow of compassionate communication.

It is important to realize that it is quite "human" to have a storehouse of ineffective paradigms hidden away in our unconscious mind because as a child we experienced most of these communication blocks. It is imperative that we don't beat ourselves up when we hear ourselves making blocking statements. The productive approach is to see the experience as an opportunity to be aware of our false paradigms and learn a new way to express ourselves so that we can maintain a flow of compassionate communication with our children.

Compassionate Expression

When we want to make a statement to our child that will keep the possibility of heart to heart communication alive, we can share an "I" message with him. The difference between an "I" message and a blaming "You" message is that in an "I" message we take full responsibility for our observations, feelings and needs. To share a message in this manner we must: 1) describe what happened (or is happening), 2) share what we are feeling, and 3) express the need we have that is not being met and 4) request what we need. Each of these areas will be explored in greater detail.

- **Describe the Incident**: When we observe something happening, our first reaction is to make an instant evaluation about what we are seeing. Our evaluation is our interpretation or story about the event. When describing an event it is important to do our best to separate our story about the event from the actual description of the event. For example, a child is playing with his food. We may make a statement like, "Playing with your food is not good." Because this is a judgment statement, we will most likely evoke an ego based reaction from the child. Instead we can refrain from any evaluation and just describe what we see, *"When I see you playing with your food instead of eating it...."* By doing this we avoid the opportunity for the child to take our observation personally.

- **Share Feelings**: The second step is to share how we feel about what we observe. This, of course, requires that we recognize our emotional reaction and name it. For very young children it is helpful to label our emotions as simply as possible using such words as: "mad," "sad," and "afraid." As children mature it is helpful to expand our emotional vocabulary to more clearly describe our feeling. To continue our observation about the child playing with his food we might say. *"When I see you playing with your food instead of eating it, I feel annoyed...."*

- **Express the Reason for Feelings**: What we feel is directly connected to what we are thinking or how we interpret an event. Our interpretation of what we see happening brings up negative emotions in us if the activity goes against a need we have. For

215

example, when we see our child playing with his food, we might interpret the child's activity as wasting food. If we have a strong need to conserve food, his actions may trigger a negative emotional reaction in us. Our "I" message based on this scenario might be, *"When I see you playing with your food instead of eating it, I feel annoyed, because I don't like to see food wasted."* A second scenario might be that we interpret the child's playing with food as keeping him from getting the nutrition he needs. Our feeling might change from being "annoyed" to one of being "worried" because we have a need to make sure that our child eats enough healthy food. Our "I" message based on this scenario might be, *"When I see you playing with your food instead of eating it, I feel worried, because I want you to get enough healthy food in your body."*

- **Request What We Need**: To complete the "I" message it is important to request what we would like to see happen to fulfill our need. When making the request it is critical to frame it in positive language and refrain from putting it in a negative framework such as, "Please do not play with your food." A more effective way to express the request might be, *"Please finish eating your food."* Our request is more likely to be honored if we make a clear concrete statement of what we need and our tone of voice and delivery are respectful.

It is not necessary to use the complete "I" message every time we are disturbed by something our child is doing. Sometimes, going right to the respectful, clear request is a sufficient reminder of what we would like to see happen. Another approach is to ask a question to the child to bring his attention to the situation. "Are you aware of how loud you are playing your music?" Once the child responds, we can make our request. If these two approaches fail to bring satisfactory resolve, it is helpful to take a deep breath and go through the three steps of the "I" message to make it clearer to the child. If the child continues to ignore the request, his behavior may be rooted in an unfulfilled need of his own and will require another approach from us. Chapter 16, Understanding Children's Behavior, addresses various ways to address children's unfulfilled needs.

The "I" message is also an effective tool to express appreciation for what our child has done. So many times we respond to our child by saying things like, "I like what you are doing," or "You did a good job on that." On the surface these seem like positive, harmless statements; however, they are actually statements of judgment. (If this is "good" this time, it might be "bad" next time). Too many judgment statements will encourage our child to do things for our accolades rather than for his own inner satisfaction. An alternative to judgment statements is to use the first three steps of the "I" message: 1) describe the incident, 2) share feelings, and 3) express the reason for our feelings. An example might be, "When I see how thoughtfully you have cleaned the kitchen, I feel happy because having an orderly home is important to me."

When we share an "I" message with our child it is helpful to ask him what he heard us say. By doing this, we know if the child received our message accurately or if we need to repeat or change it in some way. Through the process of asking our child to feed back what he hears we help him develop his listening skills and the ability to tell another what he has heard. A child is capable of doing this around the age of four or five.

Roadblocks to Listening

How many times have you been emotionally distraught and felt the need to share your thoughts and feelings with a friend only to have the friend listen to the first few sentences of your story and then say something like, "That happened to me and this is what I did about it." All of a sudden the focus shifts and your friend is telling her story while you are left hurting and unfulfilled. Learning how to truly listen is an art.

Empathetic understanding is the art of listening so that the other person feels respected and understood at the deepest level of authenticity—heart to heart communication. It is so easy to think we are listening, but frequently we unknowingly actually stop the flow of authentic communication. Following are some common road blocks that we put up when our child comes to us with a problem. We take on the persona of:

- **The Teacher**: In this persona we listen to our child's problem and then begin to tell him what we think he needs to do about it. "This is what I think you need to do about this...."

- **The Red Cross Nurse**: In this persona we listen to the child's problem and then proceed to feel sorry for him and see if we can fix the problem. "Oh I am so sorry that happened. Don't worry I will fix it for you."

- **The Big Boss**: In this persona we listen to the child's problem and then proceed to boss him around by telling him what to do. "That behavior is uncalled for. You need to just hit him back next time."

- **The Judge**: In this persona we listen to the child's problem, make a judgment about the situation and pass sentence. "Your friend was in the wrong and you are right. Don't have him come over again."

- **The Interrogator**: In this persona we listen to the child's problem and continue to question him in an interrogating, almost accusing manner. "Now tell me—When did this happened? Who was involved? What did the teacher do?"

- **The Politician**: In this persona we listen to the child's problem and then suggest the best strategy to deal with the situation. "I think the best thing for you to do in this case is to ignore him for a few days and play with other children so that he will see what he is missing by not being your friend."

In each of these scenarios we rob the child of three things: 1) his need to express himself and be heard, 2) his need to be understood at the heart level, and 3) his ability to think through and decide on a solution to his problem. Following is an effective alternative to the above listening scenarios. It is called "Empathetic Understanding."

Empathetic Understanding

To be able to listen with compassion requires that we listen with our whole being. We must be totally present in the moment and listen not for just a child's words, but for the meaning behind the words and his nonverbal clues. We do our best to "walk in another's moccasins" or understand what they are saying from a place of empathy. The word empathy means that we respectfully receive what another is sharing so that we can understand from his point of view. Intellectual understanding is different than empathetic understanding. Intellectual understanding is listening with our mind and empathetic understanding is listening with our heart and mind. To be able to receive another with empathy, we must come with an open mind—with no preconceived ideas or answers. Our three tasks are: 1) to be present and focus on what is being said, 2) do our best to understand the meaning of what is being shared, and 3) check to see if we understood. The power of love emanating from our empathetic energy opens the door to compassionate communication.

It is not an easy task to totally attend to the process of listening. We often find our minds wandering or thinking about what we are going to say in response. This has the effect of breaking the compassionate connection between us. Many of us hold a faulty paradigm that when someone comes to us with a problem he wants us to fix it. This is absolutely not the case. People don't want to be "fixed," they want to be heard and understood. When effective listening takes place, people feel affirmed and receive clarification about their difficulty so they can find solutions on their own.

Once we listen and receive what our child is sharing with us it is important that we let him know what we *think* we hear him saying. The process of feeding back what is being said is our process of checking in to see if we have heard our child accurately and understood the meaning of his words. To accomplish this, we need to listen from our heart rather than our mind. This is not a matter of parroting the words we hear for that is only annoying to the individual. Our purpose is to listen for the *meaning* of what is being said. A helpful guideline is to listen for the components of the "I" message: 1) the child's description of what happened, 2) his resulting feelings, 3) the unmet need the child is experiencing, and 4) what he would like to receive. When we **"get"** the essence of his discomfort, his heart is touched. An example might be, "What I hear you say is that when David wouldn't play ball with you today you felt sad because he is your best friend and you really wanted to play with him. Is that right?"

It is amazing to watch the joy that registers on a child's face when we successfully feed back to him what we hear him saying. When he is heard and feels understood, he generally wants to continue and go deeper into his thoughts. As he continues sharing we continue to feed back what we think we have heard him say. A phrase that is helpful during the feed back process is: "What I hear you say is...." If we are on target we will usually see a recognition response from the child. If we don't see this, we may want to ask him to repeat what he said. Our intention is to understand what our child is saying to us. Our process of asking him if we have understood him is our way of determining if we are on track.

During this listening process we can also interject open-ended statements such as, "Tell me more," "I'm listening," "Is there anything more?" This process continues until the child reaches a place of feeling understood and accepted. Watch for a deep sigh or other sign of relaxation in the child. It is at this point, and not before, that he is open to being asked what he thinks would be a good solution to the situation. From this point on, he is on his way to considering alternative solutions and deciding on one that he feels will work. If he asks for our advice or suggestion at this point, it is fine to share our ideas.

For a young child who may not be able to articulate what is wrong, we can empathetically observe and share with him how we think he may be feeling. For example we might say, "Are you feeling sad?" or "It looks like you might be feeling sad." If we see a recognition response or a positive response, we might follow up by saying, "Would you like to tell me what happened?" From this point we can continue making open-ended statements to encourage him to tell his story. When we have an understanding of what is bothering the child, we can summarize what we think he is struggling with. If we see that we have received his message accurately, then we can engage in the process of helping him come up with a solution to his problem. Sometimes this entails our making one or two suggestions of what he can do. It is important to give him a choice if at all possible. Sometimes there is nothing that needs to be done—the child just needed to be heard and understood.

Empathetic understanding works well when our child comes to us with a problem and wants to share it with us. It also works well when our child comes to us because **we** are his problem. For example he might say to us, "You are being unfair to me." When we hear such a message we have several response options. We can either:

- Accept blame—Accept the blame. "I guess I am being unfair to you."

- Blame others—It's not my fault. "It isn't me who is being unfair, you don't understand."

- Share our own feelings and needs—Use an "I" message. "When you tell me that I am not being fair to you, I feel concerned, because I want to be fair with you."

- Sense the other's feelings and needs—Use empathetic understanding. "Are you feeling mad because I told you that you couldn't go to the movies with your friend and you really want to do this?"

The first three responses are limited because they only satisfy our need to express our feelings. The fourth option is generally the most effective because we provide an opportunity for our child to share his feelings. When we use the fourth option of empathetic understanding in response to our child's negative message to us, it helps to take a deep breath and do our best not to take the statement personally. We can then observe how he looks and reflect on what he just said to us. At that point we might say, "Are you feeling _____because_____?" From this point, we can enter into the mode of reflecting back to our child what we are hearing him say as described above.

Problem Solving

The word "problem" has a negative connotation for many of us. We see problems as something to avoid, but avoiding them is impossible because of the very nature of life. The best we can do is to learn how to effectively work with problems when they arise and learn from them. The first step is to determine who has the problem and the best approach to resolve it.

1. If the child has a problem with someone else, or with you, use empathetic understanding.

2. If you have a problem with the child, or someone else, use the "I" message.

3. If both you and your child have a problem with each other, or if two children have a problem between them, use conflict resolution.

CONFLICT RESOLUTION PROCESS

In the home, it is quite common that two children have a problem that needs to be resolved peacefully. In this case, we can serve as mediators until the children are capable of going through the conflict resolution process on their own. It is important to remember that a mediator is not a judge but rather an objective facilitator. If the conflict is between you and your child, follow the same procedures below, but instead of being the mediator, be one of the participants.

The process of conflict resolution combines the use of both "I" messages and empathetic understanding between the two participants. We have found it helpful to have an artificial "Peace Flower" to help facilitate the following process.

- Bring the Peace Flower (in a vase) to a rug or table where you will be discussing the problem. Invite the children to sit facing one another so they can make eye contact. It is best if you sit as the third person in the triangle.

- Take a deep breath and invite the children to do the same. Let them know that, "No one is in trouble," and that you are there to help them resolve their difficulty. Get a commitment of participation from them, "Are you willing to do this?"

- Briefly explain (or remind them of) the problem solving process they will experience so they each understand that they will have an opportunity to both share their issue and be listened to. Here is an example:

"Johnny, I am going to give Susie the Peace Flower so she can tell you 1) what happened and 2) how she feels. (With older children include the 3rd and 4th step—the reason for the feeling and the request for what is needed) You will then be able to tell her what you heard her say.

Susie, once Johnny has heard what you said, it will be his turn to hold the Peace Flower and tell you what happened and how he feels. You will then be able to tell him what you heard him say. OK?" (As above add the third and fourth component of the "I" message with older children)

- Ask the children if they understand and agree to participate in the process. By establishing the process ahead of time, the children are less likely to interrupt each other because they know they will have a turn to share.

- Begin the process of "I" messages and empathetic understanding. Give the Peace Flower to Susie and ask her to tell Johnny what happened and how she feels. (For older children add steps 3 and 4.) Make sure that Susie talks *directly to Johnny* in a clear "I" message.

- When Susie has delivered her message, ask Johnny if he understood what she said. Ask him to tell her what he heard her say. If he has difficulty doing this, have Susie repeat what she said and again ask Johnny to let her know what he heard. Once he gives the feedback to Susie, ask Susie if he heard her accurately. This is her time to say "yes" or give Johnny further clarification. When Johnny does "get it," Susie gives Johnny the Peace Flower. (When Susie feels heard by Johnny, her emotional tensions begin to relax.)

- Invite Johnny to repeat the same process just described until he also feels heard.

- When both children complete the process of expressing what happened, how they feel, (for older children), the reason for the feelings and a request for what is needed, place the Peace Flower in the vase on the floor or table. Sum up the difficulty, as you understand it. This helps to clarify the situation so that problem solving can begin.

- Ask the children if the way they handled the situation in the first place was the best or most peaceful way. Usually they will recognize that it was not. This is the time to ask them what ideas they have to solve the problem and work it out in a peaceful way.

- Encourage the children to come up with ideas to make the situation better. This may include agreements to meet each other's requests, a promise to do something differently in the future or some form of restitution. A specific apology is not necessary. If it is a natural expression, that is helpful, but it is not meaningful if a child just says "I'm sorry" because it is expected of him.

- Once the conflict has been resolved, ask them if they are ready to "declare peace." Have them put their hands alternately on the stem of the Peace Flower and say, "We declare peace!"

- Thank them for their willingness to participate and express confidence in their ability to make positive choices in the future.[2]

SEEKING WIN/WIN SOLUTIONS

Steven Covey describes the fourth habit of "effective" people as the ability to, "Think Win/Win."[3] This means that when we are seeking resolution to a problem with our child or someone else it is important to seek a solution that will work for all people concerned. This requires moving from a position (I am right and you are wrong) to a shared principle (what we hold in common.) For example, if a teacher asks a parent to come to a conference because she needs to discuss a challenge she has with a child; and if the parent comes into the conference feeling a need to defend her child, the chances of the two of them coming to a satisfactory solution is questionable. However, if both can talk about the situation from a common principle (the interest they both have in helping the child be successful) there is a much greater chance that they will come up with a plan they can both embrace. The following diagram illustrates Win/Win and the alternatives of Win/Lose or Lose/Lose.

When there is a power struggle and no one is willing to listen or make compromises, the end result is that everyone loses, everyone is emotionally distraught and in a defensive posture. (Lose/Lose) When one person uses power to get his way and the other person loses, the end result is that one person may be temporarily happy that he got his way, but the other person is emotionally angry and will most likely seek ways to get even. (Win/Lose) Searching for a Win/Win solution to a problem leaves each person feeling respected and understood.

These three concepts can be compared to the Parenting Styles discussed in the previous chapter. The Lose/Lose model is the Permissive style. The Win/Lose model is the Autocratic style. The Win/Win model is the Montessori Parenting style.

Conclusion

Communication is much more than the words we say to one another—it is the presence we bring to any situation. The more we let go of preconceived notions of reality and just "show up" in the present moment, the more we will experience our compassionate nature and the more our children will be able to reveal their authenticity. In this state our language is naturally compassionate.

When we do speak to our children it is important that we use compassionate language as much as possible so that we keep the heart connection between us strong. When we slip and make harmful statements, we can observe the result and make amends. If an apology is necessary we need to be humble enough to recognize our error. We can then rethink how we might handle the situation in a more compassionate manner and do that. For example, if we have made a judging statement, "Your room is a mess," we can observe the physical and emotional reaction of our child. Recognizing that our child has put up a wall, we can apologize and tell him that we would like to try again to say what we mean. At that point we give an "I" message such as, "When I see your clothes all over the floor, I feel frustrated, because you are not taking care of them. Would you be willing to pick them up and put them away?"

When our children come to us with a problem, they want to be understood. Developing the ability to empathetically listen will be healing and satisfying for them. Carl Rogers describes the power that empathy has. "When I have been listened to and when I have been heard, I am able to reperceive my world in a new way and go on. It is astonishing how elements which seem insoluble become soluble when someone listens. How confusions which seem irremediable turn into relatively clear flowing streams when one is heard."[4]

Suggestions for Follow Through

▨ Be aware of your child's reaction when you use judging, criticizing or comparing statements with him. Reflect on this in your journal.

▨ Practice giving "I" messages when you are upset with your child. Record the experience in your journal.

▨ Practice Empathetic Understanding with your child. Record the experience in your journal.

▨ Facilitate Problem Solving between two children. Record the experience in your journal.

CHAPTER 15

Facilitating Inner Discipline

"If a child has to be rewarded or punished,
it means he lacks the ability to guide himself."[1]

—MARIA MONTESSORI

Montessori discovered that when children are meaningfully engaged in their Unveiling Cycle of self discovery and healthy boundaries are in place, the use of rewards or punishments are not necessary and can actually interfere with children's natural development of inner discipline.

Inner discipline requires balancing children's freedom with responsibility and encouraging them to make choices based on an awareness of the consequences of their behavior. To help children develop inner discipline it is important to replace rewards with meaningful work and honest acknowledgement, establish reasonable and consistent boundaries and replace punishment with natural or logical consequences.

In this chapter we discuss ways to encourage children to be intrinsically motivated toward positive behavior and point out how using rewards for positive behavior actually interferes with the development of inner discipline. We explore the importance of establishing reasonable boundaries and how to help children take responsibility for their actions through the use of natural or logical consequences. Finally, we look at how the use of punishment blocks the development of a child's ability to assume responsibility for his actions and make thoughtful choices from his inner guide and conscience.

Encouraging Children's Positive Behavior

As stated in Chapter 5, each time a child engages in meaningful work, he strengthens his ability to eliminate unnecessary stimulation so he can concentrate on his chosen work. As he concentrates, he develops the power of his inner will and experiences the joy and peace of his Authentic Self. In this place positive behavior is all there is. Montessori discovered how children's negative behavior disappears when they are engaged in meaningful work. "One of the facts that made our first schools remarkable was the disappearance of these defects.... Once some interest had been aroused, they repeated exercises around that interest, and passed from one concentration to another."[2]

In our homes we can provide many opportunities for our children to involve themselves in activities that interest them and then refrain from interrupting them. At the beginning children may need encouragement, but as they engage, we need to step back and let them follow their unfolding interests. It is important to remember that children need mental food, as much as physical food, because it constructs their inner life. The more engaged our children become the more inner discipline they develop.

Children are more likely to follow what they see us do than follow what they hear us say! What we model for our children is much more important than what we say to them. No matter how fancy our words or how persuasive our arguments, children follow our example. Because they absorb our behaviors and make them their own it is important that we "walk our talk." While none of us is perfect in the practice of living harmoniously from our authenticity, we can demonstrate humility to our children by recognizing our short comings and resolving to do better the next time. "Errors divide men, but their correction is a means of union."[3] It is appropriate and healthy for adults to recognize their mistakes with the children and be humble enough to admit them. We can show children how coming from our place of authenticity is possible and preferable to living from our lower mind of ego-based mentality. When we are operating from our Authentic Self, our deep love attracts that in others—especially in our children. As stated earlier, children come from love, are love and want to follow love. Love motivates positive behavior!

Another important way to encourage positive behavior in our child is to appreciate his thoughtful behavior when we see it. By doing this, we add to his emotional bank account and increase his desire to do more of the same in the future. Of course, to be able to "see" positive behavior, we must clear our own lens of perception. If we have a tendency to see our child through the lens of judgment and criticism that is what we will see because he will continue to act as we see him. However, if we look through the lens of respect and appreciation, we will see our child engaging in positive actions. When we see positive behavior, it is important to make note of this and at the appropriate time acknowledge our appreciation of his actions.

If our child helps us fix dinner, it is important to let him know how much we appreciate his help. A simple acknowledgment of his work and a thank you will do. "Thank you for your help. It made preparing dinner much more fun for me!" We might witness our child sharing his toys with a friend. The first step is to take a deep breath, smile inside and affirm the natural loving nature of the child. Then, when the time is right (perhaps after his friend has left and you are saying good night to him) say something like, "When I saw you sharing your toys with Tim today, I felt happy because you both had such a good time together." Taking the time to recognize and acknowledge our child's positive behavior naturally reinforces the pleasurable experience for him and makes it more likely that he will want to repeat similar experiences in the future.

Honest encouragement for our children is another key factor in helping them have the confidence to make constructive behavioral choices. When children are struggling they are more likely to make choices that will lead to negative behavior. Their struggle may be about how they see themselves, another person or a pending difficulty they may be facing. When we see a struggling child, we can graciously inquire into what is happening and ask if we can be of service to him. If he is open to talking to us about his issue, it is a perfect time to use our empathetic listening skills so that we can fully understand his story. Once we have heard all that he has to say, we can ask him what he thinks he can do about the situation. We can help him weigh the consequences of his choices and encourage him once he makes a decision about what to do. If he asks for our opinion, we can give some suggestions, but leave the decision to him. Our encouragement comes in the form of our support and unconditional regard for the child.

Providing opportunities for our children to give of themselves and experience the joy from helping others is a powerful way to build lasting memories that will serve to motivate them toward selfless service throughout their lives. When I was a young girl, my family decided to provide food, clothes and toys for a family in our town that would not have had much at Christmas time. It was such a magical experience for me because it was going to be a surprise to them and we were going to be Elves for Christmas. Most of the fun was preparing for the delivery in "Santa's workshop." To this day, I smile when I remember that experience and I still love to surprise others with "gifts."

The Downside of Using Rewards to Motivate

While there are appropriate times to use rewards, it is important that we understand both their positive and negative impacts on children's natural development of inner discipline. Research shows that rewards tend to enhance performance when the task is specific and limited in scope as opposed to creative and open-ended.[4] Rewards also motivate performance in groups of people when they are working together for a specific common cause such as a contest or sports event. While it is motivating and exciting to offer rewards for the above activities, rewards can actually stifle our child's internal motivation and satisfaction to learn and behave in thoughtful ways.

When we offer rewards to motivate our child's good behavior we actually detract from his authentic response of wanting to contribute to the family or group. Instead of spontaneously following his natural inclination to contribute to the whole, he learns to act in certain ways to receive a reward. To say, "If you behave at school today, I will buy you a soda on the way home," may seem innocent enough; however, we are planting the seed that good behavior equals reward. Instead of the child enjoying the natural "fruits" of positive behavior in school he begins to expect rewards for it. If this practice continues he may become extrinsically rather than intrinsically motivated to behave thoughtfully.

Rewards can also be a hindrance to a child's natural learning process. In many schools children are encouraged to learn for stars, credits to the school store, pizza and grades. Too many times, they memorize material for a test so they can get the reward of a good grade, but soon forget what they have learned and are not motivated to pursue further study on the subject. Instead of being able to naturally respond to the unfolding needs and interests that compel them to delve deeply into subjects of interest; children are stifled by being limited to assigned lessons at a specific time for an outer reward or punishment. With too much emphasis on rewards children learn to look for outside reward rather than inside satisfaction. When they are given the opportunity to learn something because it has meaning to them, they experience satisfaction and are more likely to process the information at a deeper level, retain the information and have a sustained interest in the subject. Lillard reports that "Research shows that if a person was already motivated to do an activity to begin with, expected rewards actually interfere with their subsequent interest in that activity."[5] An intrinsically motivated child does not require rewards.

Giving children praise is closely related to the concept of giving children rewards. If we are not mindful, praise can teach young children to do things for adult approval. Praise is different than honest acknowledgement and appreciation. We can say, "You did a good job!" (praise) or "I appreciate the work you did on that!" (acknowledgment and appreciation) The first expression sets us up as the judge of the child's work and the second response is an honest expression of appreciation for the work of the child. It is a subtle difference, but over time it can make a difference in whether or not the child becomes extrinsically motivated to do well because he wants to have our praise, or intrinsically motivated to do his best.

Establishing Healthy Boundaries

Children need reasonable limits and boundaries so that they can focus their energies on constructive activities. Giving a child freedom without limits is disastrous for the child, the family and those engaging with the child. When a child is pampered and receives whatever he wants he comes to believe that the world owes him. He becomes self absorbed and generally acts from his lower mind of ego rather than his Authentic Self. He comes to expect instant gratification and has a difficult time being patient and controlling his impulses. He learns to manipulate others to get what he wants. Swami Rama comments that "Such a child builds boundaries around himself by gratifying his own senses and not becoming aware of the obstacles or the conflicts when his interest clashes with the interest of others. He wants to take and does not want to give. He forms the habit of taking only."[6]

When children are struggling and their behavior is destructive, it must be curtailed by using both firmness and kindness. We need to restrict their choices until they are able to settle and make thoughtful choices that come from their inner guide. The general guidelines for setting healthy boundaries are based on whether or not the child's behavior respects: himself, others and the environment. Behavior that violates either of these criteria must be stopped or redirected. Montessori made this statement.

> *The liberty of the child should have as its limit the collective interest; as its form, what we universally consider good (behavior). We must therefore; check in the child whatever offends or annoys others, or whatever tends towards rough or ill-bred acts.*[7]

There are a variety of ways to stop a child's behavior. We can ask a question about his intention, redirect him, request that he stop, order him to stop or physically force him to stop. Each of these responses has its own consequences. In the first example, we can ask a question to engage his thinking about what he is doing and hopefully bring him back to a state of focus. In the second scenario, he may successfully engage himself in a more constructive activity. In the third example, if our tone of voice is firm and kind, the child is quite likely to at least pause and be open to listening to us. In the fourth scenario, of ordering the child to stop, we will most likely get the child's attention, but also risk triggering his ego responses of defensiveness or rebellion. If we physically force the child, we most definitely will trigger resistance, anger and possible future revenge. Each of these scenarios depends on our taking control and guiding the child. It is important to establish clear boundaries in our home and at the same time allow the child freedom to make constructive choices. However, when he goes outside the established limits, we must help him realize his error without blaming, shaming or humiliating him.

As discussed in Chapter 9 establishing boundaries in the home is most effective when the full family is engaged in the process of creating the ground rules and defining the responsibilities of each family member. When children are engaged in the establishment of boundaries they are more likely to abide by them. Both the boundaries and responsibilities must be reasonable, simple and recorded for all to see. Once all of the family members are clear about the expectations and rules of the home, it is important that the boundaries and responsibilities are consistently enforced and periodically revisited to evaluate and refine them.

From this point on, our job is to model the ground rules ourselves and communicate our appreciation when we see our child following them. When we see him struggling with a task, it can be helpful to help him refine his skills so that it is easier for him. For example if his responsibility is to make his bed and he isn't doing it, it might be because it is too difficult for him. This is a great opportunity to ask him if he would like some assistance in learning how to do it more easily. However, when the child's behavior is violating the agreed upon boundaries, and it doesn't seem like a lack of the appropriate skill sets, we can help him develop inner discipline and make better choices in the future by incorporating natural or logical consequences.

Let's imagine that one of the ground rules in the family is that clothes are put away whenever they are changed. Your child, Johnny, gets ready for bed and throws his clothes on the floor. The first step is to take a deep breath and let go judgment or irritation and ask if he might need some help with the task if we sense it might feel too difficult for him. If this is not the case we can respectfully request that he put his clothes away. If he does, all is well. Let's say that he ignores your request. It is important not to nag, demand or beg him to pick them up as this engages attention getting or power struggle behavior. Continue to breathe deeply and calmly and ask that he come sit by you. Once he is settled use an "I" message to express your feelings. "When you leave your clothes on the floor, I feel sad, because it is important to me that you learn to take care of your clothes." "Would you be willing to put them away?" If he does, thank him and recognize how much nicer his clothes will be when he wears them again.

Let's say, however, that he ignores your request to pick up his clothes and you start to feel angry. At this point it is important that you walk away rather than get involved in a power struggle. Once a power struggle begins, there is no healthy solution because both of you are experiencing an amygdala attack. The best action you can take when this happens is to go to a place where you do not see or hear your child and breathe deeply to regain control of your thinking mind. Once you calm down, you are better prepared to decide what to do about the situation.

You might decide to ignore it because it is one of the first times it has happened and, if he resumes the practice of picking up his clothes, you may be able to let this one go all together. However, if he continues to leave his clothes around, you may want to use either natural or logical consequences to help him recognize the consequences of leaving his clothes on the floor.

Children continually make choices about whether or not they will follow the guidelines that are established in the home. For them to develop inner discipline it is imperative that we allow them to live with the consequences of their choices. Using natural or logical consequences helps children become aware of the consequences of their behavior and recognize that their freedom is related to their willingness to accept responsibility. The ultimate goal is to have responsible self-disciplined children who use their conscience or inner guide to direct their action.

Natural Consequences

Natural consequences are just what they say—the natural consequence of a behavior. For example, if a child falls on the sidewalk and scratches his knee, he has just suffered the natural consequence of not paying better attention. If he goes out in the cold without a coat the natural consequence of being cold may motivate him to wear a coat the next time it is cold outside. While it is often hard for us to see our child suffer by experiencing the natural consequence, it is the best teacher.

Our role in this scenario is to observe what has happened and refrain from shaming, lecturing, or saying things like, "I told you not to...." As caring adults, we are inclined to rescue them and prevent them from learning that their behavior has consequences. H. Stephen Glenn and Jane Nelsen, co-authors of *Raising Self-Reliant Children in a Self-Indulgent World*, succinctly say it this way, "Rescuing works directly against creativity, self-actualization and self reliance."[8]

The best thing we can do when a child is suffering from a natural consequence is empathize with the child's pain without trying to take it away from him by saying, "You poor boy, let me take care of that for you." We do need to be there to assist if necessary and, at the same time, help him recognize why he fell down. Once he has calmed down and received any help he might need, we might say, "Wow, you took quite a fall, what do you think you can do next time to prevent that from happening to you?" By doing this, we recognize the child's painful consequence, help him where necessary and encourage him to reflect on what he can do in the future to prevent it from happening again. During this time it is imperative that we refrain from blaming, shaming and or criticizing for this will put the child in a defensive posture and make it hard for him to reflect on the consequences of his behavior. When he recognizes the reasons for his accident, he is much more likely to make a conscious choice to be more careful in the future.

While natural consequences are preferred, there are times when allowing a child to experience natural consequences is dangerous or not practical. In those cases we can use the process of setting up logical consequences. Both natural and logical consequences help children learn from the inside out.

Logical Consequences

Logical consequences are established by adults to help children become aware of how their behavior affects them, others or the environment. They are designed to help them learn from the reality of the social order and are used when natural consequences are not appropriate or practical. The process of implementing logical consequences is designed to help the children recognize and experience the consequences of unacceptable behavior. Logical consequences are not to be used to punish or shame a child. To be successful in the implementation of logical consequences we must remember that for a logical consequence to be successful it must be: 1) Related, 2) Respectful and 3) Reasonable.[9]

RELATED

The specific behavior and consequence must be related. A related scenario might be. If the child doesn't come to dinner on time (the behavior) he misses dinner (the consequence). If this is administered in a compassionate manner, the child will most likely give some internal thought to being late the next day. An unrelated behavior and consequence would be that if the child doesn't come to dinner on time (the behavior) he can't go play with his friends (the unrelated consequence). When we use an unrelated consequence, the child sees it as a punishment and can easily go into defensive thinking because his trust in us is threatened. If our child trusts us, he can more easily let his defense or ego guard down and that opens the pathway for him to be self-reflective and respond to his inner guide.

REASONABLE

Logical consequences are not meant to shame or blame a child. They are designed to help children recognize that they have the ability to make choices and the responsibility to live with the consequences of their choices. The consequences that are decided upon must therefore be reasonable and certainly not punitive. Children need to be involved in the setting of the consequences prior to implementing them. This process needs to be done when both the adult and the child are in a calm state so the discussion can be reasonable. We might introduce this session by referring to a prior unpleasant experience between us and then invite the child to talk so we can both understand what happened and see what can be done to avoid a similar situation in the future.

For example, let's go back to the scenario of the child leaving his clothes on the floor and assume that an unpleasant pattern has developed and we feel a need to help the child realize that there are consequences related to his leaving clothes on the floor. We can begin the conversation by acknowledging our negative behavior (if that happened) and say that we were upset and acted in inappropriate ways for which we wish to apologize. (By letting our child know that we see the error of our ways, he is better able to let go his frustration and engage in the conversation with greater reason.)

The next step is to let the child know that we hope to work out a reasonable plan that will help us both avoid this discomfort in the future. At this point we can share our thoughts and feelings in an "I" message form, "When you leave your clothes on the floor, I feel sad because it is important to me that you learn how to take care of your clothes." At this point we can ask the child to let us know what he heard us say.

Once we know that he has heard us we can ask him to tell us what happened for him and how he feels. He might say, "When I take time to put my clothes away, there isn't any time for a story and I feel sad." We acknowledge what we hear him say. "What I hear you say is that you don't want to put your clothes away because it takes up your story time and that makes you feel mad. Is that right?" The child has an opportunity to accept or clarify his statement.

At this point we can restate what we see as the problem. "It looks like our problem is that you don't want to put your clothes away because it takes away your story time and I want you to put your clothes away so that you learn how to care for your clothes. Is that how you see it?" At this point, it is time to engage the child in some possible solutions to the problem. As various solutions are suggested, we need to engage the child in thinking about the positive as well as negative consequences of each solution. Once a solution is agreed upon, it is important for both the child and parent to agree to act accordingly.

Let's say that the agreed upon solution is that the child will begin getting ready for bed 15 minutes earlier so that there will be time to both put his clothes away and have a story. As the adult it is important to acknowledge and appreciate the child's willingness to engage in this problem solving process, be willing to begin getting ready for bed 15 minutes earlier and put his clothes away. At this point we also need to commit to being prepared to do a story each night after the clothes are put away as long as it is before 8:30. The final step is to let the child know that we have confidence in his ability to follow through on this agreement. However, in case he doesn't put away his clothes, we will not be able to read him a story that night because that is the agreed upon consequence when he fails to put his clothes away.

RESPECTFUL

We must implement the selected logical consequence respectfully or the child will see it as a punishment and that will most likely trigger a defensive reaction. If the child becomes defensive it will be difficult for him to reflect on the reason he lost his bedtime story and what he can do in the future to again have a story as he goes to bed. This reflection time is necessary so the child can recognize his unacceptable behavior and its consequences and then make his own decision about what to do about this in the future. Self-reflection is a key component in the development of a child's inner discipline.

As previously stated the process, of the adult and the child reaching an agreement about the nature of the logical consequence, must be carried out from a place of mutual regard and respect. Additionally, when the occasion arises that the child fails to pick up his clothes, we must implement the logical consequence from our place of empathy and love. *What* we do is not as important as *how* we do it. We must *never* chastise, blame or say disrespectful things like, "I told you I wouldn't read you a story if you left your clothes on the floor" as this breaks the mood of self-reflection for the child. Instead, we can empathize with how disappointed the child must be not to hear a story and reassure him that we are confident that he will make the choice to pick up his clothes next time so he can enjoy a story before bedtime. It takes thought, patience and self-control on our part. We need to be understanding, encouraging and respectful for logical consequences to work.

We might ask if being patient and understanding actually rewards misbehavior. Actually, it is just the opposite. Being respectful keeps the child's heart open and lessens his desire to misbehave. Our goal is "Not to win over children, but win children over."[10] Establishing an atmosphere of respect in our family allows children to experience personal control over their environment, recognize their power to make decisions and face the resulting consequences. By empowering children to discipline themselves from the inside out, we help them develop into people who will one day make the right choices and behave thoughtfully when there is no one around to tell, supervise or punish them. "When they choose an option, they do the thinking, they make the choice, the lessen sticks with them."[11]

The Downside of Using Punishment

"Punishment! I had not realized that they were an indispensable institution holding sway over the whole of child-humanity. All men have grown up under this humiliation."[12]

—MARIA MONTESSORI

Please take a moment and imagine being with a child in a public place and he begins begging you to buy him something. In your best judgment you tell him "no," but he continues to whine and beg for the item. You ask him to stop whining which he does for a moment and then resumes the irritating whining once again. This pattern of his whining and you asking him to stop persists for a period of time until your nerves begin tingling and you order him to stop.

At this point your child looks at you and yells, *"No, I hate you!"* You feel yourself becoming angry at this response and threaten him by saying, "If you don't stop this behavior immediately, I will take you home." The child just smiles and says, "I don't care!" At this point you grab his arm and pull him to the car chastising him along the way. On the ride home you are deciding what punishment is appropriate for this offence of talking back to you. Once you are home you immediately tell him he is in trouble and must spend one hour of "time out" in his bedroom.

During this hour, you continue to think about what happened and experience a great deal of frustration because you don't know how to handle your child's annoying and disrespectful behavior. In the meantime, your child is in "time out," also thinking about what just happened and may well be "plotting" ways to get even in the future. Hopefully, this scenario stops here. You calm down and the child's revenge phase does not happen. However, if we don't learn how to turn *our own behavior* around, our child's pattern of attention getting, power struggle, revenge and giving up will continue to spiral down into more and more periods of misbehavior on the part of our child.

You may ask: "Why do I need to change my behavior? My child is the one with bad behavior and it is my responsibility to straighten him out." Actually, it is not our responsibility to straighten our child out. Our responsibility is to see him as the beautiful person he is and guide him in non-punitive ways to make better choices in his life. Our child needs to understand that while we may not like what he does, we love and respect who he is. Montessori recognized that adults often think, "The child belongs to one's private life—it is something claiming duties and sacrifices from the adult and deserves punishment whenever it disturbs him."[13] When we get into a mode of feeling like our child needs to be punished (for his own good), we actually send him the message that we don't respect him and that our need to be in control is greater than his need to be respected. Montessori spoke about the harm punishment can do to the child when she said,

> To tell a child he is naughty or stupid just humiliates him; it offends and insults, but does not improve him. For if a child is to stop making mistakes, he must become more skillful, and how can he do this, if being already below standard, he is also discouraged.[14]

Punishment can take many forms such as yelling, name calling, spanking, grounding, removal of privileges and taking things away. Each of these responses is harmful to the child. When he interprets our reaction to him as punishment he immediately becomes resistant and defensive and his ability to learn stops because he is emotionally upset, discouraged and perhaps afraid. If, instead, we recognize that the child is struggling in some way, we are more likely to look deeper to see what the root cause of his misbehavior might be. When we get mad and punish him he gets the idea that the consequence for his mistake is our reaction to his behavior. He does not look deeper within himself to discover what created the difficulty for him in the first place or how he can improve his skills in the future.

Every interaction we have with our child carries two aspects: it not only says something *to* the child, it says something *about* the child. When we punish our child we threaten the natural bond of love and trust between us. He not only hears what we say to him, he comes to believe that our love for him is conditional. He begins to think that our love is based on what he does, rather than who he is. Additionally, a child who is pressured to obey is vulnerable to becoming a victim of other people because he develops a fear that he will lose love if he is not obedient. He then begins to make behavior choices that will please us and avoid our negative reactions such as anger, threats and punishment. This false sense of identity and security can affect how he makes choices in the future. Instead of making thoughtful choices that require reflection and discernment, he bases his decisions on whether or not his choice will please other people. In most situations, the only choice he can make is whether or not to comply with the wishes of others.

Our need to punish is based on our fear rather than our love. Subconsciously, we are afraid that if we don't control our child's behavior, he will go astray. We think that the best way to do this is to threaten and or punish him if he does not follow through on what we say. The old saying, "Spare the rod and spoil the child," is based on the belief that adults know what is best and must tell children what to do because children cannot be trusted to make thoughtful choices on their own. This statement negates the inner life of the child that is complete with a vital life force, inner guide and a Spirit to guide him through his natural path of development. Rather than helping children learn how to behave in appropriate ways, punishment actually blocks the natural path of thoughtful behavior that emanates when a child is engaged in his Unveiling Cycle of learning. Montessori put it this way, "A child naturally obeys an adult. But when the adult asks him to renounce those instincts that favor his development, he cannot obey."[15] She goes on to say that often times temper tantrums are a result of "a vital conflict between his creative impulses and his love for an adult who fails to understand his needs."[16] His misbehavior is based on his struggle to manifest his Authentic Self.

Children are naturally drawn to and respond to love. They are motivated by the love for their parents as well as their environment which furnishes them with a means for their growth. Fear inhibits this process of responding to both with love. Punishment may get quick results and the behavior may stop momentarily, but this does not have long-range benefits. Jane Nelsen put it beautifully when she said, "We want to inspire children to improve their behavior not make them suffer or feel worse. What is our goal—what is our attitude?"[17]

There is another downfall to using punishment to control our child's behavior—he comes to rely on us or others to make his decisions for him. If he grows up having adults tell him what to do, how will he be prepared to make thoughtful decisions when he is alone and under pressure? If we do not provide sufficient opportunities for him to make decisions and live with the consequences of his decisions, he becomes dependent on others to make his decisions. He becomes directed by outside sources rather than directed by his own inner wisdom. He becomes outer-directed rather than inner-directed.

One last note: While "time out" was not originally seen as a punishment, it has been misrepresented by most adults. Originally, it was intended to be used as an opportunity for the child to calm down and think about the consequences of his behavior. However, parents too frequently administer it in a punitive way so that most children see "time out" as a punishment. A better way to help a child calm down is for us to remain calm and request that he take some time to calm himself. (Refrain from using the word "time out.") This can be in his room or in a specified quiet place where he will not be distracted. Respectfully invite the child to return when he is calm and ready to talk about what happened. This is one of those times when both firmness and kindness is necessary.

Conclusion

A few years ago, we asked a group of parents to reflect on the pros and cons of using punishment to discipline their children. We then asked them to reflect on the pros and cons of using natural and logical consequences to promote inner discipline within their children. Following is a list of how they viewed the results from using both practices:

Outer Discipline—Punishment

Pros	Cons
Gets immediate results	Causes resentment from child
Modifies behavior in the short term	Fear based
Quick and easy	Not effective in the long run
Children remember the incident	Loss of respect for parents
Requires little thought	Creates sense of separateness
Reactive behavior of parents	Deteriorates self-esteem
Many people do it	Fosters shame
Works in some cases	Control comes from outside
Boundaries are clear	Fosters rebellion
	Judgmental
	Comes from lack of patience
	Can cause harm to children

Inner Discipline—Natural and Logical Consequences

Pros	Cons
Child becomes responsible	Hard to analyze
Child becomes empowered	Takes more time
Strengthens bond between parent & child	Requires emotional maturity
Fosters respect	Defines difference
Mutual working it out	Allows mistakes
Gentler	
Fosters self-esteem	
Encourages communication	
Emotional detachment possible	
Lessens parent's burden	
Trusts in child's desire and ability to learn	
Removes much of child's emotional reaction	
Promotes honesty and openness	
Provides a safe climate	
Learning based	

These two lists sum up the advantages and disadvantages of both outer-directed and inner-directed discipline. Clearly, from these parents' point of view, inner-directed discipline is much more effective in helping children develop the qualities of confidence, thoughtfulness and authenticity.

Suggestions for Follow Through

- As a family make a plan to do something nice for another person or family. Make sure that the entire family is involved in the planning and implementation. When it is over, process the experience with your family.

- Have a family meeting to create a shared vision for the family and home. Make sure that the entire family is involved in this process. Ask all family members to share what they value most in a family and home. You might begin the process by writing: We would like to have our family and home be…and then add the qualities each person desires. Some words might be: clean, orderly, peaceful, fun, thoughtful. Once the list is complete, see if all members of the family support the vision. When a shared vision is agreed upon, publish it in a nice form and put it in a prominent place for all to see regularly. This can be the basis for the family to begin establishing ground rules and responsibilities to ensure the realization of the vision.

- Reflect on a difficult situation between you and your child. Determine whether or not you are using punishment or reward to attempt to correct the situation. If so, observe your child's reactions and record it in your journal. Ask yourself if the child is thoughtfully reflecting on his behavior and learning from the experience. Record your feelings about the experience.

- Reflect on a difficult situation between you and your child. If you can get out of the way and allow natural consequences to take their own course, let it be and observe the results. Record this in your journal. If natural consequences are not reasonable, go through the process of establishing logical consequences. Record what happens in each of the phases: 1) discussion of the problem, 2) agreement on the logical consequence, 3) affirmation of your trust in the child's ability to follow through on the agreement, and 4) implementation of the consequence if and when the child fails to follow through.

CHAPTER 16

Understanding Children's Behavior

"The child who needs love the most
is often the child who is the most unlovable."[1]

—JANE NELSEN

As described in the previous chapter, there are two basic approaches to dealing with children's behavior. One is to use outer-directed training techniques such as reward and punishment to entice or even manipulate the child to obey our will. This outer-directed approach describes the basis of behaviorism theory which sees the child as someone to be trained by using outside stimulus to provoke a desired response from the child. The second approach is the inner-directed approach advocated by humanistic psychology and is consistent with Montessori philosophy and practice. The inner-directed approach is not about manipulating behavior but about understanding it. To be able to change children's behavior we must first understand it. To do this we need to relate to their essential nature rather than their behavior.

"Behavior" is defined as the way a person conducts himself. While it may seem like a child's behavior is random and unpredictable, it is actually based on some specific, predictable patterns. Behavior is seldom an isolated event as it occurs in a context of physical, mental, emotional and social activity. This means that for us to understand our child, we must consider what is going on around him and how he might be interpreting the activity. When the child behaves in unacceptable ways, we must learn how to discern the root causes of the misbehavior and make adjustments that will help him return to his centered state of authenticity.

There are two general reasons for children's misbehavior. The first is when the child doesn't know any better and we show him what behavior is acceptable. For example, a child is running around the house with a sharp knife. We stop him and show him the danger and ask him to put the knife away. The second and most prevalent cause of a child's misbehavior is that he is frustrated in his attempts to get his authentic needs met and consequently behaves in unacceptable ways. In this scenario, it is easy for us to get caught in our own emotional reactions to his behavior. If we do, we add to the drama of the situation. To thoughtfully respond to our child's unmet need and the corresponding misbehavior requires that we also observe our own reactions to see how our thoughts and behaviors might be contributing to our child's negative behavioral pattern.

Children's behavior is intricately connected to whether or not they *experience* their needs as being met. In Chapter Four we discussed Maslow's, Hierarchy of Needs and the necessity to fulfill children's: (1) Physiological, (2) Safety, (3) Love and Belonging, (4) Esteem and (5) Self-Actualization needs in that order because each need builds upon another. For children to experience a sense of self-actualization they must first have their physiological, safety, love and belonging and esteem needs fulfilled. Children's needs fluctuate depending on the situation surrounding them. If they become hungry and tired, their behavior will most likely be cranky and uncooperative. Until their physiological needs, such as food or sleep, are met, their safety, love and belonging, esteem and self-actualization needs take a back seat. Once the unmet physiological needs are fulfilled children naturally move to the next level of need satisfaction, that of safety. If children feel safe, they continue to move up the Hierarchy of Needs pyramid unless they "get caught" in another need level. Once caught, they struggle to get what they need and this struggle often takes the form of unacceptable behavior.

Misbehavior is a signal that a child is caught in an unmet need and is struggling to have it met. Understanding a child's behavior is the first step to changing it. By carefully observing the situation from a calm and centered place, we can help a child successfully move through his block to the next level of need fulfillment. To do this requires that we also observe our reactions to his misbehavior and determine if we are contributing to his misinterpretation of how to get his needs met. When we detach from our own emotional reactions to the child's misbehavior, we alter our automatic behavioral response patterns that often contribute to the challenge. By changing our behavior, our child's misbehavior will also begin to change.

In this chapter we incorporate some of the wisdom of the Native American Medicine Wheel, as seen in Black Elk's vision, to illustrate the relationship between positive behavior and need fulfillment as well as the relationship between negative behavior and unmet needs of the child. We examine the difference between what a child needs and what a child may want. We illustrate how a child's five basic needs are met when he is encouraged to move through his natural Unveiling Cycles and why his behavior is most likely to be positive. We also examine how ignoring or interrupting the child's natural Unveiling Cycles creates stumbling blocks on his natural path of need fulfillment and often results in negative patterns of behavior. We offer concrete ways to use firmness and kindness to redirect children's misbehavior into thoughtful behavior while consciously transforming our own stumbling blocks into stepping stones of wisdom to support our child's natural path of unveiling his Authentic Self.

Native American Wisdom

None of us are perfect parents. We are, so to speak, learning as we go. Most of us have had little formal schooling to prepare us for this most important task of parenting and our teachers are often, "trial" and "error." Realizing this, Montessori once said,

It is apparent that everyone makes mistakes. This is one of life's realities and to admit it is already to have taken a great step forward....So it is well to cultivate a friendly feeling towards error, to treat it as a companion inseparable from our lives, as something having a purpose, which it truly has.[2]

In our experience as parents we came across the book, *Black Elk Speaks* where we read about Black Elk's Great Vision.[3] Upon reading the vision our attitudes about errors or life's challenges changed. Instead of seeing difficulties as something to be ashamed of, guilty for, or angry about, we came to see them as opportunities to learn something new. Black Elk's vision placed the continual process of learning and changing into a meaningful non-judgmental framework and helped us let go of our ineffective habit patterns so we could more thoughtfully guide our children through their natural processes of unveiling their authenticity.

Following are some of the key components of the vision as seen by Black Elk in 1872 as a young nine year old boy. Growing up, he saw much destruction to his people and their way of life which grieved him deeply. He became very ill and during this time received a vision that gave him and his people hope for a more harmonious and peaceful world. Following is a paraphrase of a portion of the vision that will be used to illustrate the root causes of children's behaviors.

Black Elk felt as if he was floating and his body was being raised into the air on a cloud. As he looked down he saw a great circle or hoop. In this hoop he saw all of life's creations. He saw the sun, the moon, the stars, the planets, the earth, the water, the air and the soil. He saw all of the plants and animals including the four legged, the two legged, the fish, the birds and even the creepy crawlies. He saw that everything was good.

Then he looked around and saw four directions: West—North— East—South. Next, he saw a Black Road running from West to East. He saw that this was the Road of Difficulties or the Road of Lessons. He saw that all people sometimes walk this road. Black Elk then saw a Red Road running from North to South. He saw that this was the Road of Right Action or the Road of Peace. He saw that all people sometimes walk this road.

Black Elk's attention was drawn to the center of the hoop where the two roads crossed and there he saw a Sacred Tree. He saw that when people walked the Road of Right Action by taking care of themselves, others and the gifts of the Earth, the tree flowered and birds came to sing.[4]

Just as Black Elk was seeking understanding and clarification of life and its purpose, so we as parents seek to understand how we can best guide our child in the fulfillment of his potentials and purpose. We can see the giant hoop with all of life's creations as the family and its many influences in our child's life. As Black Elk realized that all of life's creations are necessary and important so can we recognize that the family is the strongest influence in our child's life and that all that our child experiences in the family can be used to help him unveil his Authentic Self. The sacred tree is the love in our home and the flowers represent each precious moment when a family member is manifesting peaceful behavior.

The Black Road of Difficulties or Lessons represents the challenges of life that we and our children experience. This is not necessarily a "bad" road if we use it as an opportunity to learn from our challenges. For the sake of our parenting metaphor we will call this road the "Rocky Path" because it is covered with stumbling blocks that can be turned into stepping stones as we learn from our mistakes.

The Red Road of Right Action or Peace represents the joy and satisfaction that comes when we and our children are centered in authenticity acting from our inner guides of wisdom. We call this road the "Natural Path" because when we are centered in our authenticity and encourage our children to follow their natural path of development they manifest positive behaviors which symbolically represent flowers being added to the sacred tree at the center of the family hoop. As each family member walks the Natural Path flowers bloom on the sacred tree and birds come to sing. Joy and peace abound in our family and, like the birds, others are attracted by the feelings of love in the home.

Another aspect of the Medicine Wheel metaphor that gives clarity to life's process and purpose is the concept of recognizing life's lessons as opportunities to develop our quality of life and broaden our way of seeing things. In doing this we receive deeper wisdom and understanding. Many native people identify positive qualities and perspectives with specific animals. They see these animals at each point on the great hoop of life. At the points of the four directions we often see: East = Eagle, South = Mouse, West = Bear and North = Buffalo. Eagle often represents the overview perspective, Mouse the attention to detail perspective, Bear the introspective perspective and Buffalo the knowledge perspective. At each point of the Medicine Wheel, there are numerous other wisdom perspectives and qualities such as gentleness, joy and patience that are represented by other animals such as Deer, Hummingbird and Ant.

As we encounter life's challenges and find ourselves walking the Rocky Path, we can see it as either a curse or an opportunity to receive additional wisdom from the lesson waiting to be learned. Once we change an ineffective habit or behavior and accept a new way of being, we gain a new awareness and understanding that automatically moves us to the Natural Path. As we move from being ineffective to effective in our actions, we turn what was a stumbling block on the Rocky Path into a stepping stone on the Natural Path. Each time we add a stepping stone our inner wisdom increases and another flower is added to the sacred tree. The more we can see our mistakes, and those of our children, as lessons to be learned rather than offences to be punished, the easier it is to remove guilt, judgment and blame from our thinking process. We can replace our harmful emotions with understanding, patience and courage. Montessori recognized this fact. "If we seek perfection, we must pay attention to our own defects, for it is only by correcting these that we can improve ourselves. We have to face them in the full light of day and realize their existence as something unavoidable throughout life."[5]

When a child's authenticity is seen, his needs are met and he is encouraged to engage in his dynamic Unveiling Cycles, his corresponding behavior reflects the affirmative qualities of respect, cooperation, respect, joy, curiosity and love. These are the natural behavioral qualities of a child who is operating from his Authentic Self. At these times we can say that he is walking on the Natural Path and so might we be.

Conversely, when a child's authenticity is not recognized, his needs are not met and his natural developmental processes are interrupted, he has to struggle to be recognized. At times like this his behaviors frequently take the form of disrespect, ignoring, disruptiveness, destructiveness, meanness and defensiveness. These qualities are based on a child's false assumptions and beliefs that in order to be recognized and belong he needs to act in misbehaving ways. At these times we can say that he is on the Rocky Path and so might we be.

Montessori clearly saw the relationship between children's misbehavior and their natural path of development being blocked. "We can now state with certainty that the naughtiness of young children represents a disorder regarding the natural laws of psychic life in the course of construction."[6] After discussing the difference between needs and wants we will revisit children's five basic needs and see how their Natural Path of development, through the Unveiling Cycles, fulfills their needs so they can manifest positive behaviors. We will next examine what happens when children's needs are not met and they begin to manifest misbehavior. Finally, we will explore how we can help children move from the Rocky Path back to the Natural Path by changing how we see and react to their misbehavior.

The Difference between Needs and Wants

Most parents enjoy making their child happy by giving him what he needs and wants. Half of this is a positive thing and the other half can be harmful. What do we mean? Fulfilling our child's needs is imperative if we want him to be fulfilled, engaged in constructive activities and displaying positive behavior. However, fulfilling every want our child has is harmful and counter-productive to the above goal.

Children's needs originate within their Authentic Self and must be met for their authenticity to come forth. However, children's wants originate from their lower mind of sensory stimulation, ego and past memory. Children's wants can be endless as they are continually bombarded by outside sources giving them messages that they won't be happy unless they have this and that item. They see their friends have things and their ego suggests to them that they must have the same to be happy. They watch television and see hundreds of ads that also give them the suggestion that they must have the item to be happy. These impressions embed themselves in children's memory banks and pop up independently when something retriggers these thoughts.

Of course, fulfilling some of our child's wants some of the time is fun and fine, but it is important that we recognize the importance of moderation. It is important to examine what is a real need and what is an arbitrary want. If our child comes to see us as the ever-open treasure chest, he will keep coming for more treats and come to expect instant gratification. He may become very upset when his wants are delayed or unmet. We can easily get caught in the trap of feeling guilty if we can't give our child what he wants and being afraid that he will not like us if we deny his wishes. The sad thing is that his wants will never be satisfied, while his needs will. If we continue to focus on meeting the child's wants, rather than needs, we actually encourage him to identity with his ego rather than his Authentic Self. Following is a list of the five basic needs and examples of wants that are often mistaken for genuine needs.

Basic Human Needs

Needs	Wants
1. Physiological and Preservation Needs	
Food	Junk food
Clothing	Brand names
Shelter	Fancy bedroom
Touch	Cling
Water	Soda Pop
Sleep	Stay up late and sleep in late
Health	

Needs	*Wants*

2. Safety Needs

Security and protection	Over protection
Stability and reliability	Smothering
Structure and consistency	Constant reassurance
Freedom from fear	

3. Love and Belonging Needs

Recognition and appreciation	To be number one
Acceptance and inclusion	To be the center of attention
Affection and bonding	To be served
Understanding and support	
Ability to contribute	
Empathy and compassion	
Trust and reassurance	
Cooperation and community	

4. Esteem Needs

Self-respect	To be the center of focus
Self-confidence	To be right
Mastery	To be the best
Identity and authenticity	To have it our way
Autonomy	

5. Self-Actualization Needs

Wholeness	To have material goods
Competence	To be excessive
Consciousness and wisdom	To be famous
Creativity and self-expression	
Equality and mutuality	
Meaningful engagement	
Inspiration and celebration	

Physiological Needs

The basic physiological needs are related to preservation and survival. Some of the key elements at this level of need are: food, water, sleep, clothing, shelter, touch and health. If any of these are missing, children have a difficult time operating from their authenticity because their physical needs tend to take over their thinking and emotional systems that, in turn, overshadow the connection with their inner guide. The child's basic physical needs must be satisfied before he can focus on satisfying his next need level of safety.

THE NATURAL PATH

When a child's basic needs for physical preservation are fulfilled, he is most likely to have the ability to focus his energy on what is before him. To make sure that this first and most basic need is fulfilled, we must do our best to see that each of his physical needs is met. For example, it is important that our child get enough sleep each day to meet his individual sleep requirements. We have all experienced the unsettled, cranky behavior of an overtired child. Nothing satisfies him until he can "catch up" on his need for sleep. A similar situation exists with all of the other physiological needs listed above. When a child is "out of sorts" the first place to look for understanding as to what might be causing the child's behavior, is to take a quick inventory to see if one or more of his physical needs can be taken care of. An example of this might be to give our child a little snack before dinner so that his hunger can be abated while we complete the preparation of the dinner meal. This small act can help him calm down and have the patience to wait.

THE ROCKY PATH

When our child's physical needs are not met he can become irritated, restless and not centered. We may find it challenging to get his attention because he is struggling to focus his energies and become engaged in an activity. When we react to our child's unnerving behavior by becoming irritated or cranky ourselves, it only worsens the difficulty and puts us on the Rocky Path. Now, the child is not only upset because he is overtired, too hungry or otherwise physically uncomfortable, he now feels insecure and disrespected by us. In this scenario, instead of helping to meet the need of the child, we create more stumbling blocks that keep him from being on the Natural Path.

TRANSFORMING STUMBLING BLOCKS INTO STEPPING STONES

Of course, we have our own feelings and needs that must be met—especially the need for peace and quiet. If at all possible, instead of displaying our feelings of irritation, it is best to remove ourselves from the immediate situation and find a place of solitude where we can do some deep breathing and re-center ourselves. From this calmer place we will have a better chance of knowing what to do to meet our child's need. The first place to look is to see if our child might need something to eat, a rest or nap, of even a tender hug. If our child's behavior is stemming from an unmet physical need, the best way to move from the Rocky Path back to the Natural Path is to regain our own center of wisdom and satisfy his physical need.

Safety Needs

Once the physical needs of a child are met the second level of safety needs come into focus. For a child's need for safety to be fulfilled he must feel that he is secure and protected, experience stability and dependability, and have clear and consistent boundaries in the home. Ultimately, he needs to be free of fear and experience emotional safety.

NATURAL PATH

When our child's need for safety is met he more readily displays enthusiasm, curiosity and courage because he feels secure within himself. He is better able to access his Authentic Self, inner guide and respond to the natural impulses of his life force. He can walk the Natural Path and engage in the process of unveiling his authenticity.

A child's need for safety begins with his physical safety. It goes without saying that when we are walking the Natural Path we protect our child from any physical threat or abuse so that he can naturally move through this level of need and continue to pursue his quest for love and belonging, self-esteem and self-actualization. In addition we ensure that his mental, emotional and spiritual lives are also free of harmful influences that might threaten our child's need to feel safe.

When we are following the Natural Path as it relates to meeting our child's need to feel safe, we refrain from shaming, blaming or making our child feel guilty. Instead, we see his misbehavior as being motivated by feeling afraid, uncomfortable and possibly discouraged. We do what we can to reassure or encourage him and, if needed, assist him in something he is hesitating to be involved in. It is important that our child feel safe enough to reveal his vulnerability and comfortable enough to ask for and receive assistance. Helping him understand his feelings and learn to constructively express his emotions, gives him the tools to move through fears that come up.

This is the place where we pay attention to communicating with respect and compassion so our child feels secure in knowing that we are sincerely interested in him. This is the place where we establish agreed upon reasonable boundaries in the home so that the child knows what to expect from us and can rely on our consistency. This is the place where we let the child know ahead of time when there is going to be a change so he can prepare for it. This is the place where we monitor the messages that our child is receiving through the media and other people in his life to make sure that his emotional safety stays intact. This is the place where we stop any of his behaviors that are harmful to him, others or the environment. This is the place where we help him reconnect to his place of calm so he can make healthier choices.

When walking the Natural Path we look for ways to enjoy one another, celebrate and have fun together. When doing this we make deposits into our child's emotional bank account as well as our own emotional bank account. It is important that we do this regularly so that when we inadvertently walk on the Rocky Path and make withdrawals from each other's emotional bank accounts, we don't bankrupt the emotional trust we have established with our child.

THE ROCKY PATH

A few of the signs that might alert us to the fact that we are dealing with our child's unmet need for safety are that he hesitates, clings, whines or becomes shy. If we recognize that our child's behavior is rooted in some anxiety or fear, we have a better chance of helping him move through his temporary block. On the other hand if we become frustrated or even angry at his hesitant behavior we will find ourselves on the Rocky Path.

Three harmful responses we might fall prey to are blaming, shaming or criticizing. All three of these culprits further undermine our child's sense of confidence, and trigger additional feelings of inadequacy, discomfort and fear within our child. If our frustration deepens to anger we may resort to threats or punishments. If we select this response, we not only raise our child's anxiety level but trigger his ego as well. Our child's ego then sends up red flags of protection which may trigger even worse behavior than the original unmet safety need did. If it goes too far, it might trigger the child's amygdala and put him into a flight or fight mode.

If we consistently fail to meet our child's need for safety he may begin to experience increased stress, fear and even a sense of abandonment. His ego may work over time to attempt to justify to him that if people are mean to him he has the right to be mean to others. Too much of this can plant the seeds for future bullying behavior.

TRANSFORMING STUMBLING BLOCKS INTO STEPPING STONES

When we find ourselves on the Rocky Path, it is best to stop what we are doing, find a place to calm down and reflect on our own behavior to see how it might be adding to the child's problem. Once we recognize our error it is important to find a time when the child is calm and apologize for our over reaction to his behavior. This might be a good time to open a discussion about what he might be feeling about the situation that seems to trigger his anxious behavior. This is an excellent opportunity to encourage him to use an "I" message and for us to empathetically listen to him. Once we have a better idea of what is bothering him, we can constructively help him work through the issue and be more patient when and if it reoccurs.

Love and Belonging Needs

A child's need to be loved and belong to the family or group is one of the strongest. When this need is not fulfilled, the child acts out in ways that he *thinks* will meet his need to experience love and belonging in the family. His behavior is not necessarily based on the reality of a situation as much as how he *interprets* the situation. If he perceives or interprets that he doesn't belong or isn't loved, he misbehaves to get what he thinks will satisfy his need to be a valued member of the family.

THE NATURAL PATH

For a child to experience the satisfaction of having his need for love and belonging met, he must feel accepted, appreciated and included in the on-going family activities as well as experience the family as a community of support and cooperation. For him to get the message that he is valued, he needs to be treated with compassion, honesty and consideration. In addition, there are four positive goals that a child needs to meet to fully experience himself as a valued member of the family. We call these goals: 1) Contribution, 2) Empowerment, 3) Justice and 4) Withdrawal from conflict.

1. *Goal of Contribution*: When a child is walking the Natural Path he has a natural desire to not only be valued but to be involved and contribute to the family. For this reason it is important that we establish a family vision, give our child specific responsibilities that he can successfully accomplish, and thoughtfully acknowledge his contributions to the family. As discussed earlier, meaningful work for the child in the home is vital to his realizing his potential and making contributions to the family. When he successfully completes a task, he experiences joy and satisfaction that flow from his Authentic Self. This sense of satisfaction strengthens his desire to continue to contribute to the betterment of the family. He comes to believe that he belongs by contributing. Letting our child know that we appreciate his contribution reinforces his sense of belonging and being loved.

2. *Goal of Empowerment*: A child's natural desire to be empowered is accomplished when he can do things for himself, make choices

and take responsibility for his actions. This sense of autonomy and power is essential. We can help our child accomplish this goal in positive ways by encouraging him to be independent and giving him the skills so he can do more and more things by himself. Where possible we can refrain from correcting him so that he can discover his errors on his own. Further, we can give him as many opportunities as possible to make choices and allow him to take responsibility for the outcomes of his choices. When this happens we empower our child to select and participate in meaningful work, make thoughtful choices and develop self-discipline. He comes to believe that he has the power to decide and be responsible for his behavior. All of this contributes to his sense of being loved and an important part of the family.

3. *Goal of Justice*: When a child is walking the Natural Path and responding to his authenticity, he naturally wants things to be fair and just and prefers working things out in a cooperative manner rather than fighting. In fact, seeking justice and fairness is one of the sensitive periods during the elementary years when children's moral development begins to take shape. It is also a time when children are sensitive to and prefer to work cooperatively. When a child recognizes an injustice, either to himself or another, and he is listening to his inner wisdom, he does his best to see if the injustice can be worked out. As parents we can model this behavior so our child will learn how to handle difficulties by our example. We can also encourage peaceful behavior by engaging in compassionate communication and problem solving so that he will be familiar with the process and the positive results that can come from this practice. As our child recognizes that we are sincerely committed to working things out in the home in a fair and just way, his goal is reached and he continues to know that he is a valued member of the family.

4. *Goal of Withdrawal from Conflict*: The ability to withdraw from conflict is crucial. When a child is centered in his authenticity, walking the Natural Path, he gradually learns to ignore provocations, avoid power struggles and still know that he belongs and is loved. This takes a combination of experience, courage

and inner wisdom. Again, the best thing we can do as parents is to be an example to our child and engage him in conversations about alternatives to violent behavior. Of course this ability must be nurtured and developed over time. If continued, our child will come to know that he is capable of withdrawing from conflict when he chooses to do so. Each time we see him successfully resist returning violence with violence, it is important that we let him know we recognize his ability to act in such a mature manner.

THE ROCKY PATH

Rudolf Dreikurs, an Adlerian psychologist, researched the root causes of children's misbehavior and identified four goals that children mistakenly think they must pursue if the above four authentic goals are not fulfilled. These four mistaken goals are: 1) Attention, 2) Power, 3) Revenge and 4) Display of Inadequacy.[7] When children's authentic goals to satisfy their need to belong and be loved are blocked they begin to resort to pursuing inauthentic goals based on their ego's direction rather than inner wisdom.

The four authentic goals of the child do not change; but when he walks on the Rocky Path, he interprets the goals differently and ends up with a different set of behavior patterns that we often refer to as "misbehavior." When a child's genuine Goal to Contribute is frustrated, he mistakenly gets the idea that the way to feel that he belongs is to engage in behavior to get our Attention. This may take the form of acting helpless, drawing us in to serve him or acting out to get us to pay attention to him. When his authentic Goal of Empowerment is not realized, he begins to believe that he belongs only when he has the Power and is in control. When his Goal of Justice is frustrated, his ego takes over and he begins to seek Revenge for what he perceives as unfair. Finally, when his authentic Goal of Withdrawal from Conflict doesn't happen, he can become discouraged and come to believe that he is Inadequate and must keep others' expectations of his capacities low. If we are not careful in how we handle our reactions to these mistaken goals for love and belonging we may inadvertently escalate them.

1. *Goal of Attention*: When our child does not successfully satisfy his goal of realizing his value by contributing to the family, he gets the mistaken idea that what he needs to do to be loved and belong is get our attention. He delights in putting on a little show for us called, "Get mommy and daddy's goat." He purposely does things to upset us so we will notice him. Our attention takes many forms such as reminding, repeating, lecturing, or even threatening. If we continue to respond to his game, he reaches his mistaken Goal of Attention. The more we fall into this trap, the more our child repeats it. To deal effectively with this situation we need to ask ourselves who the audience for the show is. Of course, it is us. When the child plays to our weakened emotional state where we let our own anger, annoyance or fear cause us to placate our child's misbehavior, he knows he has, "got our goat." In this game, neither the child nor the parent reaches the authentic Goal of Contribution.

If we give attention to our child when he is attempting to get it through negative behavior, he will continue to repeat it and develop habitual patterns of this behavior. This does not imply that we should ignore our child's genuine requests for assistance or for private time with us. We can discern the difference between genuine requests and attention-getting behavior by observing our own reaction to it. If it is a genuine request, coming from the heart of the child, we feel it in our heart and are naturally there for him. However, if we feel irritated or annoyed by his behavior, or feel like we want to remind, serve or coax him, we can be quite certain that he is acting out of his faulty belief that says "I belong only when I am being noticed or served."[8] This is the time when we do not give the child what he is asking for.

To cope with our child's attention-getting behavior we must switch our attention *from* the child's naughtiness *to* our own emotional reaction to it. For many of us this "gotcha game" has become a long established pattern between our child and our self. To break this unhealthy situation we must first change our behavior by simply not allowing the game to be entered into and repeated over and over. Specific ideas for doing this are covered when we discuss how to transform this stumbling block into a stepping stone.

There is another stumbling block we need to be aware of. If we continue to reinforce our child's negative attention-getting behavior, it will continue to escalate over time until our frustration and irritation turns to stronger emotions and we begin to demand his obedience. As soon as we do this we risk the danger of pushing our child's ego buttons and activate his faulty belief that to belong he must have power and be in control.

2. *Goal of Power*: We will know that our child is acting from the mistaken Goal of Power and control when we feel like our authority is being threatened. When our child's authentic need to be empowered is blocked, his ego takes over and encourages the child to believe that he is important and valued only when he is in control. This mistaken belief of the child is easily triggered when we come from our own ego place of power and control. In other words, when we reach an intense level of frustration and begin to order, boss, threaten or punish our child, we open the door to our child's artillery of power. We set off his amygdala reaction and open the gates to a potential power struggle between us.

If we engage in frequent power struggles with our child, it not only negatively impacts his behavior but our relationship as well. The child's quest for power and control intensify and his attitude of defiance can permeate many areas of his life. He continues the "gotcha game" and enjoys doing things that make us angry because he is satisfying his faulty belief that he belongs when he is in charge and in control. The more we react from our position of power, the worse the situation becomes.

3. *Goal of Revenge*: If our child has been involved in a habitual pattern of power struggles where he comes to view himself as the victim, he resorts to engaging in revengeful behavior. In this case our child feels hurt and comes to believe that he has the right to retaliate and hurt back.

We will know that our child has reached this stage when we feel like we want to be revengeful ourselves. Our immediate impulse will be to retaliate by escalating the stakes or increasing our punishment. Escalating our revenge only strengthens the child's resolve to seek ways to satisfy his Goal of Revenge. This stage of misbehavior can be extremely trying for us and to get through it we must remember that at the heart of this misbehavior is a discouraged child who needs our help. We need to draw on our inner resources of self-control and find ways to transform this stumbling block into a stepping stone.

4. *Goal of Displaying Inadequacy*: When our child becomes extremely discouraged, he actually turns the positive goal of being able to withdraw from conflict upside down and thinks that he is inadequate and should withdraw all together. This can easily take the form of giving up on himself and doing what he can to have others give up on him as well. We will know if our child is experiencing these feelings if we begin to feel concern and despair about him and consider giving up on him. It is imperative that we do not do this. Just the opposite needs to be done.

TRANSFORMING STUMBLING BLOCKS INTO STEPPING STONES

1. *Switching the Goal of Attention back to the Goal of Contribution*: To move from the Rocky Path to the Natural Path it is helpful to do whatever we can to ignore our child's attention-getting behavior. This is a perfect time to leave the scene as calmly as possible or do something he doesn't expect. Whichever we choose we must show no outward evidence that we are aware of or reacting to his misbehavior. We must not speak or display non-verbal clues that give him satisfaction that he has successfully distracted us and gotten our attention. This is the time to go outside, into the bedroom or even the bathroom. Dreikurs suggests going into the bathroom where we can turn on the water and even listen to music (and we suggest breathe). This will help us let go of our knee-jerk amygdala reaction because we are out of sight and sound of our child. Our child's attempt to "get our goat" will be frustrated for the time being. Of course if it is an unsafe situation, as calmly as possible, remove the hazardous object or person

who might need to be protected and then leave the room without saying anything. If the child begins to react by crying or yelling or some other outburst, we need to ignore it. One word from us will satisfy our child's need to have us pay attention to him.

Once we have calmed down and see that our child has gotten involved in something else, we can look for ways to engage him in an activity where he can authentically contribute to the family. We can look for a good time to ask him if he would like to help us with a task such as preparing dinner or watering the plants. It is important not to discuss the episode of behavior at that time; however when the air is clear, discuss the situation using "I" messages and empathetic listening, problem solve and establish agreed upon logical consequences. If the behavior occurs in the future, we need to remember to carry out the logical consequence with genuine love and empathy. Another action that will strengthen our child's need to feel valued is to create a regular special time to be together with our child.

As much as possible we need to facilitate and appreciate our child's engagement in meaningful work at home so that he will gradually realize that the way to experience authentic love and belonging is to be a contributing member of the family. He will gradually change his belief that, "I belong when I am getting attention" to "I belong when I am contributing." When we give our child opportunities to practice contributing behavior we affirm his authenticity and our love for him. This will not happen overnight, it may take many repeated positive experiences and patience on our part for the child to switch his faulty thinking to authentic thinking. Whatever it takes, it is worth the effort! Jane Nelsen reminds us that "behind the misbehavior is a child who just wants to belong and is confused about how to accomplish this goal."[9]

2. *Switching the Goal of Power Back to the Goal of Empowerment*: When we sense that our child's misbehavior is based on the goal of seeking power, we must refrain from getting engaged in his attempt to show that he is the boss. We must avoid getting angry or using power techniques such as, ordering, threatening

or punishing because he will interpret it as his win which will increase his desire to engage us in power struggles. A better alternative is for us to walk away, and when our child has calmed down, look for ways to enlist his cooperation and experience his authentic empowerment. At a later time, when it is calm, it is good to engage our child in compassionate communication using "I" messages and empathetic understanding, problem solving and the establishment of logical consequences for future misbehavior that might occur.

If we do find ourselves involved in a power struggle it is imperative that we disengage as soon as possible. As discussed earlier, it helps to find a place where we do not see or hear our child so we do not continue to receive the sensorial stimulation of our child's misbehavior. Simultaneously, it is important to consciously do deep breathing and calm those irrational thoughts racing through our mind. Once we are able to regain our composure, it is important not to re-engage our child on the issue at that time. We need to wait to process the situation, as suggested above, until there is an atmosphere of mutual respect between us.

Our main focus needs to be finding ways to help our child experience the satisfaction of fulfilling the authentic side of this goal—Empowerment. Gradually we will see an improvement in our relationship and in our child's behavior.

3. *Switching the Goal of Revenge back to the Goal of Justice*: The most important thing we can do when our child is displaying revengeful behavior is to refrain from retaliating, not take his behavior personally and focus on improving our relationship. For us to turn around our child's goal of revenge, we must detach from our own emotional reactions and remember that our child is responding to his mistaken belief that, he belongs only by hurting others who he feels have hurt him. There are things we can do to help him let go of this faulty belief.

While it may be challenging for us, this is the time to offer him justice and forgiveness. This is easiest to do when we remember that the cause of our child's misbehavior is largely due to his discouragement. The word, "discourage" means to be without courage. Our responsibility is to encourage our child, by reassuring him of our love and bringing him to a state of self confidence so he can more consistently connect with his authenticity. This may require clearing the air and engaging in communication and problem solving. The more we can engage our child in cooperative activities and provide significant one on one time together the faster the transformation process will take place.

4. *Switching the Goal of Assumed Inadequacy back to the Goal of Withdrawal from Conflict*: If our child is experiencing the extreme pain of feeling inadequate to the point of withdrawing from activity, we must absolutely refrain from all criticism and look for ways to point out his strengths, encourage and reassure him. We can provide opportunities for him to experience small successes along the way. Additionally, we can look for ways to support, share and value what he is interested in. For example if he loves airplanes, we can learn more about them by engaging our child in conversation, by independently learning more on our own and sharing opportunities to go to an airport or watch a special show on airplanes together. This is a time to encourage him to expand his involvement in his compelling interests.

A child caught in the Goal of Assumed Inadequacy is struggling to have confidence in himself and needs to experience our love more than ever. We must put our focus on building up his courage so he can begin to re-experience the joy and satisfaction of accomplishment and re-engage in the natural process of unveiling his authenticity.

Esteem Needs

This level of need has two components: 1) how the child sees himself, and 2) how he interprets others' view of him. He has a strong desire to be competent and self confident and to have others accept, recognize and appreciate him. When both of these aspects are in place, he experiences inner joy and satisfaction and is able to walk the Natural Path. However, when he does not experience the fulfillment of one or both of these needs, he begins to rely on his ego to satisfy his need for self-esteem. When this happens he walks the Rocky Path.

THE NATURAL PATH

When a child is walking the Natural Path he is in touch with his authenticity and is able to respond to the direction of his inner guide. He experiences greater and greater autonomy as he engages in his ongoing quest for self mastery and develops his ability to make thoughtful choices. He remains enthusiastically engaged in learning and pursuing his unfolding interests and realizes new levels of competence as he involves himself in meaningful work. He deepens his understanding through repetition and the development of concentration. In addition his physical needs are met, he feels safe and he has a secure sense of belonging. He knows that he is appreciated and loved. Generally, his behavior is respectful and cooperative.

We are walking the Natural Path when we allow and encourage our child to engage in his natural unveiling process as described in Part II. A second important component is that we are doing our best to compassionately communicate with our child and model effective communication skills. The foundational key to all of this is that we are continually clearing our lens of perception so that we can consistently operate from our Spirit of love. The more we can sincerely communicate to our child that we see his inner beauty, light and love, the greater will be his self-esteem. What a child manifests in his outward behavior is a manifestation of his inner sense of self-worth.

THE ROCKY PATH

If a child's need for authentic self-esteem is not met, his ego will take charge and do what it can to convince others that the child is not only competent, but better than others. We may see our child judge others and say mean things, and when we attempt to redirect his behavior he may become defensive. We may witness our child becoming angry when he doesn't feel respected. He may over compensate for his feelings of inadequacy by talking about himself and his accomplishments frequently. He may become very competitive and seek his self-identity through his outward accomplishments. "I am the best…."

We are on the Rocky Path when we compare our child to others and subsequently add to his shaky self-esteem. He comes to believe that to get our love he must be like someone else because he is not good enough. Another powerful stumbling block is criticizing our child. Sincere feedback is constructive but criticism destroys self-confidence. When we do too much for our child, we undermine his self-esteem because he thinks that we think he is incapable. Encouraging our child to be the best he can be is helpful, but encouraging our child to be better than anyone else, and do whatever is necessary to accomplish this, encourages his ego to lead the way. This will have a harmful effect on the development of his authentic self-esteem.

TRANSFORMING STUMBLING BLOCKS INTO STEPPING STONES

The primary key to helping our child move from the Rocky Path to the Natural Path is to see him in his strength and continually reflect this back to him. Letting him know that we see his authenticity will do more to help him meet his need for esteem than anything else. He will know that we see and respect him by what we say and how we interact with him. Another important stepping stone is to continuously encourage him to become engaged in meaningful work that engages his interest and brings forth concentration. As discussed earlier, concentration is the path to his inner guide and Authentic Self. From this place misbehavior disappears. Montessori witnessed this phenomenon. "One of the facts that made our first schools remarkable was the disappearance of these defects…Once some interest had been aroused, they repeated exercises around that interest, and passed from one concentration to another."[10]

Self-Actualization Needs

The ultimate purpose of human life is to fulfill our potentials by unveiling our authenticity. Each time we unveil a new aspect of our Authentic Self we catch a glimpse of our Divine Nature and have what Maslow called a "Peak Experience.

THE NATURAL PATH

Children on the Natural Path naturally manifest peaceful qualities such as kindness, understanding, cooperation, enthusiasm, and joy. They experience love and are motivated by love. Montessori recognized that when children are centered, and are being led by their inner guide, they are in their normal state of authenticity. She called what has come to be known as self-actualization, "normalization." Through her years of work with children around the world she discovered that "normalized children show the strongest attraction toward good. They do not find it necessary to 'avoid evil.'"[11] They naturally act from love.

The more children engage in their natural cycles of discovering their capabilities, the more they fulfill their self-actualization needs. Creativity and self-discipline are added benefits for children who are meeting their self-actualization needs. We will know when we are on the Natural Path when we also experience the qualities of kindness, wisdom and love. With these three qualities, we will support our child's quest to fulfill his potential and step by step unveil his authenticity.

THE ROCKY PATH

A child on the Rocky Path is one who is frustrated and starved for meaningful engagement within the environment. He may demonstrate behaviors such as boredom, restlessness and a general lack of interest. Montessori observed that this is a painful place and described it this way, "The 'unconscious aim' then moving ever farther from its realization creates a kind of hell in the life of the child who becomes separated from a leading source and its creative energies."[12] This leading source of creative energies is the Authentic Self that is revealed through our child's engagement in the Unveiling Cycles. Just as a child must have physical food, he must also have stimulating mental food if he is too successfully meet his need for self-actualization.

TRANSFORMING STUMBLING BLOCKS INTO STEPPING STONES

To move from the Rocky Path to the Natural Path it is important to provide stimulating environments that will engage our child in activities of interest and refrain from interrupting him so he can develop his ability to concentrate. Montessori affirmed this need when she said, "Naughtiness can also be a form of agitation caused by mental hunger when the child is deprived of the stimuli of the environment or by a sense of frustration experienced when he is prevented from acting in the environment."[13] It is important to remember that the environment of the child needs to include a healthy physical, mental, emotional and spiritual component, for it is the combination of these four environmental aspects that nourishes and supports the natural unveiling of the Authentic Self.

Conclusion

When our child is misbehaving and walking the Rocky Path he is disconnected from his Authentic Self and is responding to the impulses emanating from his ego. In contrast, when he is walking the Natural Path he is directly connected and guided by his Authentic Self. The more we understand our child's Authentic Self and facilitate his Unveiling Cycles, the more likely he is to walk the Natural Path and engage in positive behaviors. When he, and sometimes we, are walking the Rocky Path, with its corresponding difficult behaviors, it is our responsibility to do what we can to transform the cycle of negative behavior and help create new pathways that affirm our child's authenticity. Montessori sums this up by saying:

> *Here among these children, order came from mysterious, hidden, inner directives, which can manifest themselves only if the freedom permitting them to be heeded is given. In order to give this type of freedom, it was precisely necessary that nobody interfere to obstruct the constructive spontaneous activity of the children in an environment prepared so that their need for development can find satisfaction.*[14]

Our child's greatest task is to reveal his Authentic Self. To do this he must be recognized and supported in this process. We are the most influential people in our child's life because we are the ones mirroring back to him the image we hold of him. We are also the ones who provide the critical home environment that supports his growth and development. If we see our child in his authenticity, encourage the development of his authentic nature through our actions, and encourage him to follow his natural Unveiling Cycles, he will naturally grow up with his physical, safety, belonging, self-esteem and self-actualization needs met. Gradually, one step at a time, our child will gracefully unveil his magnificent Authentic Self.

Whenever we become aware that we are becoming impatient, frustrated or discouraged with our child's behavior, it is helpful to close our eyes, see our child in his pure authenticity and experience the accompanying glow of joy and satisfaction emanating from his heart. Enjoy this moment of recognizing and experiencing the shared magical feelings of love. At this point we can shine our light of love on our child and receive his light of love shining back. We can affirm that this is our child's true nature by saying, "I see your light of love and I want to encourage its continued manifestation throughout your life."

Suggestions for Follow Through

- ▪ Provide new opportunities for your child to contribute to the family. Make sure that his efforts are acknowledged and appreciated. Record what you observe.

- ▪ Become aware of what you are doing for your child that he might do for himself. Offer him the opportunity to be more empowered by making it possible for him to do the task independently. This may take a slight change in the physical environment to make it child size and child friendly as well as a demonstration on how to do the activity successfully. Record what you observe.

- ▪ When you become aware that you are emotionally upset about something your child is doing, avoid getting involved and leave the room to calm down. Be sure to remove yourself from sight and sound of your child and begin breathing deeply to regain your center of calm. Become aware of what emotions you were experiencing (annoyance, irritation, frustration, anger, revenge or discouragement) and do your best to determine which need of your child is not being met. Make a plan to transform this current stumbling block into a stepping stone by doing something to meet the authentic need of the child. Record the results.

- ▪ If you are not already doing so, make a plan to spend one on one time with your child on a regular basis. Involve your child in this plan and get his feedback as to what he would like to do. If something comes up where you cannot meet the regular schedule, share it ahead of time with your child and set an alternative date that he can look forward to. This outing does not have to be expensive or lengthy. It can be a time to go to the park or play ball together. The important thing is that the child experiences unconditional love, one on one, on a regular basis. Record the results.

REFERENCES

PREFACE

1. McFarland, Jim. Shining Mountains Press Motto.

2. Wolf, Aline D. *Peaceful Children, Peaceful World: The Challenge of Maria Montessori.* Altona: Parent Child Press, 1989.

PART I

1. Montessori, Maria, *The Absorbent Mind.* Oxford: Clio Press, 1988, p xi.

2. Montessori, Maria, *The Secret of Childhood.* New York: Ballantine Books, 1996, p. 34.

3. Ibid. p. 36.

CHAPTER 1

1. Standing, E. M., *Maria Montessori Her Life and Work.* Penguin Books, 1957, p. 35.

2. Kramer, Rita, *Maria Montessori: A Biography.* Da Capo Press, 1988, p. 32.

3. Standing, p. 22.

4. Ibid, p. 22.

5. Ibid, p. 24.

6. Ibid, p. 28.

7. Ibid, pp. 28–29.

8. Ibid. p. 31.

9. Ibid. p. 85.

10. Kramer, p. 113.

11. Montessori, *The Secret of Childhood*. p.119

12. Ibid, p. 122.

13. Kramer. p. 117.

14. Standing, p. 48.

15. Ibid. p. 50.

16. Montessori. *The Secret of Childhood*. p. 128.

17. Standing, p. 54.

18. Centenary of the Montessori Movement, (Internet).

CHAPTER 2

1. Montessori, Maria, *To Educate the Human Potential*. Oxford: Clio Press, 1989, p. 6.

2. Montessori, *The Absorbent Mind*. p. 56.

3. Montessori, *To Educate the Human Potential*. p. 78.

4. Wolf, Aline D., *Nurturing the Spirit in Non-Sectarian Classrooms*. Hollidaysburg: Parent Child Press. p. 13.

5. Montessori, Maria, *From Childhood to Adolescence*. p. 39.

6. Interview by Susan Bridle, Spring Issue 2001, *Enlightenment Magazine*, "The Divinization of the Cosmos."

7. Montessori. *To Educate the Human Potential*. p. 6.

8. Montessori. *The Absorbent Mind*. p.150.

9. Montessori. *To Educate the Human Potential*. p. 55.

10. Montessori. The Secret of Childhood. p. 207–208.

11. Shakespeare, William. *Hamlet*.

12. Montessori. *From Childhood to Adolescence*. New York: Schocken Books, 1976, p.102.

13. Christian: King James Version of the Old/New Testament. Genesis 1:27 and 31.

14. Ibid. John 17:21–22.

15. Jewish: Torah Genesis 1:27

16. Muslim Quran Chapter 1 Verses 28–30.

17. Swami Rama. *Happiness Is Your Creation*. Honesdale: Himalayan Institute Press, 2005. p. xi.

18. The Teaching of Buddha. Bukkyo Dendo Kyokai, 1966. p.154.

19. Standing. p.53.

20. McFarland, Sonnie. *Honoring the Light of the Child: Activities to Nurture Peaceful Living Skills in Young Children*. Buena Vista: Shining Mountains Press, 2004. pp. 17–19.

CHAPTER 3

1. Montessori. *Absorbent Mind*. p. 4.

2. Montessori. *The Child in the Family*. Madras: Kalakshetra Press, 1991. p. 18.

3. Montessori. *The Absorbent Mind*. p. 56.

4. Swami Rama, Rudolph Ballentine, M.D., Swami Ajaya, Ph.D. *Yoga Psychotherapy: The Evolution of Consciousness*.

5. Montessori. *The Child in the Family*. p.23.

6. Montessori. *The Absorbent Mind*. p. 56.

7. Ibid. p. 91.

8. Ibid. p. 57.

9. Swami Rama, et al, *Yoga Psychotherapy: The Evolution of Consciousness*. p. 63.

10. Montessori, *The Child in the Family*. p. 38.

11. Montessori, *To Educate the Human Potential*. p. 13.

12. Ibid. p. 13.

13. Ibid. p. 13.

14. Ibid. p. 13.

15. Ibid. p. 13.

16. Ibid. p. 15.

17. Montessori, *The Absorbent Mind*. p. 75.

18. Ibid. p. 74.

19. Abrams, Jeremiah. *Reclaiming the Inner Child*. Los Angeles: Jeremy P. Tarcher, Inc., 1990. p. 24.

20. Ibid. p. 24.

21. Ibid. p. 28.

22. Montessori, *The Child in the Family*. pp. 14–15.

23. Swami Rama. *Happiness Is Your Creation*. p. 68.

24. Montessori. *The Absorbent Mind*. pp. 25–26.

25. Ibid. p. 76.

26. Dyer, Wayne. *Inspiration*. Carlsbad: Hay House, Inc. 2006, p. 87.

27. Montessori. *The Absorbent Mind*. p. 77.

28. Ibid. p. 267.

29. Montessori. *The Secret of Childhood*. p. xxi.

30. Ibid. p. 269.

31. Montessori. *The Absorbent Mind*. p. 26.

32. Montessori, Maria. *The Formation of Man*. Madras: Kalakshetra Press, 1991, p. 20.

33. McFarland, Sonnie. *Honoring the Light of the Child: Activities to Nurture Peaceful Living Skills in Young Children*. pp.23–24.

PART II

1. Montessori. *The Absorbent Mind*. p. 80.

2. Ibid. p. 14.

3. Montessori. *The Child in the Family*. p. 68.

CHAPTER 4

1. Goble, Frank. *The Third Force: The Psychology of Abraham Maslow*. New York: Simon and Schuster, Inc, 1971, p. 40.

2. Ibid. p. 41.

3. Ibid. p. 42.

4. Montessori. *To Educate the Human Potential*. p. 82.

5. Montessori. *The Absorbent Mind*. p. 83.

6. Ibid. p. 83.

7. Ibid. p. 87.

8. Ibid. p. 84.

9. Lillard, Angeline Stoll. *Montessori: The Science Behind the Genius*. Oxford: Oxford University Press, Inc., 2005. p. 150.

10. Ibid. pp. 119–120.

11. Miller, Ron. *New Directions in Education: Selections from Holistic Education Review*. Brandon: Holistic Education Press, 1991, pp.34–35.

CHAPTER 5

1. Montessori. *The Absorbent Mind.* p. 57.

2. Ibid. p. 56.

3. Ibid. p. 24.

4. Ibid. p. 60.

5. Montessori, *The Formation of Man.* Madras: Kalakshetra Press, 1991, p. 96.

6. Montessori, *The Child in the Family.* p. 47.

7. Ibid. p. 47.

8. Montessori, *The Absorbent Mind.* p. 130.

9. Montessori, Maria. *Education for a New World.* Madras: Kalakshetra Press, 1991, pp. 52–53.

10. Lillard. *Montessori: The Science Behind the Genius.* p. 56.

11. Montessori. *The Absorbent Mind.* p. 16.

12. Montessori. *To Educate the Human Potential.* p. 5.

13. Lillard. pp. 86–88.

14. Montessori. *The Absorbent Mind.* p. 6.

CHAPTER 6

1. Montessori, Maria. *Spontaneous Activity in Education.* Cambridge: Robert Bentley, Inc., 1917, p. 68.

2. Montessori. *The Absorbent Mind.* p. 188.

3. Montessori. *The Child in the Family.* p. 63.

4. Ibid.

5. Montessori. *The Absorbent Mind.* p. 249.

6. Healy, Jane. *Your Child's Growing Mind: A Guide to Leaning and Brain Development from Birth to Adolescence.* New York: Doubleday, 1987, p. 19.

7. Goleman, Daniel. *Emotional Intelligence. New York: Bantam Books, 1995,* p. 27.

8. Ibid. p.12.

9. Ibid. p. 16.

10. Ibid. p. 79.

11. Personal notes from Daniel Goleman lecture at Association of Colorado Independent Schools Conference in Vail, Colorado.

12. Healy. p. 24.

13. Montessori. *From Childhood to Adolescence*. p. 94.

14. Lillard. pp. 235–242.

15. McFarland. pp. 18–19.

16. Lillard. p. 230.

CHAPTER 7

1. Montessori. *The Absorbent Mind*. p. 188.

2. Montessori, *The Formation of Man*. p. 47.

3. Montessori, *The Absorbent Mind*. p. 185.

4. Montessori. *Spontaneous Activity in Education*. p. 68.

5. Maslow, Abraham, *The Farther Reaches of Human Nature*. New York: The Viking Press, 1971, p.175.

6. Montessori. *The Absorbent Mind*. p.189.

7. Maslow. pp. 45–49.

8. Maslow. pp. 133–135.

9. Montessori. *The Absorbent Mind*. p.191.

10. Csikszentmihalyi, Mihaly. *Creativity: Flow and the Psychology of Discovery and Invention*. New York: Harper Collins Publishers, 1996, p. 105.

11. Ibid. pp. 110–113.

12. Ibid. p. 151.

13. Montessori. *The Absorbent Mind*. p. 191.

14. Ibid. p. 231.

15. Montessori. *The Child in the Family*. p. 66.

16. Montessori. *Spontaneous Activity in Education*. p. 179.

17. Montessori. *The Formation of Man*. p. 16.

PART III

1. Montessori. *Education for a New World*. p. 3.

2. Wolf, Aline D. *Montessori Insights for Parents of Young Children*. Hollidaysburg: Parent Child Press, Inc., 2005, p. 3.

3. Montessori. *The Child and the Family*. p. 23.

CHAPTER 8

1. McFarland. pp. 53–55.

2. Ibid. pp. 57–59.

CHAPTER 9

1. Jampolsky, Gerald. *Love is Letting Go of Fear*. Toronto: Bantam Books, 1981. Csikszentmihalyi. pp.110–113.

2. Berends, Polly Berrien. *Whole Child/Whole Parent*. New York: Harper & Row, 1983, p. 205.

3. Elkind, David. *The Hurried Child: Growing Up Too Fast Too Soon*. Cambridge: Perseus, 2001, p. 40.

4. Kosta, Arthur L. and Bena Kallick. *The Habits of Mind*. Danvers: Association for Supervision and Curriculum Development, 208, p. 27.

5. McFarland. pp. 73–76.

6. Levin, Diane and Jean Kilbourne. *So Sexy So Soon: The New Sexualized Childhood and What Parents Can Do to Protect Their Kids*. New York: Ballentine Books, 2008.

7. Elkind, p. 107.

8. Ibid. p. 106.

CHAPTER 10

1. Goleman, Daniel. *Working with Emotional Intelligence*. New York: Bantam Books, 1998, pp. 26–27.

2. Goleman, *Emotional Intelligence*. p.192.

3. Covey, Stephen R. *The 7 Habits of Highly Effective People*. New York: Simon & Schuster, 1989, p. 188–190.

4. Goleman. *Emotional Intelligence*. p. 81.

5. McFarland. pp. 87–89

6. Ibid. pp. 95–98.

7. Montessori. *The Child in the Family*. p. 91.

8. Montessori. *To Educate the Human Potential*. pp. 83–84.

CHAPTER 11

1. Montessori. *The Child and the Family*. p. 89.

2. McFarland. pp. 21–22.

3. Berend. p. 36.

PART IV

1. Montessori. *The Absorbent Mind*. p. 28.

2. Berends. p. 10.

CHAPTER 12

1. Standing, E.M. p. 298.

2. McFarland, Sonnie. *Shining Through: A Teacher's Handbook on Transformation.* Buena Vista: Shining Mountains Press. 1993, p. 3

3. Standing. pp. 300–301.

4. Ibid.

5. Hahn, Thich Nhat. *Peace Is Every Step: The Path of Mindfulness in Everyday Life*. New York: Bantam, 1992.

6. Tolle, Eckhart. *A New Earth: Awakening to Your Life's Purpose*. New York: The Penguin Group, 2005, p.2.

7. Dyer, Wayne. *The Power of Intention*. Carlsbad: Hay House, Inc., 2004. p. 38.

8. Gibran, Kahlil. *The Prophet*. New York: Alfred A. Knopf, Inc., 1923, pp. 17–18.

9. Ruiz, Don Miguel. *The Four Agreements*. San Rafael: Amber-Allen Publishing, 2001.

10. Source of chant unknown.

11. Montessori. *The Child in the Family*. p. 65.

12. Berends. p. 20.

CHAPTER 13

1. Gurian, Michael. *Nurture the Nature: Understanding and Supporting Your Child's Unique Core Personality*. San Francisco: Jossey-Bass, 2007, p.13

2. Wolf, Aline D. *Peaceful Children, Peaceful World: The Challenge of Maria Montessori*.

3. Ibid.

4. Rogers, Carl. *On Becoming a Person: A Therapists View of Psychotherapy.* Boston: Houghton Mifflin Company, 1961, pp. 31–38.

5. Ibid. p. 33.

6. Ibid. p. 36.

7. Eisler, Riane, *The Real Wealth of Nations.* San Francisco: Berrett-Kohler Publishers, Inc. 2007. pp. 111–112.

8. Ibid. p.129.

9. Montessori. *The Child in the Family.* p. 3.

10. Ibid. p. 93.

11. Tolle. *A New Earth: Awakening to Your Life's Purpose.*

CHAPTER 14

1. Rosenberg, Marshall B. *Nonviolent Communication: A Language of Compassion.* Del Mar: PuddleDancer Press, 1999, p. 1.

2. McFarland. *Honoring the Light of the Child.* pp.46–47.

3. Covey. pp. 205–234.

4. Rosenberg. p. 91.

CHAPTER 15

1. Montessori. *The Absorbent Mind.* p. 224.

2. Montessori. *Education for a New World.* pp. 82–83.

3. Montessori. *The Absorbent Mind.* p. 229.

4. Lillard. *Montessori: The Science Behind the Genius.* p. 157

5. Ibid. p. 154.

6. Swami Rama. *Marriage, Parenthood and Enlightenment.* Honesdale: Himalayan Institute Press. p.69–70.

7. Montessori, Maria. *The Montessori Method.* New York: Schocken. p. 87.

8. Glenn, H. Stephen, Jane Nelsen, *Raising Self-Reliant Children In A Self-Indulgent World.* Rocklin: Prima Publishing, 1989. p. 152.

9. Nelsen, Jane. *Positive Discipline.* New York: Ballantine Books, 1987, p. 73.

10. Ibid. p. 22.

11. Cline, Foster and Jim Fay. *Parenting With Love and Logic*. Colorado Springs: Pinon, 1990, p. 62.

12. Montessori. *The Formation of Man*. p. 39.

13. Ibid. p. 41.

14. Montessori. *The Absorbent Mind*. p. 224.

15. Montessori. *The Secret of Childhood*. p. 104

16. Ibid.

17. Nelsen. p. 76.

CHAPTER 16

1. Nelsen. p. 63.

2. Montessori. p. 225.

3. Neihardt, John G. *Black Elk Speaks*. Lincoln: University of Nebraska Press, 1972, pp.16–36.

4. McFarland. *Honoring the Light of the Child*. p.33.

5. Montessori. *The Absorbent Mind*. p. 225.

6. Montessori. *The Formation of Man*. p. 44.

7. Dreikurs, Rudolf. *Children the Challenge*. New York: E.P. Dutton, 1987. pp. 57–67.

8. Dinkmeyer, Don & Gary D. McKay. *Parent's Handbook: Systematic Training for Effective Parenting*. Circle Pines: American Guidance Service, Inc., 1976, p.14.

9. Nelsen. p. 25.

10. Montessori. *Education for a New World*. pp. 82–83.

11. Montessori, *The Absorbent Mind*. pp. 220.

12. Montessori, *The Formation of Man*. p.46.

13. Ibid. p. 46.

14. Ibid. p. 43.

INDEX

ABOUT THE AUTHORS

Dr. Jim and Sonnie McFarland have been teaching, learning, living, loving and working together for almost fifty years. They met November 22, 1963 and immediately experienced an affinity for one another. Besides sharing the love of family, they found that they shared professional interests as well.

Jim completed his Master's Degree "Interpersonal Communication" at San Francisco State College in 1968 at the same time that Sonnie discovered the educational work of Dr. Maria Montessori. They moved to Evanston, Illinois where Jim pursued his Doctorial Degree, at Northwestern University, in "Interpersonal and Group Communication" while Sonnie pursued certification to become a Montessori early childhood teacher. This time was one of exciting collaboration between Jim and Sonnie as they discovered how their two fields of interest complemented one another. It was at this time that they met the venerable Swami Rama of the Himalayas who gave them a deep understanding of human nature and development that further enhanced their personal as well as professional lives.

In 1972 they moved to Pueblo, Colorado where Jim became a Professor of Communication at the University of Southern Colorado. Their son, Christian was 2 ½ years old and ready to attend a Montessori school. To meet this need, Jim and Sonnie founded the Shining Mountains Center for Education and Consciousness that included a Montessori School, an Adult Education Center and Yoga Center. Sonnie directed and taught in the Montessori School and Yoga Center. Jim facilitated the Adult Education Center. In 1974, their daughter Jeannie was born.

The family moved to Denver, Colorado in 1980 where Sonnie joined the faculty of the Montessori School of Denver where she taught for twelve years and then became the Head of School. During this time she developed peace education activities for young children that are now published in her book, *Honoring the Light of the Child: Activities to Nurture Peaceful Living Skills in Young Children* and published a handbook on centering skills for adults entitled, *Shining Through: A Teacher's Handbook on Transformation*. Sonnie served on the national American Montessori Society "AMS" Board for eight years.

While in Denver, Jim taught "Communication" at Metro-State College. He developed the CPIR Model for Community Building in schools, businesses and homes. Throughout his career he offered a variety of workshops on Community Building, Personal Growth, Communication, and Montessori Parenting. As a team Jim and Sonnie offered parenting classes for over fifteen years. The satisfaction and experiences of working with parents to help them recognize and unveil their children's authenticity are the basis of their current book: *Montessori Parenting: Unveiling the Authentic Self*.

In 2003 they retired and currently reside in the beautiful mountains of central Colorado. Sonnie continues to travel internationally speaking and presenting on Montessori Parenting, Peace Education, Community Building and Adult Transformation. She was just named as the American Montessori Society's 2011 Living Legacy for her exemplary work throughout her career.

For information on workshops, speaking engagements and book sales, email Sonnie at Sonnie@ShiningMountainsPress.com
or visit the website at: www.ShiningMountainsPress.com

Gift of Books by
Dr. Jim and/or Sonnie McFarland
For Your Staff, Colleagues, and Friends

ORDER HERE

▓ *Montessori Parenting: Unveiling the Authentic Self*
by Dr. Jim & Sonnie McFarland

Qty:_____	$25.00 each	$_____
Shipping:	$5.00 per book	$_____
Colorado residents:	$1.85 sales tax per book	$_____

International orders must be accompanied by a postal money order in U.S. funds and include $10.00 shipping per book. Allow 15 days for delivery.

▓ *Honoring the Light of the Child: Activities to Nurture Peaceful Living Skills in Young Children* with accompanying Music C.D. Book by Sonnie McFarland and Music CD by Pat Yonka

Qty:_____	$30.00 each	$_____
Shipping:	$6.00 per book	$_____
Colorado residents:	$2.22 sales tax per book	$_____

International orders must be accompanied by a postal money order in U.S. funds and include $12.00 shipping per book. Allow 15 days for delivery.

▓ *Shining Through: A Teacher's Handbook on Transformation*

Qty:_____	$10.00 each	$_____
Shipping:	$2.00 per book	$_____
Colorado residents:	$ .74 sales tax per book	$_____

International orders must be accompanied by a postal money order in U.S. funds and include $4.00 shipping per book. Allow 15 days for delivery.

TOTAL AMOUNT ENCLOSED $_____

(over)

Name _____

Organization _____

Address _____

City/State/Zip _____

Phone_____ E-Mail _____

Please make check payable and return to:

Shining Mountains Press
P.O. Box 4155
Buena Vista, CO 81211

For information on workshops, speaking engagements
and bulk book orders,

contact Sonnie at: **Sonnie@ShiningMountainsPress.com**

or visit the website at: **www.ShiningMountainsPress.com**